High-Fashion Sewing Secrets

from the

WORLD'S BEST DESIGNERS

High-Fashion Sewing Secrets

from the

WORLD'S BEST DESIGNERS

A *Step-by-Step* Guide
to Sewing Stylish Seams,
Buttonholes, Pockets,
Collars, Hems,
and More

Claire B. Shaeffer

Rodale Press, Inc.
Emmaus, Pennsylvania

*To sewers everywhere who want to create
unique and fashionable designs*

Prop credits: Allentown Sewing Machine Outlet, Butterick Company, Clotilde, Dick Blick Art Materials, Fabric Mart of Bethlehem, Gingher, HTC-Handler Textile, Newark Dressmaker Supply, Personality Shoppe, Sawyer Brook Distinctive Fabrics, Todd Fisher Textiles, and Web of Thread. (See "Resources" on page 243 for addresses.) Also Joyce Edgar, Susan Huxley, Sandra Mugridge, Susan Nester, Sheri Rush, and Barbara Webb.

If you have any questions or comments concerning the editorial content of this book, please write to:

Rodale Press, Inc.
Book Readers' Service
33 East Minor Street
Emmaus, PA 18098

OUR PURPOSE

*"We inspire and enable people to improve
their lives and the world around them."*

**High-Fashion Sewing Secrets Editorial
and Design Staff**

Editor: Marya Kissinger Amig
Cover and Interior Book Designer: Marta Mitchell Strait
Design Assistance: Dale Mack, Jennifer Miller, Chris Rhoads, and Frank Moninghoff
Interior Illustrators: Glee Barre, Tom Moore, and Ian Worpole
Cover and Fashion Illustrator: Barbara Griffel
Cover and Interior Photographer: John Hamel
Interior Photo Stylists: Marianne Grape Laubach and Paula Jaworski
Author Photos: Mitch Mandel
Copy Editor: Erana C. Bumbardatore
Manufacturing Coordinator: Melinda Rizzo
Indexer: Nan N. Badgett
Editorial Assistance: Nancy Fawley, Susan L. Nickol, Jodi Rehl, and Lori Schaffer

Rodale Home and Garden Books

Vice President and Editorial Director: Margaret J. Lydic
Managing Editor, Sewing Books: Cheryl Winters-Tetreau
Art Director: Paula Jaworski
Associate Art Director: Mary Ellen Fanelli
Studio Manager: Leslie M. Keefe
Copy Director: Dolores Plikaitis
Book Manufacturing Director: Helen Clogston
Office Manager: Karen Earl-Braymer

Library of Congress Cataloging-in-Publication Data

Shaeffer, Claire B.

High-fashion sewing secrets from the world's best designers : a step-by-step guide to sewing stylish seams, buttonholes, pockets, collars, hems, and more / Claire Shaeffer.

p.   cm.

Includes bibliographical references and index.

ISBN 0-87596-717-5 (hardcover : alk. paper)

1. Dressmaking. 2. Tailoring (Women's) 3. Dressmaking—Pattern design. I. Title.

TT515.S484   1997

646.4'04—dc20   96-29302

Distributed in the book trade by St. Martin's Press

2 4 6 8 10 9 7 5 3   hardcover

Meet Claire Shaeffer

Internationally known sewing expert and lecturer Claire Shaeffer has studied in the high-fashion workrooms of New York and Europe, bringing together the secrets of the world's best designers for this book.

Claire first learned to sew as a child in Americus, Georgia, and has authored more than a dozen books, including *Couture Sewing Techniques*, *Claire Shaeffer's Fabric Sewing Guide*, *The Complete Book of Sewing Shortcuts*, *Sew Any Set-In Pocket*, and *Sew Any Patch Pocket*.

Known for her easy-to-follow and innovative sewing techniques, Claire is a regular contributor to *Vogue Patterns* magazine and has written many articles for *Threads*, *McCall's Patterns* magazine, *Craftrends*, *Sew Business*, *Sew News*, *Woman's Day*, *Handmade*, and *Handwoven*.

Listed in the 1997 editions of *Who's Who of American Women* and *Who's Who in the World*, Claire has been an instructor at the College of the Desert in California since 1975, teaching classes ranging from garment construction, patternmaking, and alterations to historic costume, apparel analysis, and fashion careers. In addition, she is a featured lecturer at numerous international sewing seminars and conferences every year.

Claire holds a bachelor of arts degree in art history from Old Dominion University in Norfolk, Virginia, and an associate of arts degree in fashion design and industrial sewing from Laney College in Oakland, California. She is a member of the American Sewing Guild, the American Home Sewing and Craft Association, the Professional Association of Custom Clothiers, the International Fabricare Institute, the International Textile and Apparel Association, the Fashion Group International, and the Costume Society of America.

Claire Shaeffer assists designer Charles Kleibaker in his studio in June 1985.

PART I: Fast & Fancy

FANCY CONSTRUCTION TECHNIQUES 2

SEAMS 3

Strap Seam 3 ♦ Raised French Seam 7 ♦ Raised Overlock Seam 9 ♦ Stand-Up Bound Seam 12
Piped Seam 15 ♦ Baby Seam 18

FACINGS 20

Topstitched Facing 20 ♦ Bias Facing as a Trim 25 ♦ Facing as a Trim 27

HEMS 33

Narrow Topstitched Hem 33 ♦ Gold Overlock Hem 36 ♦ Blanket-Stitched Hem 38 ♦ Chiffon Hem 40
Band Hem 43

BINDINGS 45

French Binding 45 ♦ One-Step Binding 49

FANCY DETAILS 52

POCKETS AND FLAPS 53

Piped Patch Pocket on Jacket 53 ♦ Double Welt Pocket on a Skirt 57 ♦ Windowpane Opening 60
Inseam Pocket with Invisible Zipper at Seam 66 ♦ Inseam Pocket with Faux Flap 69

COLLARS AND LAPELS 71

Tie Collar 71 ♦ Detachable Turtleneck 75 ♦ Double Flounce Collar 79 ♦ Fancy Lapels 82 ♦ Notched Collar 85

PLACKETS AND FASTENERS 88

Keyhole Opening 88 ♦ Bound Neckline Placket 92 ♦ Button Loops 97 ♦ Fly or Concealed Front Placket 101
Bound Buttonholes 105 ♦ Blind Bound Buttonholes 109 ♦ Easy Slot Zipper 111

JUST FANCY 114

TRIMS 115

Roses 115 ♦ Lace Inserts 118

WRAPS AND SHAWLS 120

Cocoon Wrap 120 ♦ Ruffled Shawl 122 ♦ Evening Wrap 124

BEHIND THE SEAMS 126

INNER SECRETS 127

Waist Stay 127 ♦ Blouse Stays 132 ♦ Cowl Stay 134

INTERFACINGS AND LININGS 136

Interfacing a Jacket 136 ♦ Drafting a Jacket Lining Pattern 140 ♦ Bagging a Jacket 143
Adding a Skirt Lining 148

PART II: Design Basics

MAKE YOUR OWN PATTERNS 154

PREPARING TO MAKE A PATTERN 155

Tools and Supplies 155 ♦ Essential Patterns 158
Basic Drafting Techniques 160

PLOTTING A PATTERN 163

Basic Patternmaking 163 ♦ Precision Patternmaking 168

COPY A GARMENT 172

PREPARE TO COPY A GARMENT 173

Tools for Copying 173 ♦ Copying Basics 176

FOOLPROOF COPYING 180

Measuring 180 ♦ Tracing 186 ♦ Rub-Off 192

PATTERNMAKING BASICS 200

ELEMENTS OF DESIGN 201

Adding a Seam 201 ♦ Eliminating a Seam 204 ♦ Transferring a Seam 207
Making a Neckline Facing 210 ♦ All-in-One Facing 213

DARTS 216

Transferring Darts 216 ♦ Converting Darts to Dart Tucks 219 ♦ Converting Darts to Seams 221

NECKLINES 225

Basic V-Neck 225 ♦ Shallow V-Neck 228 ♦ Cut-Away Scoop Neckline 229

TUCKS 230

Vertical Tucks 230 ♦ Tuck Seam 233

BUTTON CLOSURES 235

Adding Buttons and Buttonholes 235

DESIGN WORKSHEET 238

ACKNOWLEDGMENTS 239

GLOSSARY 240

BIBLIOGRAPHY 242

RESOURCES 243

INDEX 244

Introduction

From the time I learned to sew, I was captivated by the idea of creating one-of-a-kind, original garments. One of my first designs was a dress for my Sparkle Plenty doll that my mother carefully preserved in her cedar chest. Embellished with a little embroidery, the uneven stitches on the hand-sewn dress clearly reveal the awkwardness of my tiny fingers. The upside-down sleeves are more difficult to explain. I'd like to think this unusual design detail was an early sign of my creativity or the influence of the fashions of the day, but more likely it was an example of my lack of sewing expertise.

Many things have changed since I created Sparkle Plenty's dress. My hand sewing, my knowledge of garment construction, and my design skills have all improved. Sparkle Plenty has passed into oblivion, but my love for fashion and my joy in creating original garments continues to be a fascinating part of my life.

When I went to Laney College in 1966, I was a very good home sewer, and my primary purpose was to learn to make patterns for my difficult-to-fit body. Much to my frustration, I learned that I couldn't take patternmaking courses unless I also took the introductory courses in hand and industrial sewing.

I quickly learned how much I didn't know about sewing, and I discovered that sewing and design had many different facets that I had not known existed. It was the beginning of a new world for me.

By the time I graduated two years later with my certificates in Industrial Sewing and Apparel Design, I had acquired a variety of fashion industry skills ranging from factory production to haute couture. I had learned how to make original patterns by both the flat pattern and draping methods and how to create original designs from commercial patterns and rub-offs (patterns taken from ready-made garments).

Today, like most home sewers, I must use my

time as efficiently as possible. I no longer have the time to make original patterns from scratch and then spend numerous hours defining the silhouette and perfecting the fit. Instead, I rely on my library of master patterns and the techniques described in this book to create an unlimited range of original garments that express my style and personality.

Sooner or later, every home sewer wants to produce high-fashion originals that deviate from commercial patterns. You may want to incorporate design ideas from the latest ready-to-wear or couture collections before they are available on commercial patterns, or you may want to experiment with new ideas or make an individual fashion statement that expresses your personality.

No matter what the reason, creating original, fashionable garments is exciting and rewarding, and frequently it is surprisingly easy.

This book focuses on design details and construction ideas from expensive ready-to-wear fashions. It describes the methods that I use most frequently because they can be implemented quickly and easily with fantastic results, and they reflect current fashion trends from avant-garde to traditional classics.

I believe that if you can sew, you can design. Unlike other books that treat sewing and design separately, *High-Fashion Sewing Secrets* presents the two together and describes how you can use them to design and how they relate to each other.

Organized for easy reference, this book is divided into two parts. Part One: Fast and Fancy utilizes the wealth of knowledge you have acquired when sewing garments. It includes a collection of design details and fashion ideas from expensive ready-to-wear that you can use to transform simple designs into eye-catching creations or designer look-alikes. The step-by-step instructions are easy to follow and require few, if any, patternmaking skills and special tools and supplies, so you can incorporate them immediately and be assured of professional results.

Part Two: Design Basics focuses on patternmaking techniques and shows you how to use master patterns to create one-of-a-kind originals. It contains everything you need to know to begin patternmaking: the basic rules, how to use your equipment, and how to apply patternmaking techniques to master patterns. Chapter 6 details how to copy ready-made garments using three different methods—measuring, tracing, and rub-off—so you can use them as master patterns.

Designed to give you the confidence to create distinctive, one-of-a-kind fashions, *High-Fashion Sewing Secrets* was written for you. It is a timeless patternmaking and sewing techniques book. The basic principles of patternmaking and sewing can be used again and again, even though the fashions of today will only be a memory tomorrow.

Whatever your sewing experience, this book will stimulate your imagination as well as broaden your understanding of patternmaking, sewing, and design. And it will enable you to use your acquired knowledge and practical skills more creatively and intelligently.

Claire B. Shaeffer

French designer Hubert de Givenchy, a favorite of stylish women worldwide, poses with his runway models in Japan during a 1982 retrospective celebrating the 30th anniversary of the House of Givenchy.

PART I

Fast & Fancy

"Fashions fade—style is eternal."
—Yves Saint Laurent

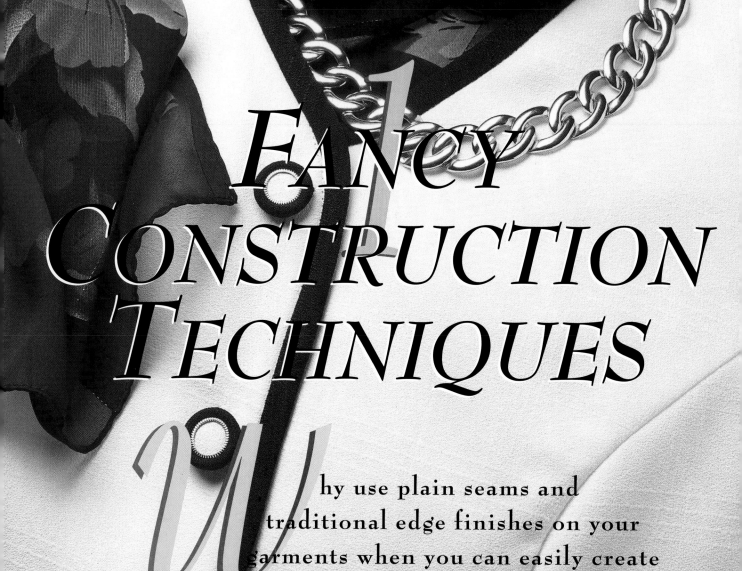

FANCY CONSTRUCTION TECHNIQUES

1

Why use plain seams and traditional edge finishes on your garments when you can easily create high-fashion designer look-alikes? This chapter will show you how to transform almost any simple garment design into a sophisticated fashion.

Seams

Today, seams aren't just functional. They embellish and accentuate a garment's design. Decorative seams can be used as simple, graceful outlines or as eye-catching accents. Use one of these seams to create a garment with a unique flair.

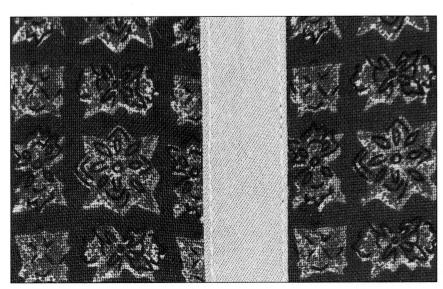

Dutch designer Koos van den Akker uses this strap seam on many of his distinctive creations.

Strap Seam

Strap seams are frequently used by designers like Koos van den Akker, Jeanne Marc, and Geoffrey Beene on their imaginative wearable art designs. Equally attractive on the inside or outside of a garment, strap seams are well suited for unlined and reversible designs. They also work well on garments that will be laundered frequently because all of the raw seam allowances are covered by the straps.

Strap seams are generally straight or slightly curved, and the straps are cut on the bias. Because bias-cut fabric is extremely flexible and easy to apply, these seams can be shaped with deep curves or angles and the straps can be cut to duplicate the seamlines. Most strap seams are ½ to ⅝ inch wide, but they can be as narrow as ¼ inch or as wide as 1 inch.

Strap seams can be made with several different methods, but these instructions are based on a Koos van den Akker design. The strap is cut on the bias and sewn into the seamline. Then the strap is pressed to one side to cover the seam allowances and is stitched flat against the garment. Depending on a garment's design, strap seams can be pressed in any direction: up or down, toward or away from the garment centers. However, paired seams should be pressed in the same direction so that the design will be symmetrical.

DESIGNER DETAIL

Koos van den Akker

Frequently called the "master of collage," Koos van den Akker is known for his imaginative combinations of unlikely fabrics and various prints, lace, and decorative tapes on simple silhouettes. His fabric-collage designs often include interesting machine appliqués with bias covering the raw edges as well as the strap seam described here.

Tools & Supplies

♦ See-through ruler
♦ Chalk wheel
♦ Serger (optional)
♦ Edgestitch foot or wide straight-stitch foot (optional)

Cut the Garment and Bias Strips

1. Cut out the garment with ⅝-inch seam allowances and transfer all pattern markings.

■ SEWING SECRET: To mark notches, foldlines, garment centers, and other matching points, clip no more than ⅛ inch into the seam allowance.

2. To make ½-inch-wide straps, cut bias strips 1½ inches wide following the instructions in "How to Cut and Join Bias Strips" on the opposite page.

3. Join the bias strips end to end to make straps that are long enough for all the seams, following the same instructions as in step 2.

■ SEWING SECRET: If you did not preshrink your fabric before you cut the bias strips, preshrink the strips now. Wrap the strips snugly around a piece of white cardboard or two index cards and pin the ends to hold them in place. Then bend the cardboard at the center.

Fill a basin with very hot water and submerge the bias strips, agitating them up and down several times to be sure all of the layers are wet. Let the strips sit in the

water about 20 minutes, then remove the bias strips and set them aside to air dry.

Stitch the Seam

1. Set your machine for a stitch length of 12 to 15 stitches per inch (spi) (2.0 to 1.5 mm). With wrong sides together, stitch a ⅝-inch seam. Check the fit of the garment as needed.

■ SEWING SECRET: For most garment sewing, a stitch length of 12 spi (2.0 mm) is preferred. Because sewing machines are often not accurately calibrated, it's a good idea to check your machine's stitch length. To do this, set your machine at 12 spi or 2.0 mm. On a scrap of fabric, stitch a line 3 to 4 inches long. Mark a 1-inch length in the middle of the line of stitching. Count the stitches between your marks. Adjust your stitch length as needed until you get 12 spi (or stitches 2.0 mm in length).

2. Referring to **Diagram 1**, place the seam on top of the bias strip. Align and pin the raw edges together. Machine baste on the seamline through all of the layers.

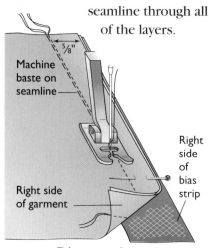

Machine baste on seamline

⅝"

Right side of garment

Right side of bias strip

Diagram 1

How to *Cut* and *Join Bias Strips*

True bias is a line located at a 45-degree angle to the selvage. Fabric is frequently cut along this line to create strips for pipings, bindings, and other trims because fabric cut on the bias is more flexible and easier to shape than fabric cut parallel or at right angles to the selvage.

The industry method described here is used to cut ripple-free bias for expensive designer fashions and in haute couture.

TOOLS & SUPPLIES

♦ Isosceles right triangle or No. 10 envelope

♦ See-through ruler

♦ Chalk wheel

MARK THE BIAS

1. With the right side up, spread and smooth the fabric so that the crossgrain is perpendicular to the lengthwise grain, which runs parallel to the selvage.
2. Locate the lengthwise grain. Mark it using a gridded see-through ruler and a chalk wheel. If the fabric has a selvage, mark the grainline ½ to 1 inch from it.
3. Use an isosceles right triangle (a triangle with one 90-degree and two 45-degree angles) to find the true bias. If you don't have a triangle, you can use a No. 10 envelope to make a bias template. Fold the envelope so that one short edge is even with one long edge.
4. Align one short edge of the right triangle or the long edge of the envelope with the chalk-marked grain. Then mark the bias along the long edge of the triangle or along the diagonal fold in the envelope, as shown in **Bias Diagram 1.**

5. To check your work, fold the fabric on the chalked bias line. Grasp the fold in your hands and pull it slightly, as shown in **Bias Diagram 2.** If the fabric twists, the line is not on the true bias.

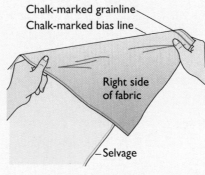

Chalk-marked grainline
Chalk-marked bias line
Right side of fabric
Selvage

Bias Diagram 2

CUT THE BIAS STRIPS

1. Using a see-through ruler and a chalk wheel, extend the true-bias chalked line, as shown in **Bias Diagram 3.**

2. Then use the see-through ruler to measure a line parallel to the chalked line at the desired width. Chalk-mark the new line. Continue marking as many strips as needed and square off the ends, as shown in **Bias Diagram 3.**
3. Chalk-mark the lengthwise grain on the ends of each rectangle.
4. Cut the strips on the marked lines.

JOIN THE BIAS STRIPS

1. With right sides together, align the short end of one strip with the long edge of another, matching the marked grainlines.
2. Set your sewing machine for a stitch length of 20 spi (1.0 mm).
3. As shown in **Bias Diagram 4,** stitch on the lengthwise grain, beginning at the lower right and stitching to the upper left. If the fabric has a horizontal pattern, arrange and join the strips on the crossgrain, stitching from the lower left to the upper right.
4. Press the seams open and trim the seam allowances.

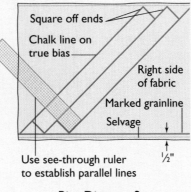

Stitch with very short stitch length
Wrong side of bias strip
Right side of bias strip

Bias Diagram 4

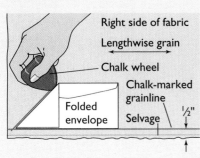

Right side of fabric
Lengthwise grain
Chalk wheel
Chalk-marked grainline
Folded envelope
Selvage
½"

Bias Diagram 1

Square off ends
Chalk line on true bias
Right side of fabric
Marked grainline
Selvage
Use see-through ruler to establish parallel lines
½"

Bias Diagram 3

■ SEWING SECRET: When machine basting, adjust the stitch length and tension so the basting will be easy to remove. Loosen the upper tension slightly and set the stitch length at 6 to 8 spi (4.5 to 3.5 mm). To remove the basting, clip the needle thread every 8 to 10 inches and pull out the bobbin and needle threads.

3. Trim the seam allowance to ¼ inch. I use my unthreaded serger to trim the edge evenly so that the seam allowances will be an even width and I can use the cut edge as a stitching guide if I have to rebaste.

■ SEWING SECRET: To trim with a serger, measure and chalk-mark the seam width in the seam allowance after the seam is stitched. Remove all of the threads from your serger or overlock machine. Place the seam under the serger foot so that the chalk-marks are aligned with the knife. Check the relationship of the chalk line to the serger foot to establish a sight line. Trim away the excess seam.

4. With right sides up, fold the strap over the seam allowance, as shown in **Diagram 2,** and press lightly. If the seam is shaped, steam and press the bias strap until it is smooth. If the bias cannot be pressed smooth, remove the strap and rebaste it.

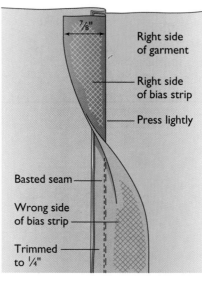

Right side of garment

Right side of bias strip

Press lightly

Basted seam

Wrong side of bias strip

Trimmed to ¼"

7⁄8"

Diagram 2

5. Stitch the seam permanently on the machine-basted line. Remove the basting stitches and press the seam.

6. Check the strap width. If it is uneven, measure and chalk-mark the finished strap width—½ inch—an even distance from the seamline. Fold under the raw edge of the bias strap on the marked line and hand baste it flat against the garment, as shown in **Diagram 3.** Following the instructions in "How to Edgestitch," below, edgestitch the strap in place.

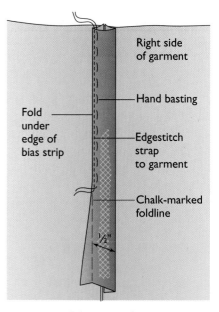

Right side of garment

Hand basting

Edgestitch strap to garment

Fold under edge of bias strip

Chalk-marked foldline

½"

Diagram 3

How to *Edgestitch*

It's easy to edgestitch evenly and close to a folded or garment edge.
1. Change your machine presser foot to a wide straight-stitch or edgestitch foot.
2. Align the folded edge or seamline with the inside edge of the foot, and set your stitch length at 12 spi (2.0 mm).
3. Stitch ¹⁄₁₆ inch from the folded edge or seamline, as shown.

■ SEWING SECRET: *If you don't have an edgestitch foot, use a zigzag foot and reset the needle so it is on the extreme right-hand side.*

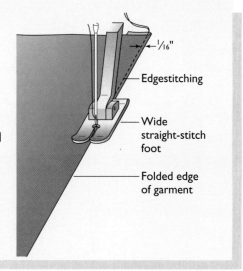

¹⁄₁₆"

Edgestitching

Wide straight-stitch foot

Folded edge of garment

Raised French Seam

Workers for Freedom

Workers for Freedom is a London-based fashion house that focuses on better day and evening-wear for "relaxed dressing, nothing formal," according to owner/designer Richard Nott. Unfortunately, this classic, understated line is sold in few American cities. When I visited this design house, I asked Mr. Nott why it was named Workers for Freedom. He explained that he and his partner had been working for other companies when they decided to start up their own, so they named the new house for themselves, since they were now "working for their freedom."

This easy-to-sew raised French seam adds an eye-catching design line to a simple silk shell.

This innovative version of the traditional French seam came from Workers for Freedom, which has used it in several of its designs. The style I liked best was a wear-anywhere silk shell with a shallow V-neck.

The edges of the neck and sleeves on the shell were first finished with a narrow bias facing on the right side of the garment. The raised French seams were then stitched at the center front, center back, and shoulder seams. You'll find this seam dresses up an ordinary shell and is very comfortable to wear.

Tools & Supplies

♦ Teflon iron shoe

Select and Prepare the Pattern

1. You can add raised French seams to almost any simple blouse pattern with a cap sleeve. However, a shallow V-neck works particularly well because the angular seam allowances are easily hidden. If your pattern doesn't have a V-neck, see "Basic V-Neck" on page 225 for instructions.

2. If your pattern doesn't have seams at the garment centers, see the instructions for "Adding a Seam" on page 201.

Finish the Neckline and Armscyes

1. Follow the instructions for "Bias Facing as a Trim" on page 25 to finish the neckline with narrow bias facing.

2. Repeat step 1 to finish the armscyes of the shell with the same bias facing.

Stitch the Seam

1. Place the blouse front sections with right sides together and raw edges even. Stitch the seam a scant ¼ inch from the edges, as shown in **Diagram 1**. All seams are ⅝ inch wide, and all stitching is 12 spi (2.0 mm).

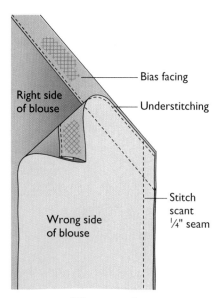

Diagram 1

■ SEWING SECRET: If there is no ⅝-inch guideline marked on

your machine base, use masking tape to mark one.

2. Press the seam flat as sewn.

3. Trim any whiskers from the raw edges of the seam. Then, with the wrong side up, press the seam to one side.

4. Refold the garment sections so that the wrong sides are together, and work the seam between your thumb and forefinger to position the seamline at the fold. Clip any curves as needed so the seam will lie flat. Press the seamline on the wrong side with the point of the iron. (This method can be used to press any French seam.)

5. Hand baste the seam as needed. Referring to **Diagram 2**, stitch a ⅜-inch-wide seam.

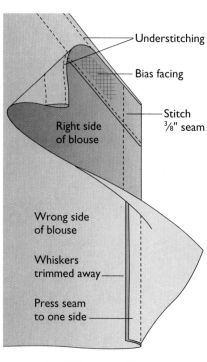

Diagram 2

6. Repeat steps 1 through 5 to stitch the center back seam and the shoulder seams.

Press the Seams and Finish the Blouse

1. Carefully press the raised French seams flat at the center front, the center back, and the shoulders.

■ SEWING SECRET: To prevent press marks from appearing on the right side of your garment, place the Teflon shoe on the sole of your iron. The Teflon shoe is designed to distribute the heat evenly across the sole of the iron.

2. Press the shoulder and side seams toward the back.

■ SEWING SECRET: It may be necessary to support the garment during pressing. This will allow you to mold and shape it easily. For support, use a tailor's ham, seam roll, sleeve board, or pressing mit.

3. Press the center front seam toward the left and the center back seam toward the right.

4. To finish the blouse, stitch the side seams and then handstitch the hem.

■ SEWING SECRET: When hand-stitching hems, avoid catching the thread on the pins by positioning the pins on the outside of the garment.

This linen bodice features a casual yet captivating asymmetrical color-blocked design created with Beau David's raised overlock seam.

Raised Overlock Seam

The raised overlock seam is frequently used on the casual fashions created by designers Andrea Jovine and Sonia Rykiel. However, in one of the most exciting raised overlock designs I've seen, Beau David used raised overlock stitching to accent the seamlines on the cropped bodice of a crisp linen dress.

The asymmetrical Beau David design featured decorative patchwork pieced from four different colors of fabric. All of the seamlines were cut on the lengthwise grain and serged with ordinary white thread.

Tools & Supplies

♦ Pattern paper
♦ White or contrasting color serger thread
♦ Serger
♦ Seam sealant

Select and Prepare the Pattern

1. Select a pattern with a short set-in sleeve and a square neckline.

2. Referring to "How to Make a Full Pattern" on page 10, use the right front pattern to make a full front pattern from pattern paper.

3. Review "Adding a Seam" on page 201 since you will have to add seam allowances to each section of the full pattern. All seam allowances are ⅝ inch wide.

4. To draw seam 1 on the true bias, see "How to Cut and Join Bias Strips" on page 5 for instructions on establishing the bias template. Draw seams 2 and 3 perpendicular to seam 1. Label the sections A, B, C, and D, as shown in **Diagram 1** on page 10. Draw the new grainlines parallel to seam 1 and, since this is an asymmetrical design,

How to *Make a Full Pattern*

When making an asymmetrical design, you need a full pattern instead of just the right half supplied by commercial pattern manufacturers.

TOOLS & SUPPLIES
♦ Stiletto tracing wheel

1. Cut a piece of pattern paper twice the width of the pattern section you plan to expand. I prefer to use paper on a roll because it is easy to store. Although you would ideally like to use pattern paper, I've used a variety of materials ranging from physician's examining paper to cheap Christmas paper to wax and freezer papers.

2. Fold the paper in half and place it on a cardboard cutting board, your dining room table pads, a large piece of cork or Celotex, or any pliable surface.

3. Place the original pattern piece on the pattern paper. Align the marked foldline on the pattern piece with the folded edge of the paper. Secure the pattern piece with pushpins stabbed through all the paper layers and the pliable cutting surface.

4. Use a stiletto tracing wheel to trace the cutting lines of the original pattern piece. Place the fingertips of one hand close to the line you plan to trace and press firmly to hold the pattern flat while you trace it. To transfer the matching points or notches, mark a line through both points of the notch with the tracing wheel.

5. Cut out the full pattern on the traced line and mark the center front.

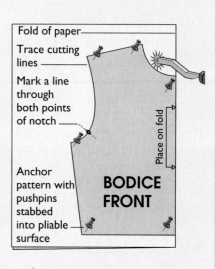

Fold of paper

Trace cutting lines

Mark a line through both points of notch

Anchor pattern with pushpins stabbed into pliable surface

Place on fold

BODICE FRONT

mark each pattern section "RSUP" to indicate that it is to be cut with the pattern and fabric right side up.

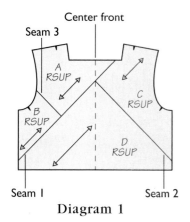

Center front
Seam 3
A RSUP
C RSUP
B RSUP
D RSUP
Seam I
Seam 2

Diagram 1

5. Trace each pattern section onto pattern paper, and add seam allowances.

Stitch the Seams

1. With wrong sides together and raw edges even, stitch the two short seams (2 and 3) on your conventional machine using matching threads and a straight stitch of 12 spi (2.0 mm). Press.

2. Thread your serger with the white or contrasting color thread for a balanced stitch using only the left-hand needle thread. Make a sample seam and adjust the tensions and stitch length until the stitch is attractive on both sides.

■ SEWING SECRET: Experiment with a variety of decorative threads when planning raised overlock seams. Threads such as polyester or rayon topstitching thread, pearl or crochet cotton, machine embroidery cotton, metallic and rayon threads, texturized nylon, fine knitting yarns, and ribbon will all produce interesting and different effects.

3. Stitch the seams again on the serger with the left-hand needle on the seamline, trimming away the excess seam allowances as you stitch, as shown in **Diagram 2.**

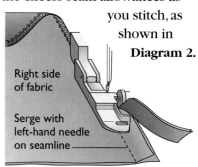

Right side of fabric

Serge with left-hand needle on seamline

Diagram 2

Tips for Decorative Overlocking

These tips will help you serge successfully when designing and stitching garments with raised overlock seams.

READY

♦ Decorative overlocked seams are designed to be ornamental and should bear little or no stress. Therefore, when adding decorative seams, place them where they will not be stressed, or use them to accent a loose-fitting design.

♦ Locate any new decorative seams on the lengthwise grain or crossgrain when possible.

♦ Never waste your time sewing with cheap or old, dry thread on either your conventional machine or your serger. This is especially important during decorative serging.

♦ Keep a record detailing the threads you use on specific fabrics (including the serger tension settings, stitch lengths, and the number of fabric layers) for future use.

♦ Clean and oil your serger before you begin a project. I use an old hair dryer to blow out the lint.

♦ Clean the cutting blade with rubbing alcohol, then apply a little sewing machine oil. Use a cotton swab to avoid cutting your fingers.

SET

♦ Insert a new needle before beginning decorative serging.

♦ Before serging, run the unthreaded serger at a slow speed and watch the hand wheel revolve. To avoid knots, never turn the hand wheel in the opposite direction.

♦ Avoid pin-basting with the pins placed perpendicular to the seamline.

♦ When possible, try to use three or four identical cones of thread to avoid differences in the way the thread unreels and to create smooth stitches.

♦ When you must serge with thread on spools instead of cones, place the spool on the spindle with the notch on the bottom.

♦ Thread the loopers first, then the needle.

♦ Always thread the needle last, even if you have to unthread it first. If a looper thread breaks when you are stitching, remove the needle thread, rethread the looper, and then rethread the needle.

♦ Avoid using needle threaders with small wire loops on the end because the wire can damage the needle eye and cause the thread to fray.

♦ Check the amount of thread on the needle and looper cones so you won't run out in the middle of a seam.

♦ Any change in the fabric type, number of layers, thread, stitch length, or stitch width can affect the tension.

♦ Before stitching your garment, adjust your tensions until the serged seam is attractive on both sides.

♦ Experiment with your serger using scraps of the fabric you will be sewing with and exactly the number of layers you plan to stitch. Always make a sample before serging decoratively on the garment.

SEW

♦ Always keep your fingers away from the serger knife and needles.

♦ Stitch slowly and at an even speed to avoid breaking the threads.

♦ Stitch with the side of the fabric that will be most visible on top.

♦ When stitching paired seams on the front of a garment, stitch one seam in one direction and the other seam in the opposite direction.

♦ Stitch with the grain, when possible.

♦ If the seam will be stressed, straight-stitch it first.

♦ If you run out of or break the thread in the middle of a seam, rip out the seam and start again.

♦ When you have to rip out serger stitches, identify the needle thread and remove it. The looper threads will then fall off.

♦ Practice, practice, practice!

---

4. Press the seams down. Generally horizontal and diagonal seams are pressed down, shoulder and side seams are pressed toward the back, and center front seams are pressed toward the left.

5. With wrong sides together and the raw edges even, stitch the long seam on the conventional machine using matching threads and a straight stitch. Press.

6. Stitch the seam again on the serger with the left-hand needle on the seamline, trimming away excess seam allowances as you stitch.

7. Secure the ends of the two short seams with a dab of liquid seam sealant.

8. Press all the seams down.

9. Stitch the remaining seams, and face or hem the edges to finish the garment.

Jeanne Marc used this stand-up bound seam to draw the eye to the hem edge of a colorful pair of full pants.

DESIGNER DETAIL

Jeanne Marc

Known for its timeless, seasonless fashions, Jeanne Marc's specialty is feminine designs in beautiful colors and coordinated prints. Masters of sophisticated embellishments, the husband-and-wife team of Marc Grant and Jeanne Allen frequently use ordinary construction details such as seams, edge finishes, and zipper plackets to transform simple silhouettes into eye-catching styles.

Stand-Up Bound Seam

Like the strap seam, the stand-up bound seam is frequently used by Jeanne Marc as decorative trim. They are equally attractive on the inside and outside of a garment. These seams are well suited for unlined and reversible garments, and they can withstand frequent laundering.

Bound seams are usually straight or slightly curved. The bindings are cut on the bias because the bias cut is more flexible and is thus easier to shape and apply. However, the bindings can also be made of ribbon or fold-over braids.

Most bindings are finished at ½ inch wide, but they can be as narrow as ⅜ inch or as wide as 1 inch. In the following instructions, the finished binding is ½ inch wide

and is applied to the garment with two rows of machine stitching.

Stand-up bound seams can be pressed in any direction, up or down, toward or away from the garment centers, depending on the garment design. Paired seams should be pressed similarly so the design will be symmetrical. Since one side of the binding may be a little neater than the other, decide how the seams will be pressed before you stitch the binding so that the last row of stitching will be the one most visible after pressing.

Tools & Supplies

♦ Edgestitch foot or wide straight-stitch foot (optional)

Cut the Garment and Bias

1. Cut bias strips four times the finished width of the binding. These instructions are for finished bindings ½ inch wide, so you will need to cut the bias strips 2 inches wide. For instructions on making bias strips, see "How to Cut and Join Bias Strips" on page 5.

■ SEWING SECRET: Through the years, designers Jeanne Allen and Marc Grant have shared many of their secrets for working with bias bindings. Here are several that I have found particularly helpful.

- Dip the fabric in liquid starch and allow it to drip dry before cutting the strips. When that isn't possible, use spray starch when pressing the bias strips.

- Examine the pattern shapes and replace corners and tight curves with more gentle, shallow curves.

- Always make a sample. Experiment with fabric scraps to determine the finished binding width and to be sure the bias strips are wide enough to produce the effect you want. You'll often need more fabric than you might expect to bind the fabric thicknesses.

- If necessary, baste the bindings to prevent rippling when you stitch.

2. Join the bias strips as needed to make enough binding for all the seams.

3. Press the bias strip, stretching it slightly.

4. Measure the width of the bias strip, and trim it to 1¾ inches.

Stitch the Seam

1. All seams are ⅝ inch wide, and all stitching is 12 spi (2.0 mm) unless otherwise indicated.

2. With wrong sides of the garment together, stitch a ⅝-inch seam. Press the seamline and trim the seam allowance evenly to ¼ inch.

3. Place the seam on top of the bias strip with the right side of the garment against the right side of the bias strip. Align the raw edges, and pin-baste the

layers together. Stitch again on the seamline, as shown in **Diagram 1.**

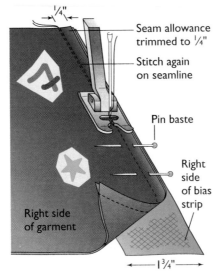

Diagram 1

■ SEWING SECRET: When binding outward curves, ease the bias to the garment section. When binding inward curves, stretch the bias slightly.

4. With the garment right side up, fold the bias strip over the seam, and press the seamline lightly, as shown in **Diagram 2.**

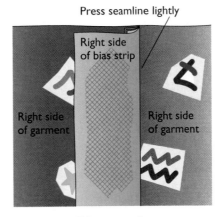

Diagram 2

5. Turn under the raw edge of the bias strip ⅜ inch. With wrong sides of the garment together,

wrap the bias strip around the seam, aligning the folded edge of the strip with the seamline, as shown in **Diagram 3.** Hand baste the folded edge in place so it won't shift position when you machine stitch. Check the bias strip width as you baste it to be sure it is an even ½ inch, and adjust it as needed.

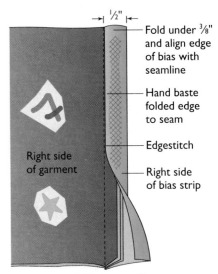

Diagram 3

6. Following the instructions in "How to Edgestitch" on page 6, edgestitch the binding to secure it permanently, as shown in **Diagram 4.**

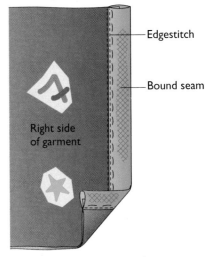

Diagram 4

7. Press the seam flat. Then press vertical seams on the front and back toward the sides.

◼ SEWING SECRET: If you decide you would prefer a flat strap seam instead of the stand-up bound seam, simply press the bound seam to one side and edgestitch it flat against the garment following the instructions in "How to Edgestitch" on page 6.

8. Examine the finished seam to make sure the binding is not puckered. If it is, carefully re-move the edgestitching and restitch.

◼ SEWING SECRET: Generally the side of the bias strip that was on top when the strip was edgestitched is a little neater. When possible, stitch the bound seams so this side will be more visible.

9. Press the shoulder and side seams toward the back, and press the horizontal seams up or down, depending on the design.

◼ SEWING SECRET: To avoid scorching the right side of your garment, always use a press cloth or a Teflon iron shoe.

10. Finish the garment.

Tips for Basting

I probably dislike basting as much as you do. But since I hate ripping even more, I use a variety of basting techniques to avoid having to rip out stitches.

♦ When I'm stitching something that will show on the right side of the gar-ment, I like to baste by hand because it is the most dependable method. Sometimes I double-baste for extra security, filling the spaces of the first basting with the stitches of the second basting.

♦ Pin-basting is quick and easy, and it works well for many applications. When pinning, I try to place pins so I won't stitch over them. When that isn't possible, I place the heads to the right or toward me so they'll be easy to remove as I sew. That way I won't be tempted to stitch over them.

♦ If you absolutely must stitch over pins, stitch very slowly or turn the hand wheel manually. Throw away any pins that have been stitched over to avoid causing an ugly pull in a future garment.

♦ Glue-basting with a washable glue is also one of my favorite basting methods. I buy glue sticks by the dozen and keep them in the refriger-ator until I'm ready to use them. When using glue, be sure it is dry before you begin stitching.

♦ Use doublestick basting tape, a narrow, double-faced tape, to position zippers and to match fabric patterns, or use it to temporarily repair a ripped seam or hem. Always position the tape so you will not stitch through it, and remove the basting tape after stitching the garment. If basting tape is left in the finished garment, it will ripple when the garment is laundered. Doublestick basting tape can be pur-chased in most fabric stores or through mail-order catalogs.

♦ Before basting a napped fabric with double-faced tape, test the tape on a scrap of fabric to be sure it won't pull off the nap when it is removed. With napped fabrics, always remove double-faced tape by pulling it down in the direction of the nap.

♦ Double-faced tape also can be used to baste suede and synthetic suede.

♦ To join large sections of fabric quickly, lengthen the stitch on your machine. Stitch five or six stitches, skip five or six inches, and repeat until you finish basting. Clip the threads be-tween the stitched sections.

♦ Use pins with large heads to pin-baste loosely woven or knitted fabrics.

♦ Use metal hair clips, pins with large heads, or hand basting to baste lace or open-weave fabrics.

♦ Always use metal hair clips, paper clips, or clothes pins to baste leather and vinyl.

♦ To baste faux fur, use round tooth-picks or pins with large heads.

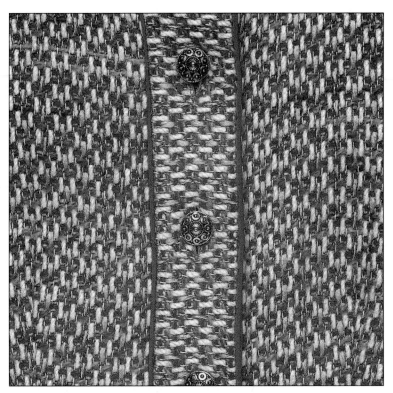

A sophisticated piped seam can turn an ordinary wool jacket into a smashing creation.

Designer Detail

Gregory Pal

Typical of many small fashion houses, Gregory Pal specializes in made-to-measure designs. At the beginning of each fashion season, the designer creates a small collection in model sizes (size 8 or 10) which is taken to specialty shops and stores like Saks Fifth Avenue. At these stores, the collection is presented at trunk shows where potential clients can place orders. The clients are measured and the garments are made by adjusting the firm's slopers for those measurements—very much like a home sewer does when using a commercial pattern.

Piped Seam

Used by designers such as Perry Ellis, Bill Blass, Jeanne Marc, Chanel, and Ungaro, piped seams accentuate the lines of a design. Piping can be made from a variety of materials including ribbon, lace, and fringe, but bias strips with or without cording are used most frequently.

Using the following technique, you can create an elegant garment with little effort.

Tools & Supplies

♦ Zipper foot

Make the Piping

1. Following the instructions in "How to Cut and Join Bias Strips" on page 5, cut and join 2¼-inch-wide bias strips to equal the length of the seams you plan to pipe.

2. Make the piping following the instructions in "How to Make Piping" on page 16. All seams are ⅝ inch wide and all stitching is 12 spi (2.0 mm).

■ SEWING SECRET: To determine the amount of piping you will need, pin seam binding to the pattern or garment pieces.

Then measure the amount of seam binding that you used. Add 2 to 3 feet to the measured amount to allow for finishing ends, curves, and corners on the seamlines.

Sew the Seam

1. With one garment section right side up, place the piping on top of the garment. Align the stitched line on the piping with the seamline on top of the garment and pin the raw edges together. Place the zipper foot on your machine and stitch on top

How to *Make Piping*

Piping is one of the easiest trims to make. It is frequently used as a contrast trim at seams and edges. It can be large or small, corded or flat. It is particularly attractive on plaids and stripes and can be used effectively on seamlines that can't be matched and on fabrics that are difficult to match precisely.

These instructions are for corded piping. The finished piping is $\frac{3}{16}$ inch wide and the seam allowance is $\frac{5}{8}$ inch wide. Both the seam width and piping can be wider or narrower. To make piping a different width, cut your bias strips three times the desired finished width plus two seam allowances.

TOOLS & SUPPLIES
- Cording or postal twine
- Zipper foot
- Serger (unthreaded)

1. Select a small-size cording and preshrink it following the instructions in the Sewing Secret under step 3 in "Cutting the Garment and Bias Strips" on page 4. I frequently use postal twine, which is a little softer than most cording.
2. Following the instructions in "How to Cut and Join Bias Strips" on page 5, cut a bias strip the desired width and length.
3. With the wrong side up, place the cord in the middle of the bias strip and wrap the bias strip around the cord. Place a zipper foot on your

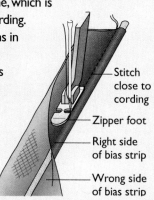

Stitch close to cording

Zipper foot

Right side of bias strip

Wrong side of bias strip

Piping Diagram 1

machine and stitch close to the cording at 12 spi (2.0 mm), as shown in **Piping Diagram 1**.
4. Measure and mark the $\frac{5}{8}$-inch seam allowance on the bias strip.
5. Using the unthreaded serger, trim the bias strip on the marked line, as shown in **Piping Diagram 2**.

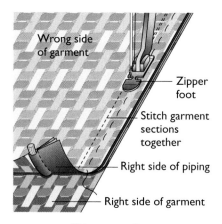

Piping trimmed evenly by unthreaded serger

Trim on marked line

$\frac{5}{8}$"

Piping Diagram 2

■ **SEWING SECRET:** *Recycle pretty bias-cut neckties to make attractive piping.*

---

of the stitched line on the piping, as shown in **Diagram 1**.

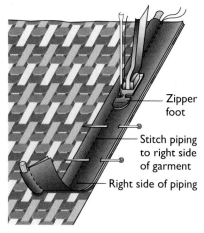

Zipper foot

Stitch piping to right side of garment

Right side of piping

Diagram 1

2. Press and examine the stitched line. If the piping is too tight or too loose or if the seam is puckered, rip out the piping and restitch it.

3. With right sides together, place the remaining garment section over the piping. Align the edges, match the notches, pin, and baste as needed. Turn the sections over and stitch permanently on the seamline, as shown in **Diagram 2**.

■ SEWING SECRET: Rub the stitched line with pure soap or chalk to make it easier to see.

Wrong side of garment

Zipper foot

Stitch garment sections together

Right side of piping

Right side of garment

Diagram 2

4. Press the seamline and finish the garment.

How to *Stitch Piping* on *Curves*

It's easy to stitch piping on curves if you remember to follow a few general rules.

♦ When sewing piping to edges with inward curves, such as necklines and armscyes, clip the seam allowances on the piping and hold the piping taut so you can shape it smoothly.

♦ When sewing piping to edges with outward curves, such as collars, pockets, and flaps, ease the piping to the seamline so the finished edge won't curl under.

♦ When piping square necklines, hold the piping taut at the corner.

♦ When piping cuffs and collars, clip the seam allowances on the piping and ease the piping at all of the corners.

How to *Use Fringe* as *Piping*

By substituting fringe for piping, you can change the look of your garment—dramatically.

Chanel, Bill Blass, and Oscar de la Renta all use fringe as an attractive novelty piping. I've seen many variations on this detail, with finished fringes ranging in width from ½ to 1 inch wide. Generally, fringes are more attractive when cut on the lengthwise grain with the crossgrain fibers forming the fringe, but they can also be cut on the crossgrain. They can be made of a single layer or doubled for a fuller fringe.

These instructions are for single fringe that is 1 inch wide when finished.

TOOLS & SUPPLIES
♦ Serger (unthreaded)

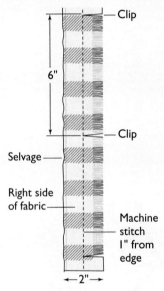

Fringe Diagram 1

1. Cut a strip of fabric 2 inches wide and as long as your seam. You can use the selvage as one long edge of the fabric strip to save time. One advantage of this is that you will be able to grip the selvage with one hand as you use the other to pull threads and create the fringe without distorting the fabric.

2. Machine stitch 1 inch from the long raw edge at 12 spi (2.0 mm).

3. To start the fringe, clip the fabric strip perpendicular to the stitched line every 6 to 8 inches, being careful not to clip through the line of stitching, as shown in **Fringe Diagram 1**. Do not clip the selvage side if you have used it as one long side of your strip. Gently pull out the clipped yarns to make the fringe.

4. Measure and mark the ⅝-inch seam allowance on the fringe strip. Then use the unthreaded serger to trim the seam on the marked line, as shown in **Fringe Diagram 2**.

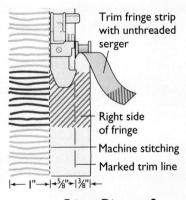

Fringe Diagram 2

The delicate but sturdy baby seam is perfect for crisp, transparent fabrics.

Baby Seam

I first saw the baby seam used on a multilayered polyester chiffon dress by California designer Bill Travilla. It is, as the name implies, a very tiny seam that generally measures about ⅛ inch wide.

The baby seam is suitable for crisp, transparent fabrics and is made using several rows of machine stitching similar to the chiffon hem that is described on page 40.

Since this method encloses all of the raw edges of the fabric, the seam is sturdy, and it wears well. However, the baby seam may be too stiff to drape attractively on soft fabrics, and it may be too bulky for heavier materials.

Tools & Supplies

♦ Edgestitch foot or wide straight-stitch foot (optional)

Cut Out the Garment

1. Cut out the garment with ⅝-inch seam allowances.

2. All stitching is 12 spi (2.0 mm).

Stitch the Seam

1. With right sides together, stitch the seam a scant ½ inch from the raw edges.

■ SEWING SECRET: To prevent the end of a seam from being pulled into the machine's needle hole, chain stitch from another garment section or a small scrap of fabric, as shown in **Diagram 1,** or begin stitching on a piece of tissue paper and then stitch onto the end of the seam.

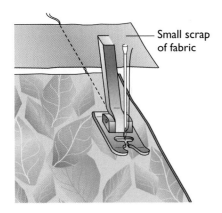

Diagram 1

2. Press the seam flat. Fold both layers on the stitched line and press again.

3. With the seam allowances toward the feed dogs, follow the instructions in "How to Edgestitch" on page 6 and edgestitch ⅟₁₆ inch from the folded edge, as shown in **Diagram 2.**

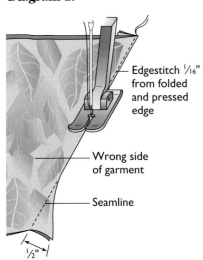

Diagram 2

4. Trim as close as possible to the edgestitching, following the instructions in "How to Trim Closely," below.

5. Fold the seam again to enclose the raw edges. Referring to **Diagram 3,** edgestitch again on top of the last row of stitching.

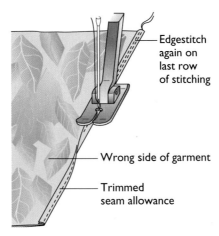

Diagram 3

6. Press the seam.

Bill Travilla

Known for his beautiful head-to-toe looks, Bill Travilla is the designer who created Loretta Young's gowns for her famous television show openers and Marilyn Monroe's most famous dress—the halter bodice with the accordion pleated skirt—for The Seven-Year Itch. *His ready-to-wear line focuses on feminine designs with style and drama to create an air of beauty and character.*

How to Trim Closely

With this "palms-up" technique you can trim close to any seam or edge. I prefer trimming with 5-inch trimmers, but you can also use larger shears.

Hold the seam in your left hand and the scissors in your right hand. Slip the lower blade under the raw edges. With both palms up and the scissors almost parallel to the garment seamline, trim close to the edgestitching.

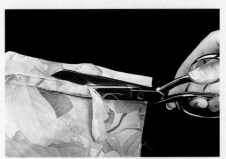

Remember to keep the scissors almost parallel to the garment when trimming closely.

Facings

Used by the world's top designers, decorative facings make dramatic fashion statements. Replace your everyday facings with one of these options for a spectacular, sophisticated style.

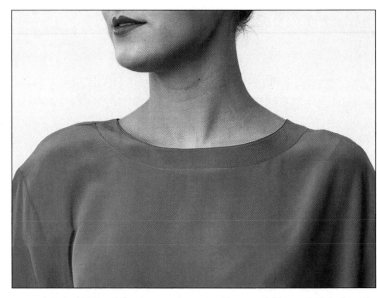

A topstitched facing enhances the neckline of this lovely silk blouse at the same time it secures the facing.

Topstitched Facing

This simple but smart topstitching detail is used by many of the world's great fashion houses. Liz Claiborne, Anne Klein, and Rodier have all used this detail in recent designs. Practical as well as decorative, the topstitching detail not only enhances the neckline but also secures the facing.

This facing is used on a variety of designs from everyday knit tops to elegant silk blouses, and it can be applied to an assortment of styles from traditional jewel necklines to cut-away scoop necklines.

Topstitching is often used to finish sleeve hems on casual garments. Generally the topstitching is placed ¾ inch to 1½ inches from the edge of the garment, but it can be as close as ⅛ inch or as

Liz Claiborne

Since the Liz Claiborne design house opened in 1976, it has consistently produced fashionable clothing lines. Liz Claiborne's specialty is translating new trends into easy-to-wear, moderately priced designs. A favorite of working women who have little time for shopping, the line's separates-based wardrobes have a casual, relaxed styling.

far as 2 inches from the edge.

These instructions are based on a Liz Claiborne cotton knit top with a cut-away neckline. The neckline and sleeve hems are top-stitched 1⅜ inches from the edge of the garment.

You can apply this technique to other neckline styles, to front and back openings, and to sleeve and blouse hems. I particularly like to use it on silk blouses with jewel necklines.

Tools & Supplies

♦ Tailor's chalk
♦ Edgestitch foot or wide straight-stitch foot
♦ Serger
♦ Fine-point marker

Select and Prepare the Pattern

1. Select a simple blouse pattern with cap or set-in sleeves.

2. If the pattern you have chosen

doesn't have a cut-away neckline, restyle it to add one. For details, see "Cut-Away Scoop Neckline" on page 229.

3. Add an opening if the neckline is small or if you don't want to pull the blouse over your head. For casual knits, I sometimes use a button/buttonhole closure or a zipper; when sewing suit blouses, I like the faced keyhole opening described on page 88.

Prepare the Neckline

1. Cut out the garment and facings. All seams are ⅝ inch wide and 12 spi (2.0 mm) unless otherwise indicated.

2. Finish the garment opening, if any.

3. With right sides together, stitch the shoulder seams on the blouse. Then stitch the shoulder seams on the neck facing.

■ SEWING SECRET: To save time and prevent thread knots from forming when stitching is

started on a piece of fabric, operators in apparel factories chain stitch from one garment section to the next, as shown in **Diagram 1.** If another garment section isn't available, they chain onto a small fabric scrap, as shown.

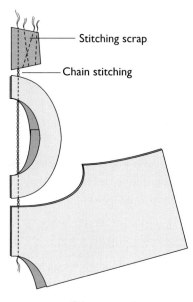

Stitching scrap

Chain stitching

Diagram 1

4. Finish the edges of the shoulder seams and press them open.

■ SEWING SECRET: To avoid unattractive pulls at the end of a seamline and to reduce bulk, trim away a triangle at each end of the seam allowance, as shown in **Diagram 2,** before crossing it with another seam.

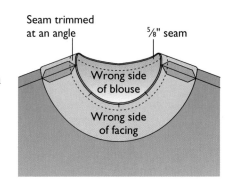

Seam trimmed at an angle

⅝" seam

Wrong side of blouse

Wrong side of facing

Diagram 2

Sew the Facing

1. With right sides together, place the neckline facing on top of the garment. Align the raw edges, seams, and notches, and pin the edges together. Stitch the seam, as shown in **Diagram 1** on page 21.

■ SEWING SECRET: When stitching curves, I shorten the stitch length to 15 to 18 spi (1.5 to 1.0 mm). Using a shorter stitch length not only produces a stronger seam but also makes it much easier to guide the fabric accurately under the needle.

2. Understitch the seam following the instructions in "How to Understitch," below.

3. Trim the seam allowances close to the understitching.

4. With the facing side up, press the neckline edge. Referring to **Diagram 3**, measure and chalk-mark a line on the facing 1½ inches from the neckline edge, which is ⅛ inch wider than the width of the finished topstitching.

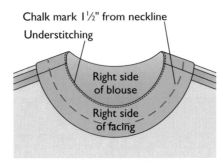

Chalk mark 1½" from neckline
Understitching
Right side of blouse
Right side of facing

Diagram 3

5. Serge the facing edge with a two- or three-thread stitch, placing your needle precisely on the chalk mark. If you trim too much, your topstitching won't catch the facing.

6. With wrong sides together, pin the facing in place. Place the pins with the heads toward the neckline so you can remove them easily as you stitch.

Topstitch the Neckline

1. Set the stitch length for 12 to 15 spi (2.0 to 1.5 mm).

2. With wrong sides together and the right side up, begin at one shoulder seam and edgestitch ⅟₁₆ inch from the edge of the neckline. Leave long thread tails at the beginning and end of your stitching. (If the blouse has an opening, begin stitching at the opening.)

3. Before you begin the second row of topstitching, use a fine-point marker to mark a point on the machine 1⅜ inches—the width of the topstitching—to the right of the needle, as shown in **Diagram 4.**

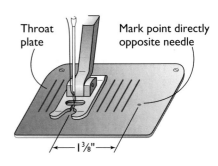

Throat plate
Mark point directly opposite needle
1⅜"

Diagram 4

4. With the garment right side up and using the marked point as a

How to *Understitch*

Understitching is a simple technique used to tame facings at garment edges. It prevents the seamline from showing on the outside of the garment and holds the seam allowances in the desired position. Follow these steps for trouble-free understitching.

1. Open the facing away from the garment, and place it on the sewing machine with right sides up. Fold both seam allowances toward the facing.

2. Place a wide straight-stitch foot on your sewing machine. Or, if you don't have a straight-stitch foot, move the needle so it is in the extreme left position.

3. Align the seamline with the inside edge of the foot, and stitch ⅟₁₆ inch from the seamline. When understitching, place your hands on either side of the presser foot and hold the layers taut, as shown. This will prevent a tuck from forming between the seamline and the edgestitching.

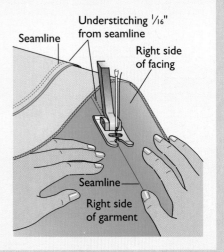

Seamline
Understitching ⅟₁₆" from seamline
Right side of facing
Seamline
Right side of garment

Tips for Topstitching

Through the years, I've examined many topstitched garments in all price ranges, including haute couture—the crème de la crème of the fashion industry, and I am regularly reminded and reassured that the topstitching from even the best designers isn't always straight. However, you will be able to improve your topstitching skills by following these pointers and by practicing.

Practice makes perfect when topstitching.

READY

♦ Begin with a clean, well-oiled machine and a needle that is new and appropriate for the fabric you are stitching.

♦ Check the amount of thread on the bobbin and the spool before starting to topstitch; replenish it if you think you will need to reload while sewing.

♦ When using polyester thread, fill the bobbin slowly—the heat of the bobbin tension discs causes the thread to heat up and stretch. Since the thread will relax after stitching, the stitching will be forever puckered.

♦ Experiment by topstitching on fabric scraps with different needle types and sizes, various threads, several machine feet, needle plates, and gauges before topstitching the garment. When you find the combination that gives you the most attractive and balanced stitching, write down the tools and thread used in your sewing notebook and keep it for future reference.

♦ Practice until you can stitch with confidence.

SET

♦ To prevent skipped stitches and thread breakage, use a needle lubricant on the thread. Apply several vertical rows of lubricant to the spool before filling the bobbin. Periodically add a drop of lubricant between the machine's tension discs and at the top of the needle. Always test the lubricant first to be sure it won't spot your fabric. Also, check your machine's

manual; some manufacturers recommend against using lubricant between the tension discs.

♦ When stitching difficult fabrics, use a needle lubricant on the needle, rub the fabric with a bar of Ivory soap, and pound thick seams with a cloth-covered hammer to soften the fibers.

♦ For straight, even topstitching, use a gauge. The presser foot is particularly handy. Use the inside of the straight-stitch foot to gauge $\frac{1}{16}$ inch and the outside of the foot to gauge $\frac{1}{4}$ inch. If you want a specific width for your topstitching, measure your presser foot before stitching.

♦ If your topstitching on tweeds and heavy fabrics looks crooked, try switching to a short, narrow zigzag stitch.

♦ Shorten the stitch length. Shorter stitches are less likely to look crooked when a stitch is out of line.

SEW

♦ Topstitch with the garment right side up.

♦ Stitch with the grain, except on fabrics with a nap or pile; then stitch with the nap.

♦ Always stitch slowly and at an even speed; if your machine has a speed regulator, be sure it is set at low speed.

♦ When stitching both sides of a seam or two corresponding seams, stitch both in the same direction.

♦ When stitching over uneven thicknesses of fabric parallel to seam-

lines, at garment edges, and around patch pockets, use a zipper foot. Align the edge of the zipper foot with the seam or the edge of the garment and "ride" the thicker layer with the foot as you stitch.

♦ When crossing thick seamlines, level the foot with a shim to prevent needle deflection and skipped stitches. As you approach the seam, insert the shim under the heel of the presser foot. As you stitch off the seam, place the shim under the toes of the foot. Although plastic shims are sold by sewing notions companies, you can make your own by simply folding a piece of cardboard to the thickness you need.

♦ If you want to emphasize the lines of topstitching, sew with two threads in the needle. If you don't have two thread spindles, fill two bobbins with the topstitching thread, and place them on the spindle. If the top bobbin feeds the thread too quickly, place a circle of felt between the bobbins.

♦ If you have only 5 or 6 inches more to topstitch and are about to run out of thread, tie the end of your thread to the thread on another spool and resume topstitching the garment. You should be able to finish topstitching the garment before the knot reaches the eye of the needle.

♦ If you run out of thread in the middle of a line of topstitching, resume stitching by inserting the machine needle precisely into the last hole stitched. Later, pull the thread ends to the underside, and knot the threads and hide them.

guide to stitch an even distance from the edge of the neckline, topstitch 1⅜ inches from the edge, as shown in **Diagram 5.** Leave long thread tails at the beginning and at the end of your stitching.

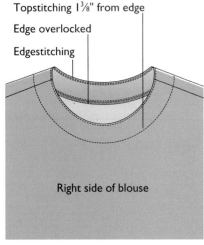

Topstitching 1⅜" from edge

Edge overlocked

Edgestitching

Right side of blouse

Diagram 5

■ SEWING SECRET: To accentuate topstitching, stitch two or three rows very close together. You can also change the look of your topstitching by using a contrasting color or different type of thread.

5. Pull the thread tails to the wrong side and give them a sharp tug.

6. Thread the ends into a needle and hide them between the fabric layers.

■ SEWING SECRET: When hiding thread ends at the end of a row of stitching, you can thread them quickly and easily into a self-threading needle, as shown in **Diagram 6.** Sometimes called a calyx-eyed, quick threading, or slotted needle, the

self-threading needle has an open end for easy threading.

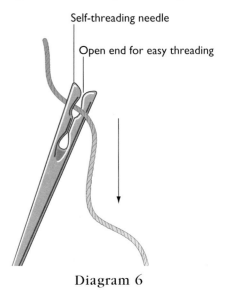

Self-threading needle

Open end for easy threading

Diagram 6

7. With the blouse wrong side up, press the neckline and finish the garment.

Bias facing can be used as an attractive and stylish trim on the outside of a lightweight silk shell.

*B*ias Facing as a Trim

Narrow bias facings are frequently used on very expensive blouses and casual tops by Yves Saint Laurent, Valentino, and Workers for Freedom. These attractive facings are used on lightweight fabrics at the neckline and sometimes on the edges of sleeves or on sleeveless armholes.

Bias facings are generally applied inconspicuously, like traditional facings, with the bias on the inside of the garment and one or two rows of topstitching on the outside. However, because they finish both the right and wrong sides of the garment neatly, bias facings can either be used on reversible garments or as a stylish trim on the outside of a garment.

These instructions are based on a silk shell from Workers for Freedom. In this exciting application, the bias facings are finished as a ½-inch-wide trim and are applied to the individual garment sections before the sections are joined with the raised French seams described on page 7. Since this approach reduces most of the shaping required for many necklines, it is easy to sew successfully.

Tools *&* Supplies

♦ Tailor's chalk
♦ Edgestitch foot or wide straight-stitch foot (optional)

Select and Prepare the Pattern

1. Select a simple blouse pattern with a shallow V-neck. If your pattern doesn't have a V-neck, follow the instructions in "Shallow V-Neck" on page 228 to restyle it.

2. Add seams at the garment centers using the instructions in "Adding Seams" on page 201.

3. Trim the neckline and sleeve seam allowances to ¼ inch.

4. All stitching is 12 spi (2.0 mm) unless otherwise indicated.

Make the Bias Facing

1. Cut six bias strips that are each 2 inches wide. Cut four long enough to bind the neckline on each garment section and two long enough to bind the bottom edges of the sleeves.

2. Fold the bias strips in half lengthwise with wrong sides together.

3. Press the folded edge, stretching the bias strips slightly. Remember that bias strips narrow slightly when you press and stretch them.

4. Measure and chalk-mark the facing width ⅞ inch from the fold on each strip. Then trim the strips on the marked line, as shown in **Diagram 1.**

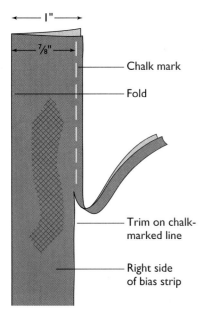

Diagram 1

(Labels: 1" · ⅞" · Chalk mark · Fold · Trim on chalk-marked line · Right side of bias strip)

Stitch the Facings

1. Cut out the garment.

2. With each blouse section wrong side up, place the bias facing on top, matching the neckline edge of the blouse to the raw edges of the facing. Pin the facing in place, easing the bias slightly so the folded edge will fit the neckline smoothly. Stitch the neckline of each facing ¼ inch from the edge, as shown in **Diagram 2.** Repeat this step to sew the remaining sleeve facings.

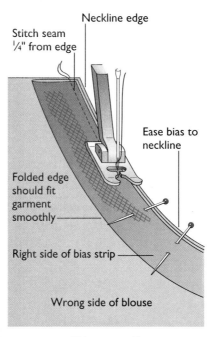

Diagram 2

(Labels: Stitch seam ¼" from edge · Neckline edge · Ease bias to neckline · Folded edge should fit garment smoothly · Right side of bias strip · Wrong side of blouse)

3. To understitch the seam, fold the seam allowances toward the blouse. With the blouse sections wrong side up, understitch through the blouse and the seam allowances. See "How to Understitch" on page 22.

4. Trim the seams close to the understitching.

Finish the Facings

1. Fold the facing to the right side, and press the neckline with the blouse wrong side up.

2. Pin or hand baste the facing in place on the right side, and edgestitch the folded edge of the facing to the garment, as shown in **Diagram 3.** (For details, see "How to Edgestitch" on page 6.)

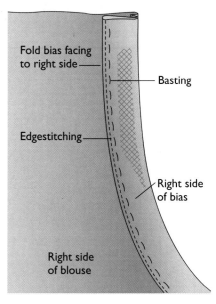

Diagram 3

(Labels: Fold bias facing to right side · Basting · Edgestitching · Right side of bias · Right side of blouse)

3. Press the edges.

Finish the Blouse

1. To join the garment centers and shoulder seams, see "Raised French Seam" on page 7.

■ SEWING SECRET: Always make a test seam to check the needle size, stitch length, thread size and color, tension, and pressure.

2. Use the seam of your choice to join the underarm seams.

3. Finish the blouse.

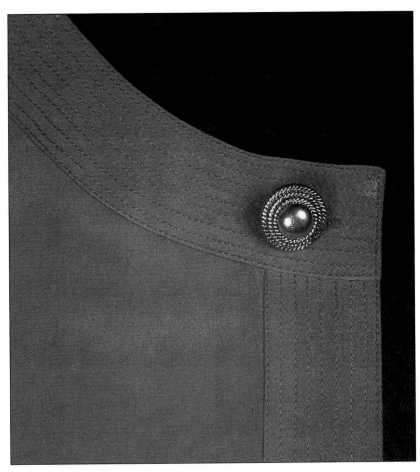

Exquisite topstitched facings like this can be found on the most expensive designer garments.

Facing as a Trim

Facings as a trim are a chic but easy finish sometimes used on very expensive designs from Chanel, Louis Feraud, Zandra Rhodes, Celine, and Bill Blass. Not only can they be used on any edge, from necklines to garment openings and hems, they can also be applied to a variety of fabrics, from chiffon and blouse-weight silks to linens, knits, and wools.

Facings can be made from an assortment of materials, such as self or contrasting fabric, leather, ribbon, or lace. They can be cut on any grain, but they are frequently cut on the same grain as the garment.

Because facings used as a trim finish both sides of the garment neatly, they are particularly attractive on scarves, reversible designs, and any edges that might be flipped back to expose the wrong side. I like them because they enclose all the raw edges, they

launder well, and you never have to worry about facings wrinkling or popping out inconveniently.

These instructions are based on a lovely silk blouse from a famous French fashion house. It is quilted at all edges with multiple rows of silk thread. The neckline facing is finished $1\frac{3}{16}$ inches wide, while the facing on the front overlap is finished $1\frac{1}{8}$ inches wide. The underlap is finished with an inconspicuous facing on the wrong side.

Instructions are included for making and sewing the facings to the blouse at the front opening, but I often eliminate this feature by using a plain button/buttonhole closure down the center front or a pattern with a neckline that is large enough to slip over the head.

Tools & Supplies

- Pattern paper
- Lightweight sew-in interfacing
- Edge guide or quilter's gauge (optional)

Prepare the Blouse Pattern

1. Select a blouse pattern with a round or jewel neckline.

2. Seams at the neckline and lower edge of the facing are ¼ inch. All other seams are ⅝ inch and all stitching is 12 spi (2.0 mm) unless otherwise indicated.

3. Trim the neckline seam allowances to ¼ inch on the pattern pieces for the front and back.

4. On the front pattern piece, draw a line parallel to and ⅝ inch away from the center front for the lap extensions. If you don't have enough space to draw this line, you may have to tape the front pattern to a piece of pattern paper. Trim the excess pattern paper. (See "Adding Buttons and Buttonholes" on page 235 for instructions.)

5. Trace the front pattern piece onto a piece of pattern paper. Mark the original pattern "Right Front" and the traced pattern "Left Front." Mark both "RSUP" to indicate that the pattern should be placed on the right side of the fabric. Draw the grainline parallel to the center front.

Make the Facing Patterns

1. On the left front pattern, draw a line parallel to the front edge and 1⅜ inches away from the

How to *Interface Facings*

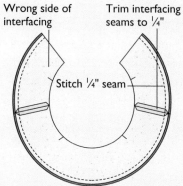

Wrong side of interfacing

Trim interfacing seams to ¼"

Stitch ¼" seam

Facing Diagram 1

Using this method you can stitch neat and tidy facings with very little effort and without having to turn under, finish, or pink any raw edges.

1. Use the garment facing patterns to cut one set of facings and one set of interfacings.

■ **SEWING SECRET:** *When a facing is used as a trim, I choose a sew-in interfacing rather than a fusible interfacing.*

2. With right sides together, join any seams first on the facing, then on the interfacing. Press the seams open.

3. On the interfacing, trim the seam allowances to ¼ inch.

4. With the interfacing on top, place the right sides of the facing and the interfacing together, matching any seams. Pin the unnotched edges of the interfacing to the facing. Stitch a seam ¼ inch from the unnotched edges, as shown in **Facing Diagram 1.**

5. Fold the seam allowances toward the interfacing and understitch on the right side. See "How to Understitch" on page 22 for details.

6. Trim the seam allowances as close as possible to the understitching.

7. Turn the facing right sides out, as shown in **Facing Diagram 2.** Press with the interfacing side up.

8. At the unfinished edge, pin and then baste the facing and interfacing together. Trim away the excess interfacing.

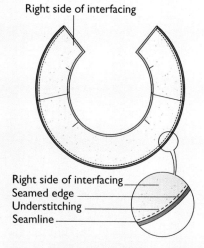

Right side of interfacing

Right side of interfacing
Seamed edge
Understitching
Seamline

Facing Diagram 2

⅝-inch extension for the underlap, or facing extension, as shown in **Diagram 1.**

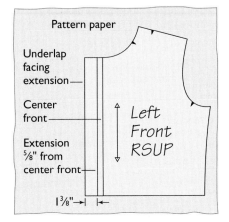

Diagram 1

2. Tape the center edge of the right front pattern to a piece of pattern paper and add a ¼-inch seam allowance to that edge, as shown in **Diagram 2.** Draw the overlap facing 1¾ inches wide, measuring from the front edge. Draw the neckline facing 1¹³⁄₁₆ inches wide. Trim the excess pattern paper.

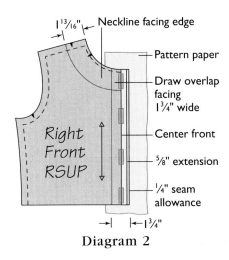

Diagram 2

3. Trace the overlap facing pattern, and draw the grainline parallel to the center front.

4. Trace the neckline facing pattern, and draw the grainline parallel to the center front.

5. To make the back neckline facing, draw the facing 1¹³⁄₁₆ inches wide on the back pattern, then trace it as you did for the front facing pattern.

6. Cut out all of the pattern pieces.

Cut Out the Blouse

1. Cut the blouse front and back pieces.

■ SEWING SECRET: If you get caught short and don't have enough fabric, don't cut off-grain. Try to fit the pattern pieces closer together or use a narrower hem allowance. You can also shorten the pattern length if the finished length measurement on the pattern envelope is longer than the measurement of a similar garment you already own.

2. Cut two front neckline facings and one back neckline facing from both the blouse fabric and a lightweight sew-in interfacing.

3. Cut one overlap facing in the same manner as in step 2.

Finish the Front Underlap

1. Fold the left front underlap to the wrong side 1⅜ inches from the raw edge and press. Fold under the raw edge ¼ inch, press, and pin it in place.

2. Edgestitch the folded edge to the blouse at 12 spi (2.0 mm), as shown in **Diagram 3.**

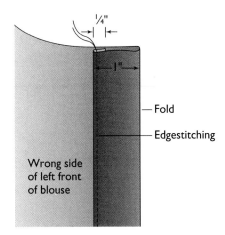

Diagram 3

Finish the Front Overlap

1. To interface the overlap facing, see "How to Interface Facings" on the opposite page.

2. To quilt the interfaced facing, begin at the seamed edge with the right side up and set your machine for 12 spi (2.0 mm). Stitch the first row ³⁄₁₆ inch from the edge. Stitch the next seven rows, spacing them ⅛ inch apart, as shown in **Diagram 4.** If your fabric extends beyond the throat plate on your machine, attach an edge guide or quilting gauge as an aid for stitching straight, even rows.

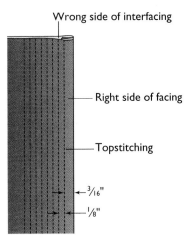

Diagram 4

■ SEWING SECRET: When top-stitching, I prefer to use two-ply, size 50 DMC embroidery thread or Mettler's 2-ply Egyptian fine embroidery thread in size 60. Both of these threads are strong and have a nice sheen.

3. With the interfacing side up, press the interfaced facing and trim away the excess interfacing at the edges. Examine the top-stitching; the last row of top-stitching should be parallel to the raw edges.

4. With the garment wrong side up, place the facing on top with the interfaced side up. Match the raw edges, and baste the layers together just inside the seam-line. Turn the facing right side out to make sure the seamline is an even distance from the last row of topstitching. Then set your stitch length at 12 spi (2.0 mm) and stitch a ¼ inch seam at the front edge, as shown in **Diagram 5.**

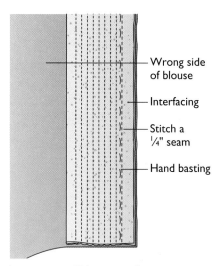

----Wrong side of blouse

----Interfacing

----Stitch a ¼" seam

----Hand basting

Diagram 5

5. Fold the facing to the right side. Press the edge with the blouse wrong side up.

6. Turn the blouse right side up, set your stitch length at 12 spi, (2.0 mm) and edgestitch the overlap edge.

7. Hand baste the free edge of the facing to the garment and edgestitch at 12 spi (2.0 mm), as shown in **Diagram 6.**

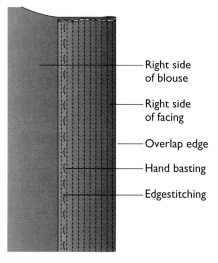

----Right side of blouse

----Right side of facing

----Overlap edge

----Hand basting

----Edgestitching

Diagram 6

8. Remove the basting. With the blouse wrong side up, press the facing area.

Prepare the Necklines on the Blouse and Facing

1. With right sides together, stitch the shoulder seams on the blouse, neckline facings, and interfacings.

2. On the blouse, serge and trim the shoulder seams to ⅜ inch. Press the seam allowances to-ward the front.

■ SEWING SECRET: To avoid an overpressed look, do not press too long with too much pressure or heat.

3. Press the seams open on the facing and interfacing. Trim the seam allowances on the interfacing to ¼ inch.

Interface the Neckline Facing

1. To interface the neckline facing, see "How to Interface Facings" on page 28.

2. To finish the ends of the facing at the opening, turn the wrong side out. Using your fingertips, gently work the seam toward the interfacing side and stitch a ¼-inch seam at each end at 12 spi (2.0 mm), as shown in **Diagram 7A**, and turn the facing right side out, as shown in **7B.**

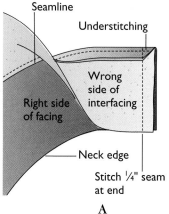

Seamline

Understitching

Wrong side of interfacing

Right side of facing

Neck edge

Stitch ¼" seam at end

A

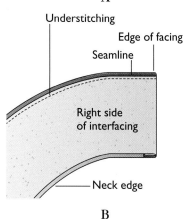

Understitching

Edge of facing

Seamline

Right side of interfacing

Neck edge

B

Diagram 7

3. Quilt the neck facing as described in step 2 of "Finish the Front Overlap" on page 29. There will be an additional row of topstitching because the neck facing is wider than the overlap facing. Leave long thread tails at the beginning and end of each row of topstitching, and pull all thread ends to the interfacing side.

4. With the blouse wrong side up, place the facing on the blouse with the interfacing side up and match the raw edges.

5. Pin and baste the layers together just inside the seamline. (For more information, see "Tips for Basting" on page 14.)

6. Turn the facing to the right side to be sure the seamline is parallel to the last row of topstitching, then stitch a ¼-inch seam.

7. Remove all of the basting stitches, and understitch the neck facing. (See "How to Understitch" on page 22.)

■ SEWING SECRET: Always remove any basting and all pins before pressing any section of a garment. Also, press as much as possible from the wrong side.

8. Press the neckline with the blouse wrong side up. If the neckline seam doesn't lie flat when the facing is pressed to the right side, trim or clip the seam allowances so that it will.

9. Hand baste the free edge of the facing to the blouse. Then edgestitch the ends and lower edge of the facing at 12 spi (2.0 mm), as shown in **Diagram 8.**

10. Finish the blouse.

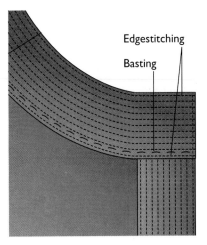

Edgestitching

Basting

Diagram 8

DESIGNER DETAIL

Louis Feraud

Louis Feraud began his career in Cannes, France, designing fashions for movie stars. His early customers included Grace Kelly, Brigitte Bardot, and Ingrid Bergman. Feraud then began designing costumes, and in 1960, he opened a ready-to-wear business in Paris. As a practicing painter, Feraud has been influenced by the art world and particularly the colors of South America. Feraud's creations are extremely popular among American women. Thus, he has become one of the most successful ready-to-wear designers in the United States.

How to *Use Ribbon* as a *Trim*

Ribbon facings are a favorite trim of many fashion houses and are used on a variety of designs, from casual linens to elegant evening wear. Ribbons can be satin or grosgrain, soft or crisp, and are available in a variety of widths, from a narrow ¼ inch to a wide 3 inches. Even though they are generally used to finish hems, ribbon facings also can be used on garment edges, from collars and pockets to garment openings.

Ribbon facings are practical as well as decorative. English designer Zandra Rhodes uses ribbons to finish the edges of her extravagant silk chiffon designs because the silk-screening process she uses to color her fabrics changes the fabric texture so that hand-rolled hems cannot be rolled evenly. Michael Novarese uses crisp grosgrain ribbons to add body and shape to the hemlines of bouffant ball gowns, and, when used on tiered skirts, the ribbon widths increase with the skirt lengths.

Ribbon facings can be applied before or after intersecting seams are joined. In the "Facing as a Trim" application on page 27, the facing is applied after the seams are sewn. In this application, the ribbon facing is applied first.

TOOLS & SUPPLIES

- ◆ Edgestitch foot or wide straight-stitch foot (optional)
- ◆ Serger

Louis Feraud uses crisp grosgrain ribbon as a facing on this blouse placket.

PREPARE THE GARMENT EDGE

1. Cut seam allowances ¼ inch wide on the edges to be faced.

2. To prevent stretching and to provide a guide for placing the ribbon, machine staystitch a scant ¼ inch from the edge.

STITCH THE FACING

1. With the garment wrong side up, place the ribbon on top of the garment wrong side down and with the edge of the ribbon barely covering the machine stitching. Pin the ribbon in place and edgestitch, as shown in **Ribbon Diagram 1**. (See "How to Edgestitch" on page 6 for detailed instructions.)

2. Fold the ribbon to the right side of the garment. With the garment wrong side up, press the ribbon in place.

3. With the garment right side up,

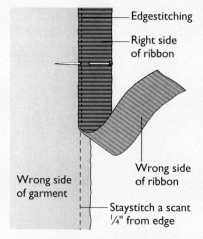

Ribbon Diagram 1

Labels: Edgestitching · Right side of ribbon · Wrong side of garment · Wrong side of ribbon · Staystitch a scant ¼" from edge

Ribbon Diagram 2

Labels: Right side of ribbon · Edgestitch ribbon in place · Edgestitching · Staystitching · Wrong side of ribbon · Right side of garment

pin the ribbon in place and edgestitch it, as shown in **Ribbon Diagram 2**.

4. With right sides together, stitch any intersecting seams and overlock the edges at 12 spi (2.0 mm), trimming them to ⅜ inch, and press.

5. Finish the garment.

▪ SEWING SECRET:

Remember, trims should have the same care requirements as the fabric you use. Preshrink all washable trims by soaking them in very hot water until the water cools. Hang the trim to dry.

Hems

Once upon a time, the only acceptable method for finishing a hem was to keep it plain and invisible. This old-fashioned tactic is still a wonderful approach for traditional fabrics and serious dressing, but it's only one of many types of hems used today.

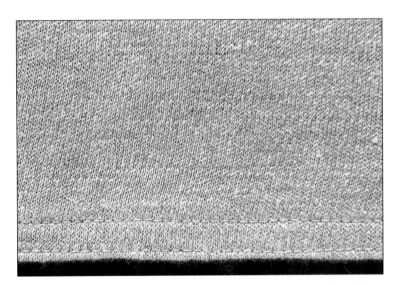

Duplicate this classic ready-to-wear topstitched hem on your next jersey creation.

Narrow Topstitched Hem

Narrow topstitched hems are used by many manufacturers on garments in all price ranges. Geoffrey Beene uses a variety of topstitched hems and stitches them in an assortment of threads, from cotton to silk. The narrow hem with two rows of top-stitching stitched in matching thread continues to be a Beene favorite, however.

Beene's technique for stitching hems in jersey fabric is unique because it eliminates those ugly tell-tale ripples and skipped stitches that frequently plague home sewers. Even though the topstitched narrow hem takes a little longer to stitch, you'll find the results achieved with this technique are well worth the effort.

Tools & Supplies

♦ Roll of fusible interfacing ½ inch wide

♦ Serger

♦ Edgestitch foot or wide straight-stitch foot

Cut the Garment and Hem Interfacing

1. Cut out the garment with a ½-inch hem allowance.

2. From a lightweight fusible interfacing, cut, on the bias or crossgrain, a ½-inch-wide strip for the hem. I prefer to use precut strips of interfacing sold on rolls, but when these are not available, I use an unthreaded serger to cut the strips from interfacing that is sold by the yard.

Prepare the Hem Edge

1. Assemble and try on the garment. If the hemline isn't level, mark the new hemline with pins, as shown in **Diagram 1.**

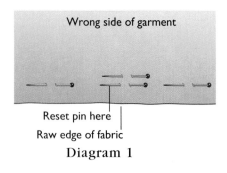

Wrong side of garment

Reset pin here

Raw edge of fabric

Diagram 1

■ SEWING SECRET: After marking a hem, always check the hemline to be sure it is straight.

DESIGNER DETAIL

Geoffrey Beene

Known for his unusual fabrications and unique garment structure, Geoffrey Beene adds little touches of fantasy and humor to his creations. Whether stitched in wool and panné velvet, linen trimmed with charmeuse, or mohair combined with lace, Beene's garments are famous for their attention to detail and quality craftsmanship.

Use a straight edge or a curved ruler to even your pin line.

2. Place the garment wrong side up on the ironing board on top of a layer of paper towels. Make sure the paper towels extend past the garment's hem edge. Place the interfacing on top of the hem allowance with the fusible side down. Align the edge of the interfacing with the pins marking the hemline, as shown in **Diagram 2.** Following the manufacturer's instructions, press the interfacing lightly to fuse it in place.

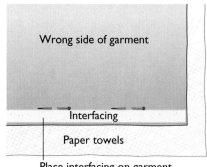

Wrong side of garment

Interfacing

Paper towels

Place interfacing on garment fusible side down

Diagram 2

■ SEWING SECRET: Always cover your ironing board with paper towels before fusing to pre-

vent the adhesive from sticking to your ironing board cover. Discard the towels if any fusible residue is left on them.

3. Serge the hem edge with the right side of the garment up, trimming the hem to ⅜ inch wide.

4. With the wrong side of the garment up, fold up and press the hem.

5. With the right side of the garment up, edgestitch the hem. (For details on edgestitching, see "How to Edgestitch" on page 6.) When you return to the point where you started stitching, overlap one or two stitches and then spot-tack. Pull the threads to the wrong side. Give them a sharp tug, and trim the ends.

■ SEWING SECRET: To spot-tack, make several stitches one on top of the other by setting your machine's stitch length to 0 or by dropping the feed dogs.

6. Topstitch the hem ⁵⁄₁₆ inch from the edge at 12 spi (2.0 mm). To topstitch evenly, adjust the needle position so that the edge of the foot is aligned with either the hem edge or with the edgestitching, as shown in **Diagram 3.**

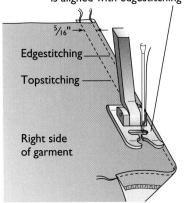

Reset needle so edge of foot is aligned with edgestitching

5/16"

Edgestitching

Topstitching

Right side of garment

Diagram 3

■ SEWING SECRET: If your machine is skipping stitches, replace the needle with a new universal ballpoint needle.

How to *Fasten Threads*

TAILOR'S KNOT

On better garments, a tailor's knot is used instead of a backtack to fasten the threads at the end of a row of machine stitching. To make a tailor's knot:
1. Pull the needle thread through to the wrong side of the garment and give both threads a sharp tug.
2. Twist the threads together once or twice so they will be easy to handle.
3. Make an overhand knot to set the knot at the end of the row of stitching, as shown. The tailor's knot won't hold securely if it isn't close to the fabric. It may take some practice to set the knot perfectly. To set the knot closer to the fabric, insert a needle into the large loop and then tighten the knot.

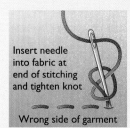

Insert needle into fabric at end of stitching and tighten knot

Wrong side of garment

BACKSTITCHES

If you find a tailor's knot difficult to tie accurately, place the thread ends into a self-threading or calyx-eyed needle and make two backstitches. See **Diagram 6** on page 24.

How to *Topstitch a Wide Hem*

An innovation of the English designer Jean Muir in the early 1970s, this attractive hem finish was used to finish her signature matte jersey dresses. Today it is widely used by many designers such as Donna Karan, Geoffrey Beene, and Karen Kane. By following these steps, you can give your garments this distinctive look.
1. When you cut out the garment, allow a 2-inch hem.
2. With the wrong side of the garment up, fold up the hem and press.
3. Set the stitch length to 10 spi (2.5 mm) and change to a wide straight-stitch presser foot.
4. Edgestitch the folded edge, using the inside of the right toe as a guide and following the instructions in "How to Edgestitch" on page 6. When you return to where you started stitching, overlap one or two stitches.
5. Topstitch ¼ inch from the hem edge, then topstitch again 1½ inches and 1¾ inches from the edge, as shown.

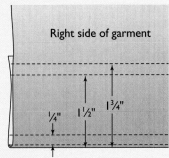

Right side of garment

1¾" 1½" ¼"

Give your garments a designer look with a top-stitched wide hem.

6. Pull all threads to the wrong side. Give them a sharp tug and fasten the threads with a tailor's knot, following the instructions in "How to Fasten Threads," above.

Gold Overlock Hem

I must admit that I was very reluctant to use serger finishes on better garments and after-five designs, but this overlock finish from Jeanne Marc is so fantastic that I've completely changed my attitude.

Jeanne Marc has used this finish on a variety of designs to hem pants, skirts, and scarves, but my favorite use of this hem is on a pair of palazzo pants made of pleated polyester chiffon (in black, of course). Stitched with a three-thread overlock and gold rayon thread, the finish has a delicate weightless quality with just a touch of glitz that floats with you when you walk. While it can be used on any color, the effect is particularly stunning when used on black.

My favorite use of the gold overlock hem is on a pair of Jeanne Marc palazzo pants of pleated polyester chiffon.

Tools & Supplies

♦ Air-erasable marking pen
♦ Size 40 rayon thread
♦ Serger
♦ Liquid seam sealant

Cut and Mark the Hem

1. Cut out the garment with a ⅝-inch hem allowance.

2. Try on the garment. If the hem isn't level, mark the new hemline with pins.

3. Check the new hemline to be sure it is straight and adjust any pins that are out of line.

4. Re-mark the hemline with an air-erasable marking pen so you can remove the pins.

Overlock the Hem

1. Remove the right needle and thread the serger with size 40 rayon thread. For instructions, see "How to Serge with Rayon Thread" on the opposite page.

2. Set the machine for a narrow flat stitch and a very short stitch (approximately 1.0 mm).

3. Tighten the tension and insert a new needle.

■ SEWING SECRET: For better thread coverage on a serged hem, place a thread palette on the upper looper thread pin. The palette can hold up to five spools of thread. Place all of the threads from the palette through the guides and the upper looper. Combine different colors or

How to *Serge* with *Rayon Thread*

Rayon thread often falls off the spool because it is fine and slippery. To prevent this, cover each spool with a thread net so the thread will feed evenly and without tangling.

Increase the tension until the threads hug the fabric edge, as shown in **Serge Diagram 1**. If the tension remains loose even though the tensions are set on the tightest setting, increase the tension manually by wrapping the thread around one or more thread guides a second time, as shown in **Serge Diagram 2**.

To thread the serger easily, use a dental floss threader or dip the thread ends in liquid seam sealant, wipe away the excess liquid, and let the ends dry before threading the machine.

Before stitching, floss the thread between the tension discs to be sure it is laid correctly.

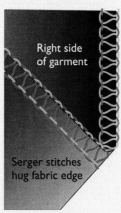

Right side of garment

Serger stitches hug fabric edge

Serge Diagram 1

Wrap threads around thread guides a second time

Serge Diagram 2

different textures of thread on the palette for a unique look. The thread palette can also be used on the conventional sewing machine.

4. Using a scrap of fabric, stitch a sample on the same grain as the garment. For a hem this is generally the crossgrain. Adjust the stitch length and stitch width as needed to achieve an attractive stitch.

■ SEWING SECRET: To prevent the edges of soft, flimsy fabrics from rolling under as you sew, always spray the edge of the fabric with spray starch and press. Always test a scrap of fabric for spotting before you spray the garment.

5. With the right side up, place the edge of the garment under

the serger foot, aligning the knife with the marked hemline. Hold the edge taut and serge, trimming away the hem allowance, as shown below.

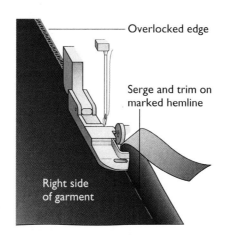

Overlocked edge

Serge and trim on marked hemline

Right side of garment

6. When you return to the point where you started stitching, overlap one stitch, raise the presser foot, and release the tension discs.

7. Pull the garment to the back of your machine until the threads are about 6 inches long, and clip the threads.

8. Hide the thread ends underneath the serger stitches.

■ SEWING SECRET: To hide the thread ends in the serged edge of the garment, insert a knit-picker, crochet hook, needle threader, or tube turner through the last ½ inch of serged loops. Latch the serger threads over the end of the turning device and pull them through the serged loops.

9. Press the edge of the hem gently and carefully.

■ SEWING SECRET: If you use metallic thread, use a Teflon press cloth or a Teflon iron shoe when pressing the hem.

This Ralph Lauren-inspired blanket-stitched hem will give your garment a stylish and sophisticated look.

Blanket-Stitched Hem

The blanket-stitched hem was popularized by Ralph Lauren's sophisticated Western designs. Suitable for many garments, it is especially attractive when used to finish the edges of wrap skirts and classic jackets with shawl collars.

These directions are based on Ralph Lauren's classic wrap skirt made in an attractive blanket-weight wool. The edges have a narrow hem to improve the shape and stability of the skirt, and they are secured with a decorative blanket stitch sewn with wool yarn in a contrasting color. The overlap is finished with a square corner.

Try this technique for a stylish look that is easy to stitch.

DESIGNER DETAIL

Ralph Lauren

Ralph Lauren focuses on classic silhouettes, sophisticated, low-key fashions, and quality workmanship. He maintains a non-fashion approach that focuses on lifestyle and the clothes you live in. Designed for women who prefer being stylish to being fashionable and who have the confidence to wear his fashions forever—or at least until they wear out—many Lauren collections are variations of Americana: homespun or denim prairie skirts worn over white cotton petticoats, full-sleeved and ruffled blouses, leather belts, hooded capes, patchwork jackets and vests, refined Western looks, or designs inspired by folk art or samplers.

Tools *&* Supplies

♦ Silk thread or cotton embroidery floss
♦ Clapper
♦ Large embroidery needle
♦ Wool yarn

Prepare the Garment

1. Cut out the garment with ⅜-inch hem allowances.

2. Assemble the garment and press.

Prepare the Hem

1. Fold the hem to the wrong side and hand baste it in place with silk thread or cotton embroidery floss. To make an attractive finish at the corner where the garment edges overlap, first fold the horizontal edge ⅜ inch to the wrong side, then fold the vertical edge ⅜ inch to the wrong side and baste, as shown in **Diagram 1.**

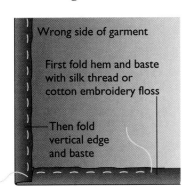

Wrong side of garment

First fold hem and baste with silk thread or cotton embroidery floss

Then fold vertical edge and baste

Diagram 1

2. With the wrong side up, press the edge. Use a clapper to flatten the folded edges at the corner.

3. Thread a large embroidery needle with wool yarn.

■ SEWING SECRET: Use a fine polyester thread as an aid when threading yarn. Fold the thread about 3 inches from the end. Crimp the thread at the fold by pressing the needle against the thread. Insert the folded end into the needle eye, as shown in **Diagram 2.**

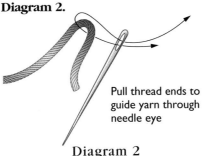

Pull thread ends to guide yarn through needle eye

Diagram 2

Thread the yarn into the thread loop and pull the thread ends, guiding the yarn through the needle.

4. Examine the raw edge of the hem allowance and trim away any thread whiskers before continuing.

5. Follow the instructions in "How to Make Blanket Stitches," below, to finish the edge of the garment, working the stitches from the top to bottom. Turn the work and make stitches to the next corner or to the end.

6. Continue stitching until the garment's hemline is covered with blanket stitches.

How to *Make* *Blanket Stitches*

Practical as well as decorative, blanket stitches are used to secure hem allowances at edges, finish raw edges of eyelets, strengthen thread chains, and secure hooks, eyes, and snaps. Follow these directions for a blanket stitch that decorates the edge of a garment and at the same time secures the hem.

1. With the garment right side up, hold the hem edge in your left hand. Secure the yarn between the layers with a backstitch and pull the needle through the fold at the hemline, as shown in **Blanket Diagram 1.**

2. Make a loop of yarn at the fabric edge. Insert the needle into the right side of the fabric, ⅜ inch from the folded edge and about ¼ inch to the right of the last stitch.

3. Loop the yarn under the point of the needle and pull it through to make the stitch.

4. Repeat to make stitches to the corner.

5. Make one stitch at the corner by inserting the needle into the last stitch, as shown in **Blanket Diagram 2.** Pass the needle between the layers, exiting at the corner on the hemline.

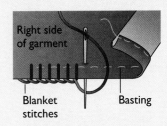

Right side of garment

Blanket stitches   Basting

Blanket Diagram 1

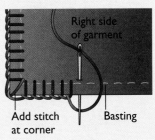

Right side of garment

Add stitch at corner   Basting

Blanket Diagram 2

Chiffon Hem

The graceful and glamorous chiffon hem is a favorite of many American designers.

The chiffon hem is a very narrow hem that can be machine-stitched without special feet or attachments. Called the machine-rolled hem in home sewing, the chiffon hem is frequently used to finish the edges of expensive ready-to-wear garments.

Attractive on both the right and the wrong side, it is easier to stitch on straight and almost-straight edges. However, it can be adapted for edges with curves and corners.

Suitable for lightweight and sheer fabrics, the chiffon hem is a favorite of many American designers. Some typical applications include Ralph Lauren's hems on full pleated silks, which help the garments to maintain a light, airy look, and Adele Simpson's finish for the curves of tulip skirts. Judy Hornby uses this hem on her cracked-ice chiffon designs, and Oscar de la Renta uses it on his polyester organza creations.

Tools & Supplies

♦ Edgestitch foot or wide straight-stitch foot (optional)

Prepare the Hem

1. Cut out the garment with a ⅝-inch hem allowance.

2. Set the stitch length on your machine to 12 spi (2.0 mm), and stitch and finish all the vertical seams.

3. To reduce bulk in the hem area, trim the seam ends on an angle and, with the wrong side up, staystitch ½ inch from the raw edge to control the material and provide a guide when turning the edge under, as shown in **Diagram 1.** If you want a fluted finish, stretch the edge as much as possible when staystitching; otherwise, guide the fabric so that it is neither stretched nor eased.

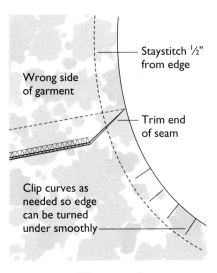

Diagram 1

4. When the edge is shaped, clip the hem allowance as needed so the edge will turn under smoothly, as shown in **Diagram 1.**

Stitch the Hem

1. Change to an edgestitch or wide straight-stitch foot, or move the needle to the right so you can align the folded edge of the hem with the inside edge of the presser foot.

2. With the right side up, fold under the edge of the hem on the line of staystitching. Following the instructions in "How to Edgestitch" on page 6, edgestitch close to the fold, as shown in **Diagram 2.**

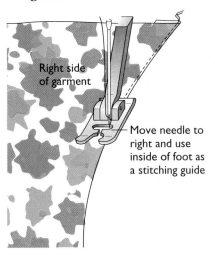

Diagram 2

3. With the wrong side up, anchor the hem under the presser foot. Hold the edge taut, and trim close to the stitched line.

4. With the wrong side up, fold up the edge again, enclosing the raw edge. Stitch again on the last stitching line, as shown in **Diagram 3,** so the second row of stitching won't be noticed on the finished garment.

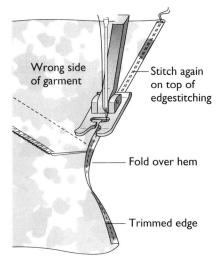

Diagram 3

■ SEWING SECRET: The finished width of a narrow chiffon hem is determined by how close to the edge of the fabric you stitch and how close to the stitched line you trim. Use an edgestitching foot or the inside edge of the straight-stitch or all-purpose foot as a guide to stitch evenly and no more than 1/16 inch from the edge. Then use the "palms up" technique for trimming described in "How to Trim Closely" on page 19. When trimming, always anchor the garment under your machine's presser foot and hold the edge taut.

5. With the wrong side up, press the hemmed edge.

How to *Stitch* a *Pin Hem*

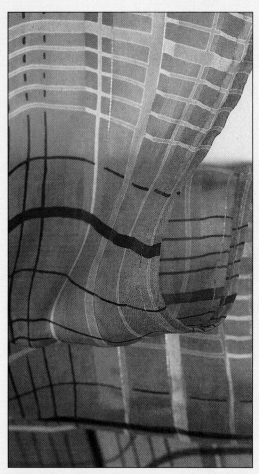

*The pin hem allows
your delicate garments
to drape gracefully.*

The pin hem is a narrow, flat hem finished by hand. It is similar to the chiffon hem, but since it is more labor intensive, and therefore much more expensive to sew, it is used less frequently in the apparel industry.

The obvious advantage of the pin hem is that there is no machine stitching on the right side of the garment. It is also softer than other hems and drapes more attractively.

1. Prepare the hem and staystitch it as you would for the chiffon hem, as shown in **Diagram 1** on page 41.

2. With the right side up, fold under the edge on the stitched line and edgestitch close to the fold. For instructions, see "How to Edgestitch" on page 6.

3. Trim away the hem allowance close to the stitched line.

4. With the wrong side up, fold the edge again, enclosing the raw edge. Use a small fell stitch to finish the hem, working from right to left, as shown in **Pin Diagram 1.** To make the stitch, secure the thread between the layers. Insert the needle into the garment directly opposite the last stitch, and pick up a single thread or portion of a thread on the garment. Insert the needle into the fold of the hem and pull the needle through. Following **Pin Diagram 2,** repeat this process to make the next stitch.

5. With the wrong side up, press the hemmed edge.

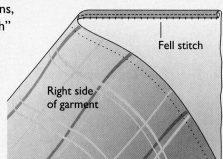

Fell stitch

Right side of garment

Pin Diagram 1

Wrong side of garment

Needle enters here

Pin Diagram 2

Use this smart band hem to accent the hemline of a casual and contemporary calf-length skirt.

Perry **E**llis

Known for his use of natural fiber fabrics, unusual proportions, wearable designs, and slightly anti-fashion approach, Perry Ellis made the preppy look fashionable in the 1970s and was one of the first design houses to make unlined classics. During the 1980s many of his successful contemporary menswear designs were modified to fit the female figure. Since Mr. Ellis's death in 1986, the firm has continued to specialize in fine-quality classics with exciting and unusual proportions.

Band Hem

This easy band hem by Perry Ellis is one of those wonderful techniques that can be used in a variety of ways. Used to finish the hem on a calf-length skirt, the band is simply joined to the lower edge of the skirt with a piped seam.

You can use the piped application on an assortment of fashions ranging from casual day wear to luxurious evening designs. Or,

you can replace the piping with a raised French seam, as shown on page 7, or a stand-up bound seam, as shown on page 12.

The instructions for this technique are based on the Perry Ellis design. The full, softly pleated skirt is 32 inches long, and the band at the hem is 9 inches wide. The band is doubled, and both raw edges are joined to the skirt with a piped seam.

Tools & *Supplies*

♦ Zipper foot
♦ Serger

Prepare the Pattern

1. To add a seam for the band, see "Adding a Seam" on page 201.

2. Make a pattern for the band front that is as wide as the skirt front and twice the finished length of the band (18 inches), plus 1¼ inches (allowing for two ⅝-inch seam allowances). In the same manner, make a pattern for the band back. For this design, each band is 19¼ inches long.

Cut Out the Skirt and the Band

1. Cut out the skirt, band front, and band back pieces with ⅝-inch seam allowances. Cut the band on the same grainline as the skirt.

2. Cut enough bias strips to make the piping with ⅝-inch seam allowances, following the instructions in "How to Cut and Join Bias Strips on page 5."

Prepare the Skirt and Band

1. Following the directions in "How to Make Piping" on page 16, make the piping for the band and set it aside.

2. With right sides together and raw edges even, stitch the vertical or side seams on the skirt. Press all of the seam allowances open.

3. With right sides together and raw edges even, stitch the side seams on the band, and press the seam allowances open.

Sew the Piping to the Band

1. With wrong sides together, fold the band in half lengthwise, matching the raw edges. Set the stitch length on your machine to 12 spi (2.0 mm), and stitch the raw edges together ½ inch from the edge, as shown in **Diagram 1.**

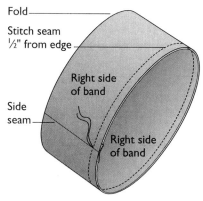

Diagram 1

2. With the band right side up and beginning at one side seam, align the raw edges of the piping and the band. Pin the piping to the band, as shown in **Diagram 2.**

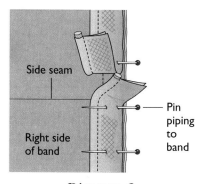

Diagram 2

3. At the beginning, lap the piping over the seamline. At the end, lap and pin the piping over the beginning end by about ¼ inch.

4. Place a zipper foot on your machine and stitch the piping in place, as shown in **Diagram 3.**

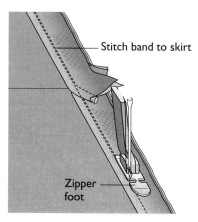

Diagram 3

■ SEWING SECRET: When piping a straight edge, lay the piping flat without stretching it or easing it to the garment section.

Sew the Band Seam

1. With right sides together and the band on top, match and pin the skirt and band together with the seamlines and the raw edges aligned. Stitch the band to the skirt, using the last stitched line as a guide.

2. Serge the seam, and press it toward the waist.

3. Finish stitching the skirt.

Bindings

An attractive substitute for traditional facings, bindings accentuate the edges of a design as well as conceal the raw edges of your fabric. Use a variety of materials such as contrasting textures and colors to create interest on a simple silhouette, or use self-fabric for a refined tone-on-tone combination.

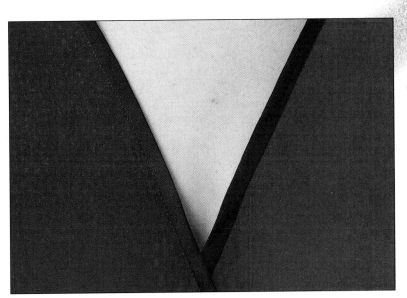

This exquisite French binding is favored by designers worldwide as a decorative detail and practical finish.

French Binding

A favorite of American and European designers alike, French binding is frequently used as a decorative detail as well as a practical finish.

Sometimes called a double binding, the French binding begins with a wide bias strip that is folded in half with wrong sides together. Then the bias strip is stitched to the right side of the garment, wrapped around the raw edge, and machine stitched on the right side to secure it permanently.

With a little practice, you'll be able to master this high-fashion binding technique.

Tools & Supplies

- Fusible or nonfusible interfacing
- Chalk wheel
- Zipper foot

DESIGNER DETAIL

Oscar de la Renta

Oscar de la Renta is known for his smartly defined suits and his sophisticated, opulent evening designs. In addition to designing the luxury ready-to-wear collection for his own New York fashion house, he also designs the French haute couture for Balmain.

Prepare the Garment

1. Referring to **Diagram 1,** trim away the seam or hem allowances on the edges to be bound, set your machine for a stitch length of 12 spi (2.0 mm), and staystitch the edges just inside the new seamline. The staystitching should be slightly narrower than the finished binding width.

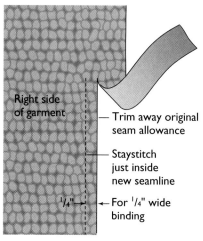

Diagram 1

2. Interface the edges of your garment as needed so they will maintain the desired shape. You may want to use a heavier interfacing on your facing to maintain the shape of the garment edge or when using heavier bindings. With lightweight fabrics and bindings, you may not need any interfacing.

■ SEWING SECRET: To ensure that garment edges hold their shape, Jeanne Marc uses facings and bindings on the edges of jackets made of soft fabrics. First a fusible interfacing is applied to the wrong side of the facing. Then, with wrong sides together, the facing and garment are stitched at the edge, as shown in **Diagram 2,** and the binding is applied.

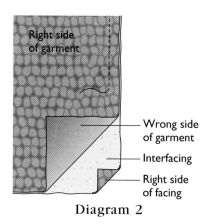

Diagram 2

3. Stitch, press, trim, and finish any seams that will be crossed by the binding.

Prepare the Binding

1. Cut the bias strips about ten times the finished width. For ex-

ample, for a ¼-inch-wide binding, cut the bias strips 2½ inches wide. Then, with right sides together, join the bias strips to make a strip long enough to bind the entire neckline. For instructions, see "How to Cut and Join Bias Strips" on page 5.

2. Fold the bias strips lengthwise with wrong sides together and raw edges even, and press, stretching the strips slightly.

3. Measure from the folded edge three and a half times the finished width of the binding. Use a chalk wheel to chalk-mark the desired width and trim away any excess fabric.

4. Hand baste the raw edges together ¼ inch (the width of the binding) from the edge.

Sew the Binding to the Garment

1. With the garment right side up, place the folded bias on top of the garment. Match and pin-baste the raw edges together and, if needed, hand-baste the layers together just inside the seamline.

2. Stitch the binding in place by

Tips for Binding a Neckline

Since a neckline binding is the most visible binding on a garment, it should be as flawless as possible. Here are some secrets I've learned from the professionals:

♦ Try to avoid having a seam on your bias strip, particularly on a neckline. You can do this by cutting the bias strip for the neckline in one piece.

♦ When binding a jewel neckline, trim away an additional ⅛ inch to avoid having the finished neckline fit too tightly.

♦ To preserve the neckline shape, Los Angeles designer Michael Novarese taught me to use a paper shaper when staystitching the edge. Trace the neckline sections of the garment front and back on wax paper, nonwoven interfacing, or tear-away stabilizer. Identify the cutting edges and seamlines on the paper shaper. Stitch the shoulder seams together on the garment and then on the paper shaper, as shown. Place the garment on the paper shaper and staystitch the neckline a scant ¼ inch from the edge. Remove the paper shaper. If you make your paper shaper out of tear-away stabilizer, you won't tear the stitching and the shaper will be easy to remove.

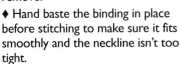
Marked seamline

Paper shaper

♦ Hand baste the binding in place before stitching to make sure it fits smoothly and the neckline isn't too tight.

♦ Hand baste the binding before ditch-stitching to prevent the underlayers from shifting when they are stitched.

♦ Ditch-stitch by hand, using a very short running stitch.

baste it in place, as shown in **Diagram 4.**

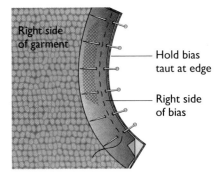

Right side of garment

Hold bias taut at edge

Right side of bias

Diagram 4

When binding outward or convex curves such as the edges of collars, flaps, or pockets, the garment edge is longer than the stitching line. To prevent the edge from cupping under, ease the binding at the staystitching so it will fit the edge smoothly, as shown in **Diagram 5.**

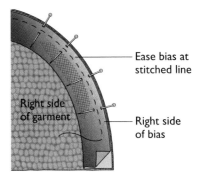

Ease bias at stitched line

Right side of garment

Right side of bias

Diagram 5

3. Press the seam flat. Then fold the binding toward the raw edges and press it lightly.

4. Wrap the binding around the raw edges to the wrong side. Measure the binding, and check the width on the wrong side. The binding should overlap the seamline slightly. The finished binding on the right side will probably be a little wider than you had

stitching a seam the width of the finished binding, as shown in **Diagram 3.** For example, for a ¼-inch-wide binding, stitch ¼ inch from the edge.

■ SEWING SECRET: When binding inward or concave curves such as the neckline or armscyes, the garment edge is shorter than the stitching line. To avoid having excess fullness at the edge, hold the binding taut when you pin and hand

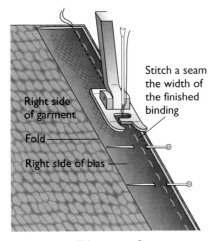

Stitch a seam the width of the finished binding

Right side of garment

Fold

Right side of bias

Diagram 3

planned because of the bulk of the fabric. This won't usually matter, except on jewel necklines and when the underside of the binding is not wide enough to overlap the seamline. In either case, you can trim the seam allowance as needed before wrapping the binding to the wrong side to ensure an even binding on the right side and a neckline that will fit comfortably.

5. With the right side up, hand baste close to the binding seam to secure the binding, as shown in **Diagram 6.**

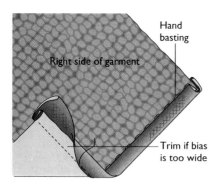

Diagram 6

6. Place a zipper foot on your machine and ditch-stitch next to the basting, as shown in **Diagram 7.**

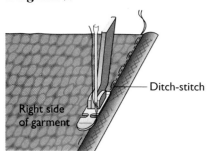

Diagram 7

■ SEWING SECRET: Ditch-stitching is a technique where you stitch in the well or the ditch of the seam on the right side of the garment. It is frequently described as stitch-in-the-ditch or stitching in the crack. For techniques such as binding and banding, which have a ridge on one side of the seamline, you stitch next to the seamline instead of in the well of the seam.

How to *Finish Binding Ends* at an *Opening*

Here's a quick way to finish bindings at the openings of a garment.

1. When you get close to the garment opening, stop hand basting the binding in place.

2. Unfold the binding at the end of the garment opening, as shown in **End Diagram 1,** and fold the right sides of the binding together, as shown in **End Diagram 2.**

3. Align the folded edges of the binding and stitch a seam in the ends of the binding ¹⁄₁₆ inch from the edge of the garment, as shown in **End Diagram 3.** (I frequently sew this little seam by hand with a short backstitch.) Trim the seam allowance to ¼ inch.

4. Repeat steps 1 through 3 to sew the binding on the other side of the garment opening.

5. Turn the bindings right side out, as shown in **End Diagram 4.** Fold the raw edges under, readjust the bindings, and finish the basting in preparation for ditch-stitching.

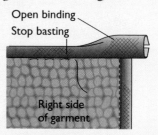

End Diagram 1

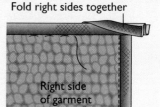

End Diagram 2

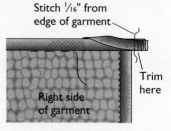

End Diagram 3

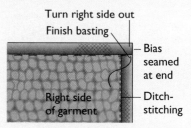

End Diagram 4

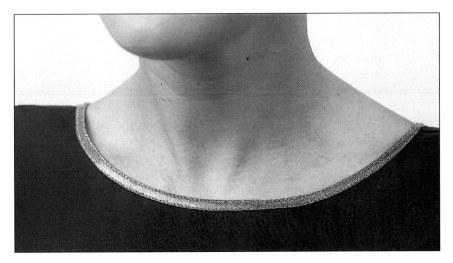

This metallic silver binding provides a luxurious accent to basic black evening wear.

One-Step Binding

Two of my favorite designers—Geoffrey Beene and Jeanne Marc—use one-step binding applications. Often cut from metallic gold or silver fabric, Beene's bindings are generally a narrow ¼ inch wide, while Jeanne Marc uses several widths ranging from ¼ to 1 inch and makes them in fabrics similar to the garment fabric. In this application, the finished binding is ½ inch wide.

One-step bindings, or one-run applications as they are called in the apparel manufacturing industry, are sewn with only one row of stitching or one run under the presser foot. I particularly like this application because it's easy to shape the bias to fit curved edges, even though I don't always like the topstitching that is visible on the finished binding.

In the industry, a one-run binding begins with a roll of the unfolded binding material that is fed into an attachment in front and to the right of the presser foot. Called a folder, this attachment folds and positions the binding at the fabric edge directly under the needle. The operator guides the binding material into the folder, then inserts the garment into the folded binding and stitches the two together. This sounds easy, but it requires practice to stitch the binding successfully, especially on curves and corners.

Folders are available for some home sewing machines, but they are expensive and a little more time-consuming to operate if the binding material isn't packaged on rolls. Also, the binding will ripple if the rolled bias isn't cut precisely on the true bias, no matter how skilled the operator of the folder.

Tools & Supplies

- ♦ ½-inch-wide roll of fusible interfacing
- ♦ Pattern cloth or nonwoven interfacing
- ♦ Padded press board
- ♦ Zipper foot

Prepare the Garment

1. Trim away the seam or hem allowances on the garment edges to be bound.

2. Set your machine for 12 spi (2.0 mm), and staystitch the edges just inside the seamline. The staystitching should be slightly narrower than the finished binding width.

3. Following the instructions in step 2 of "Prepare the Garment" on page 46, interface the edges.

4. Stitch, press, trim, and finish any seams that will be crossed by the binding.

■ SEWING SECRET: Bindings made from soft fabrics tend to ripple and shift more than crisp bindings do. Many of the bindings at Jeanne Marc are made of soft cottons or rayons, which are very difficult to sew. To give these fabrics body, this house cuts them into lengths several yards long, dips the yardage into liquid starch, and hangs it to drip dry.

When dry, the starched yardage is sent to a cutting contractor. There the fabric selvages are stitched together, and the fabric is cut into wide bias strips, which are rolled onto a long tube. Finally, the rolled bias strips—tube and all—are cut into rolls the desired widths.

Prepare the Binding

1. Cut bias strips five times the finished width of the binding. For finished binding ½ inch wide, cut the bias strips 2½ inches wide. Then join the strips as needed to make enough binding for all edges. See "How to Cut and Join Bias Strips" on page 5 for details.

2. To make the bias tape, see "How to Make Bias Tape" on this page.

■ SEWING SECRET: The one-step application is often used for a variety of other materials, such as leather, suede, ribbon, and braid. Some applications that I've seen include Ralph Lauren's leather-trimmed wools and French designer Nina Ricci's braid-trimmed silk suiting, where the braid was finished ¼ inch wide.

Shape the Binding

1. Trace the original paper pattern onto pattern cloth or non-woven interfacing. Mark the finished edge of the garment on the traced pattern. This is generally the facing seamline.

How to *Make Bias Tape*

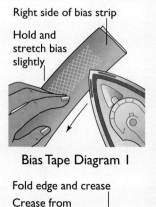

Right side of bias strip

Hold and stretch bias slightly

Bias Tape Diagram 1

Fold edge and crease

Crease from first press

Wrong side of bias

Bias Tape Diagram 2

There are several ways to make bias tape. I particularly like this method for double-fold tape.

1. To determine the width of the bias strips, begin with the measurement for the finished binding, add 1 inch, and double the total. For example, if the finished bias will be ½ inch wide, cut the strip 3 inches wide.

2. With wrong sides together fold the bias strip lengthwise, and press the folded edge, stretching it slightly, as shown in **Bias Tape Diagram 1**.

3. From the folded edge, measure twice the finished width plus ⅛ inch. For ½-inch bias tape, measure 1⅛ inch; for a ¼-inch bias, measure ⅝-inch. Mark and trim the raw edges.

4. Fold one raw edge in to meet the fold at the center and press, as shown in **Bias Tape Diagram 2**. Repeat to press the other side.

2. Pin the traced patterns together on any seams that will be crossed.

3. Place the pattern on a firm but well-padded press board. Place the binding right side up on top of the pattern with the folded edge of the binding aligned with the finished edge of the garment (the marked seamline on the pattern).

4. Pin the binding in place at one end by stabbing the pin into the binding, the pattern, and the press board, as shown in **Diagram 1**. Steam the binding and finger-press it, shaping it to fit the edge of the garment. Stab pins into the shaped binding section and leave the binding to dry.

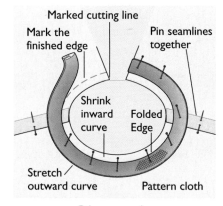

Marked cutting line

Mark the finished edge

Pin seamlines together

Shrink inward curve

Folded Edge

Stretch outward curve

Pattern cloth

Diagram 1

Set the Binding

1. Insert the edge of the garment into the bias tape so the edge of the tape covers the seamline. If you have not steamed and shaped the bias, ease the binding around outward curves and stretch it slightly on inward curves. Hand baste through all the layers so that the bias won't shift and ripple when you stitch permanently.

2. Edgestitch the bias in place. To eliminate skipped stitches caused by uneven layers when edgestitching bias tape, stitch it with a zipper foot, positioning the foot so it rides on top of the bias, as shown in **Diagram 2A**. Most of the Geoffrey Beene bindings are edgestitched again on the outer edge, as shown in **2B**.

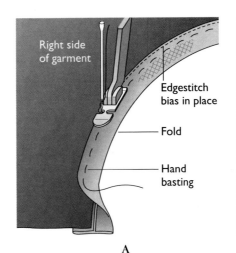

A

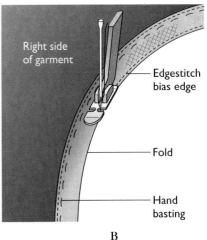

B

Diagram 2

How to *Stitch Double Binding*

As the name implies, a double binding is one binding applied on top of another. These instructions describe the double binding sewn to an edge, but it can also be applied to a seam.

In this technique, the first binding is ½ inch wide and the second is ¼ inch wide, but you may prefer to make the second binding ½ inch wide instead.

PREPARE THE GARMENT AND BINDINGS

1. Prepare the garment following the directions in "Prepare the Garment" on page 49.
2. Cut the bias strips five times the finished width. So, for the wide (½ inch) binding, cut the bias strips 2½ inches wide, and for the narrow (¼ inch) binding, cut the bias strips 1¼ inches wide. However, make a sample before cutting all the strips. Narrow bindings tend to "shrink" more than wider ones, especially when the fabrics are bulky.
3. Join bias strips as needed to make enough bias tape binding for all the edges. To make the bias tape, see "How to Make Bias Tape" on the opposite page.

4. To reduce bulk, trim the seam allowances on the wide binding and the garment edge to ³⁄₁₆ inch.
5. Shape the binding following the directions in "Shape the Binding" on the opposite page.

SEW THE BINDINGS

1. Insert the garment edge into the wide binding so the edge of the binding barely covers the staystitching. Baste the binding in place and edgestitch permanently, following the instructions in step 2 of "Set the Binding," above.
2. Insert the folded edge of the wide binding into the narrow binding. Baste the narrow binding in place, and edgestitch it permanently, as shown.

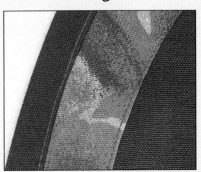

Make a dramatic statement with double binding.

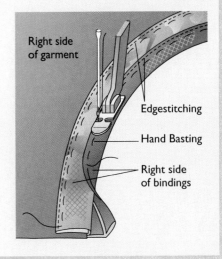

FANCY DETAILS

2

You can develop many new designs by simply applying your sewing expertise to create different pockets, assorted closures, and various collars. And, even though a knowledge of patternmaking is certainly helpful, it really isn't necessary if you are adventurous and a careful observer.

Pockets and Flaps

Re-create a designer look by adding simple flaps or handsome pockets to your basic design.

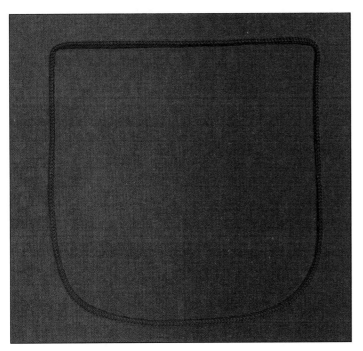

Black piping is the perfect accent for a smartly tailored red wool crepe jacket.

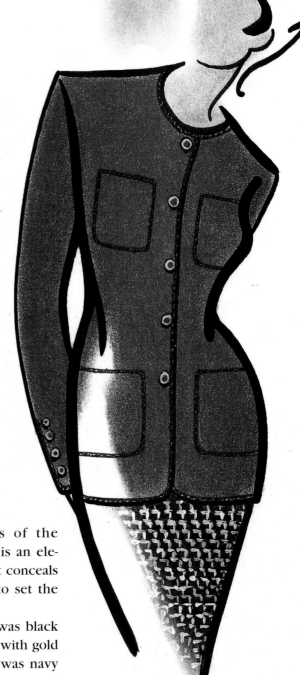

Piped Patch Pocket on Jacket

This touch of elegance belies the notion that creating high-fashion garments must be time consuming and arduous. I first saw this patch pocket on a marvelous jacket from Escada. More recently, Yves Saint Laurent used it on a terrific tailored jacket. The piping on the edges of the pocket and the jacket is an elegant, attractive trim that conceals the topstitching used to set the pockets.

The Escada jacket was black wool and was trimmed with gold piping. The YSL jacket was navy

db
DESIGNER DETAIL

Yves Saint Laurent

Yves Saint Laurent is known for designing simple, wearable fashions in beautiful fabrics. A master tailor, his menswear-inspired pantsuits are a favorite of fashionable women all over the world. In addition to haute couture, Saint Laurent designs several ready-to-wear lines. The most expensive line—Rive Gauche—is particularly well made, and each collection is filled with exciting design and sewing ideas.

and was trimmed with navy rayon piping similar to many trims available at your local retailer. Both designs had four pockets—two large pockets at the hips and two smaller ones at the bust. On the YSL design the piping outlined all of the pocket edges, while on the Escada design the piping did not extend across the pocket opening. I like both pocket designs, but since the ends of the piping are easier to finish when all of the pocket edges are piped, I use that technique more often.

I also like the look of custom piping (see "How to Make Piping" on page 16) when it coordinates with the skirt or contrast trim. I try to avoid purchased fabric pipings, except for use in children's wear, because the fabric quality is often poor. Often the weave is coarse and the fabric is fuzzy.

In the following technique, however, the pockets are piped on all edges with a purchased rayon piping because it is readily available in most fabric stores.

Tools & Supplies

♦ Pocket patterns
♦ Pattern paper
♦ Lightweight fusible knit or weft-insertion interfacing
♦ 3 yards of purchased rayon piping

Plan the Design

1. Draw a sketch of the design you'd like to make (you may want to begin by making only one pair of large pockets), and select a commercial pattern that closely matches your design.

2. Press the pattern pieces.

■ SEWING SECRET: For most designs, I separate the pattern pieces into three stacks: (1) the pieces that won't be used, (2) the sections that require some preparation, and (3) the remaining pieces. After returning the first stack to the pattern envelope, I press the rest with a dry iron to avoid damaging the tissue paper.

Prepare the Pocket Patterns

1. If the jacket doesn't have patch pockets, draw the patterns below onto pattern paper. The **Piped Patch Patterns** include ¼-inch seam allowances. If the seam allowance on your piping is wider than ¼ inch, increase the seam allowance on the patterns as needed.

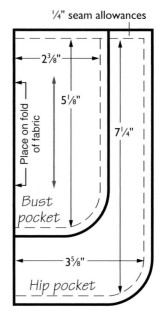

Piped Patch Patterns

2. Trace the pocket patterns.

■ SEWING SECRET: To copy small patterns, I simply make photocopies instead of tracing them. To copy larger patterns, I spread the pattern paper on a cardboard cutting board or a Space Board. Then, I place the patterns on top and trace them using a stiletto tracing wheel or pattern tracer. One of the advantages of using the stiletto tracing wheel is that you can make several copies simultaneously. (See "Resources" on page 243 for sources.)

Cut Out and Interface the Pockets

1. From the fashion fabric, cut two large pockets and two small pockets.

2. From a lightweight fusible knit or weft-insertion interfacing, cut two large pockets and two small pockets.

3. From the lining fabric, cut two large pockets and two small pockets. Do not round the corners.

4. With the pockets wrong side up, place the interfacing pieces—fusible side down—on top of the pocket sections. Fuse the interfacing in place.

Sew the Piping to the Pockets

1. With one fabric pocket right side up and beginning at the center of one long edge, align the seam allowance of the piping and the edge of the pocket and pin them together, as shown in **Diagram 1.** (The following diagrams show construc-

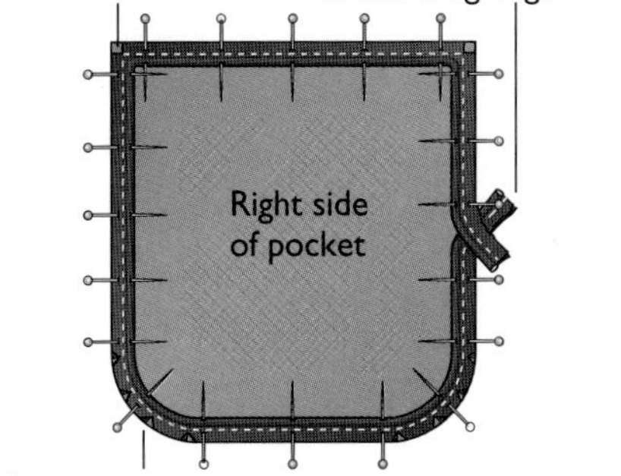

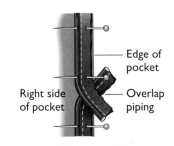

Clip piping and ease at corners   Start piping at center of one long edge

Right side of pocket

Ease piping at curves and clip piping so it will lie flat

Diagram 1

tion of a pocket for the left side of the jacket. To construct a pocket for the right side of the jacket, start pinning the piping to the opposite long side of the pocket.)

■ SEWING SECRET: At curves and corners, ease the piping to the pocket so the pocket edges will not cup under when the pocket is finished. Clip the piping seam allowance as needed so it will lie flat at curves and corners, as shown in **Diagram 1.**

2. Overlap the ends of the piping, as shown in **Diagram 2.**

Edge of pocket

Right side of pocket   Overlap piping

Diagram 2

3. Set your machine for 12 stitches per inch (2.0 mm), and use a zipper foot to stitch the piping to the pocket as close to the piped edge as possible.

■ SEWING SECRET: When applying piping, I prefer to use a generic zipper foot because the zipper foot for my machine cannot be adjusted to stitch close to the cord. Generic feet are available for most machines, and your local retailer can help you select one to fit yours.

4. Before proceeding, fold the seam allowances to the wrong side, as shown in **Diagram 3,** and examine the pocket. If the seam allowance shows, restitch that area.

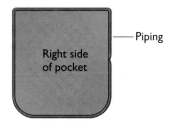

Right side of pocket   Piping

Diagram 3

5. Following step 1, pin the piping to the remaining large pocket, but start on the opposite long side. Follow steps 2 through 4 to sew the piping to the pocket. Examine the pockets to be sure they appear to be identical mirror images of one another.

■ SEWING SECRET: If your body is larger on one side than the other, experiment with making the pocket for the smaller side a little narrower to create the illusion of a symmetrical figure.

6. Repeat steps 1 through 5 to apply the piping to the two small pockets.

Line the Pockets

1. With right sides together, place the lining on top of the piped pocket. Pin the centers together, as shown in **Diagram 4.**

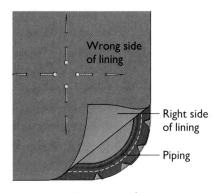

Wrong side of lining

Right side of lining

Piping

Diagram 4

■ SEWING SECRET: When pinning pockets to their linings, I place the pins with the heads near the center so I can stitch the pieces together without removing the pins.

2. Check the pocket lining to be sure it is flat and unwrinkled. Don't worry if the edges of the lining and the edges of the pocket don't match, as long as the lining itself covers the piping/pocket seamline.

3. Turn the pocket over so the piped pocket section is on top. Then, beginning on one long edge of the pocket, stitch again on the piping/pocket seamline, as shown in **Diagram 5**, to join the pocket to the lining. Stop stitching about 1 inch from where you started.

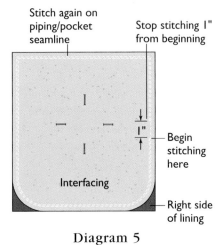

Diagram 5

4. Trim away the excess lining fabric.

5. Turn the pocket right side out and press with the lining side up, as shown in **Diagram 6.**

6. Turn the pocket over and admire your work. Repeat steps 1 through 5 to line the remaining jacket pockets.

Diagram 6

Sew the Pockets to the Jacket

1. With the right sides up, pin the large pockets on the jacket front. The piping joint for each pocket should be toward the side seam, and the opposite edge should be 2⅜ inches from the center front, as shown in **Diagram 7**. The lower edge of each pocket should be about 1¼ inches from the hemline, as shown.

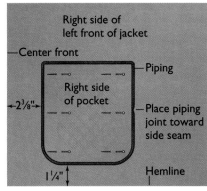

Diagram 7

■ SEWING SECRET: The pockets are usually sewn in place before the jacket is assembled. However, when adding pockets to a pattern that doesn't call for pockets, I like to check the placement before stitching them permanently.

To check the pocket placement, pin the pockets in place, then pin-baste the vertical seams and shoulders together. Put the jacket on a dress form to examine the pocket placement. Repin the pockets as needed until you are pleased with their placement.

■ SEWING SECRET: If you don't have a dress form, you can easily make one that is inexpensive and portable. Place a T-shirt on a hanger and stuff it with balls of net. Then pin or sew the bottom of the shirt closed so the balls won't fall out.

2. Pin the small pockets in place about 5¾ inches above the large ones and 2⅜ inches from the front edge.

3. As shown in **Diagram 8,** baste all of the pockets in place with a large X, starting each leg of the X with a knot at a corner of the pocket. This will prevent the pockets from shifting as you stitch them to the jacket. Then, using a zipper foot, ditch-stitch the sides and bottom of the pockets close to the piping.

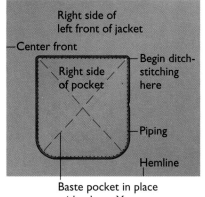

Baste pocket in place with a large X

Diagram 8

4. At the opening of the pockets, pull the threads to the wrong sides and knot.

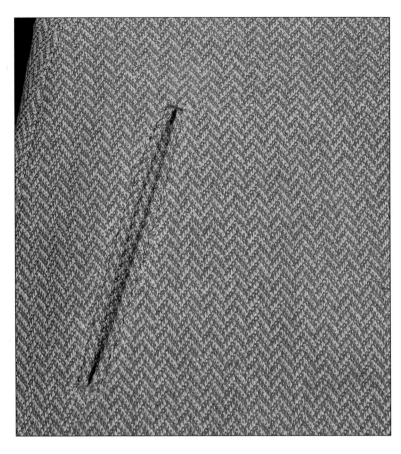

Create the illusion of a slimmer figure with a pair of these classic Calvin Klein double-welt pockets.

Double-Welt Pocket on a Skirt

Calvin Klein used a pair of these double-welt pockets to transform a simple, lightweight, wool crepe skirt into a stunning, figure-slimming design. The pockets are set at an angle high on the hips to break the width of the skirt front, and they flatter almost any figure.

The finished pocket opening is 5½ inches long and ⅜ inch wide. The distance between the pockets is 2 inches wider at the bottom than at the top, and the distance between the pockets at the top is four times the distance between the tops of the pockets and the side seams. The pocket sacks are sewn into the seam at the waistline to prevent the pockets from sagging when they are used.

Tools & Supplies

♦ Pattern paper
♦ Silk weight or lightweight fusible interfacing, such as Touch 'o Gold (see "Resources" on page 243)
♦ Chalk wheel

Plan the Design

1. Draw a sketch of the skirt design you'd like to make, and select a skirt pattern that closely matches your design.

2. Press the pattern pieces with a dry iron.

3. Draw the pocket opening on the skirt front pattern, as shown in **Diagram 1**.

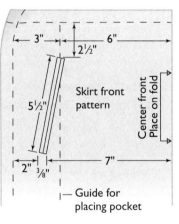

Diagram 1

4. Before proceeding, "try on" the paper pattern to see how you like the pocket location. Experiment with the location by moving the pattern right and left and up and down to determine if another pocket position would be more flattering for your figure.

Make the Pocket Patterns

1. Draw the patterns for the upper pocket, underpocket, and pocket on the skirt front pattern, as shown in **Diagram 2**. Draw the grainline parallel to the skirt front on each pocket section.

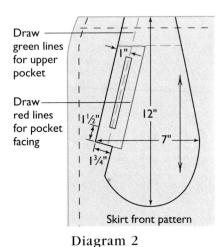

Draw green lines for upper pocket

Draw red lines for pocket facing

1"

1½"

12"

7"

1¾"

Skirt front pattern

Diagram 2

■ SEWING SECRET: To avoid confusion, use a different colored pencil or marker to draw the upper pocket, underpocket, and pocket on the skirt front pattern.

2. Trace the pocket sections and their grainlines onto pattern paper, and cut out the patterns, as shown in **Diagrams 3A, 3B, and 3C**.

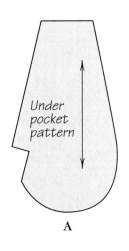

Under pocket pattern

A

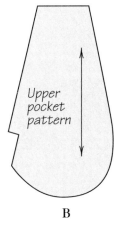

Upper pocket pattern

B

Pocket facing pattern

C

Diagram 3

3. Cut two upper pockets and two underpockets from the lining fabric.

4. From the skirt fabric, cut two pocket facings, which are applied to the underpocket to hide the lining when the pocket is used.

Mark and Interface the Pocket Openings

1. Cut out the skirt front.

2. On the right side of the skirt front, use a chalk wheel to mark the mouth—the opening between the welts—of each pocket, as shown in **Diagram 4**. Mark the ends of the openings with short, perpendicular lines.

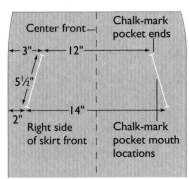

Center front

Chalk-mark pocket ends

3"

12"

5½"

2"

14"

Right side of skirt front

Chalk-mark pocket mouth locations

Diagram 4

3. To transfer the marks for the pocket openings to the wrong side of the skirt, insert a pin into the chalk-line at each crossmark. Turn the skirt so the wrong side is up, and use the chalk wheel to mark the ends of the openings and a line between the two pins.

4. For each pocket, cut a 1-inch-wide rectangle from the silk weight or lightweight interfacing that is 1 inch longer than the pocket opening. So, for a pocket 5½ inches long, cut the interfacing 1 inch wide and 6½ inches long.

5. With the skirt front wrong side up, center the interfacing strips over the chalked lines and baste-fuse them in place.

■ SEWING SECRET: To baste-fuse interfacing, steam press it only 3 to 5 seconds; then pat the interfacing gently with your fingers to fuse the interfacing to the fabric.

6. Make the double-welt openings using your favorite method. If you don't have a favorite method, try using the window-pane opening or magic window method described on page 60, or use the strip method—my favorite—described in "Bound Buttonholes" on page 105.

Prepare the Pocket Sacks

1. With the pocket facing right side up, serge the long edge.

2. With the right sides up, place the pocket facing on top of the underpocket, matching and pinning the raw edges together. Then stitch a seam ¼ inch from the raw edges. Machine stitch again through the serging at the other long edge of the facing, as shown in **Diagram 5**.

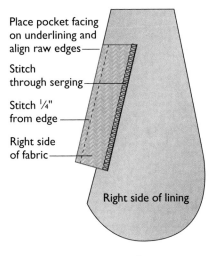

Place pocket facing on underlining and align raw edges

Stitch through serging

Stitch ¼" from edge

Right side of fabric

Right side of lining

Diagram 5

3. Repeat steps 1 and 2 to stitch the facing to the remaining underpocket.

4. Press the underpockets and set them aside.

Sew the Pocket Sacks

1. Begin with the pocket on the right-hand side of the skirt. With the skirt and upper pocket wrong side up, place the upper pocket on top of the welts. Match and pin the edges toward the center of the skirt. Stitch a ½-inch seam, as shown in **Diagram 6**.

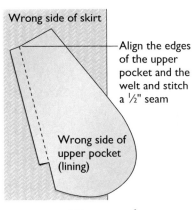

Wrong side of skirt

Align the edges of the upper pocket and the welt and stitch a ½" seam

Wrong side of upper pocket (lining)

Diagram 6

2. Open the layers so the upper pocket is right side up and the skirt is folded back out of the way. Understitch the seam, as shown in **Diagram 7**.

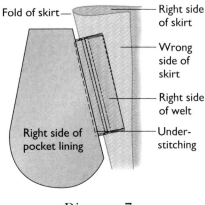

Fold of skirt

Right side of skirt

Wrong side of skirt

Right side of welt

Understitching

Right side of pocket lining

Diagram 7

3. With the skirt and underpocket wrong side up, place the underpocket on top of the welts

and upper pocket. Match and pin the edges of the underpocket away from the center. Stitch ½ inch from the long, straight edge of the underpocket, as shown in **Diagram 8**. Smooth the underpocket over the welts and upper pocket, and pin the curved edges together, as shown. Don't worry if the edges don't match.

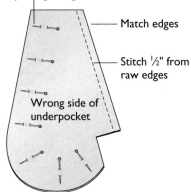

Smooth underpocket over upper pocket and pin edges together

Match edges

Stitch ½" from raw edges

Wrong side of underpocket

Diagram 8

4. With the skirt right side up, fold the skirt back so you can stitch around the pocket sack with a ¼-inch seam, as shown in **Diagram 9**.

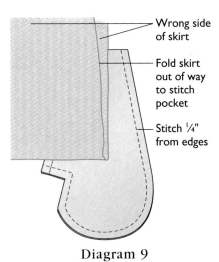

Wrong side of skirt

Fold skirt out of way to stitch pocket

Stitch ¼" from edges

Diagram 9

5. Repeat steps 1 through 4 to stitch the left pocket sack.

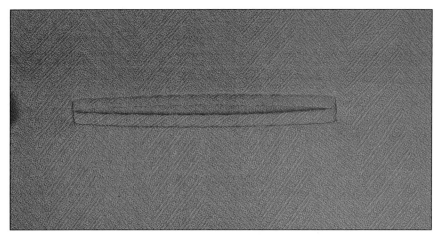

This sleek pocket is made by stitching two welts behind a simple faced opening.

Windowpane Opening

The windowpane opening is a favorite of many home sewers because it is easy to sew successfully. I like to call it the Magic Window because you can do so many things with it.

It begins with a simple faced opening, and the welts are stitched in place behind the opening. There are several advantages to this method.

The opening can be any shape. A pocket can be made with one or two welts or even without welts. The welts can be the same size or different sizes. They can meet at the center in the usual manner, have a space between them, or they can overlap for security.

The windowpane opening can be used successfully on a variety of fabrics, and when used on plaids and prints, the fabric patterns can be matched. For the facing material, I prefer to use silk organza, silk broadcloth, China silk, or a lightweight rayon lining.

Tools & Supplies

♦ Chalk wheel
♦ Lightweight fusible interfacing for the welts
♦ Lightweight fusible web
♦ Lightweight fabric for the opening facing
♦ Paper-backed fusible web

Make the Windowpane Opening

1. Follow steps 2 through 5 of "Mark and Interface the Pocket Openings" on page 58 to mark the pocket and to cut and fuse the lightweight fusible interfacing to the pocket opening. Then cut a rectangle of facing 2 inches wide and the length of the interfacing.

■ SEWING SECRET: When using a fusible interfacing on a portion of a garment, use pinking shears to cut the edges. The pinked edges will soften the edges of the interfacing so they are not visible on the outside of the garment.

2. Using pins and the chalk-marked line that marks the pocket opening on the right side of the garment as a guide, transfer the chalk-marked lines to the interfacing by following the instructions in step 3 of "Mark and Interface the Pocket Opening" on page 58. Then draw a ⅜-inch-wide rectangle on the interfacing with the marked opening at its center.

3. With the garment right side up, center the facing over the chalk lines. Pin the ends of the facing to the garment.

4. With the wrong side up, stitch around the pocket opening on the marked rectangle, as shown in **Diagram 1.**

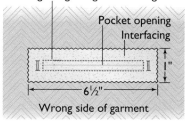

Stitch around pocket on marked rectangle beginning on one long side

Pocket opening
Interfacing

1"

6½"

Wrong side of garment

Diagram 1

■ SEWING SECRET: To stitch a perfect and durable rectangle, shorten the stitch length to 15 to 18 spi (1.5 to 1.0 mm). Change to a straight stitch foot so you can see the marked lines better. Begin at the center of one long side. Stop with the needle in the fabric at each corner, and then pivot. Count the stitches to the center, then stitch an equal number on the other side. Repeat to stitch the other end. Continue stitching and overlap the beginning stitches about ¼ inch.

5. Cut the center of the pocket opening along the chalk mark, stopping ½ inch from each end. Then cut to the corners, as shown in **Diagram 2.**

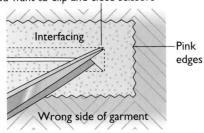

Diagram 2

■ SEWING SECRET: To cut the corners precisely without clipping the stitches, use scissors with very sharp points. Position the scissor points exactly where you want the clip to be, and close the scissors.

6. Turn the pocket opening facing to the wrong side.

7. With the wrong side up, straighten the facing so you can barely see the seamline at the opening.

8. Set the stitch length for 12 spi (2.0 mm), and understitch the long sides of the pocket. Then understitch the ends, as shown in **Diagram 3.**

■ SEWING SECRET: To make sharp, well-defined corners when understitching a faced rectangle,

understitch each side of the rectangle separately.

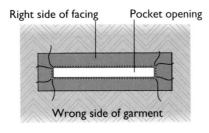

Diagram 3

9. Press lightly and trim the thread ends.

Make the Pocket Welt

1. To make the pocket welt, cut two fabric rectangles 2 inches wide and 1 inch longer than the pocket opening. Clip-mark the center of each short end.

2. If the fabric is soft or loosely woven, interface each welt with a strip of lightweight fusible interfacing ¾ inch wide. With the welt wrong side up, place the interfacing on it so one long edge of the interfacing is aligned with the clips at the short ends of the welt. Fuse the interfacing in place, as shown in **Diagram 4.**

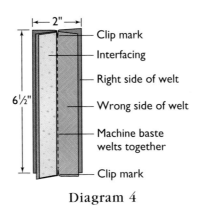

Diagram 4

3. With right sides together, stack the welts so the long cut edges of the interfacing meet. By hand or machine, baste the welts together using the clip marks as guides, as shown in **Diagram 4.**

4. Open the welts so the right sides are out and the basted seam is at the center, as shown in **Diagram 5.** Press lightly.

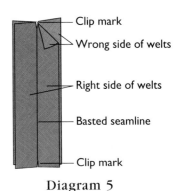

Diagram 5

Sew the Welt

1. Cut two strips of paper-backed fusible web that are ¼ inch wide and 1 inch longer than the pocket opening.

2. With the garment wrong side up, place the fusible web strips on the long sides of the facing about ¼ inch from the opening. Fuse them in place and remove the paper backing from the strips.

■ SEWING SECRET: If the opening facing is organza or tulle, place a piece of paper between the facing and garment to avoid fusing the facing to the garment itself.

3. With the garment right side up, carefully mark the center of the pocket at each end with a straight pin.

4. With the right sides up, center the welt under the opening, aligning the basted seam with a chalk mark at the ends of the pocket opening, as shown in **Diagram 6.**

Cut-away view

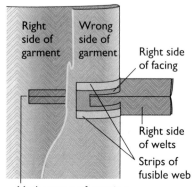

Diagram 6

5. Cover the opening with a press cloth, and baste-fuse the welt in place. (For instructions on how to baste-fuse, see the Sewing Secret under step 5 of "Mark and Interface the Pocket Opening" on page 58.)

6. Examine the pocket welts. If you are not pleased with the baste-fusing results, steam the pocket area to loosen the strips of fusible web. Then remove the welts and reset them.

7. With the garment right side up, fold the facing and welt back to expose the long seam on one side of the pocket to secure the welt.

8. Stitch again on the seamline that outlines the window, as shown in **Diagram 7,** to secure the welt.

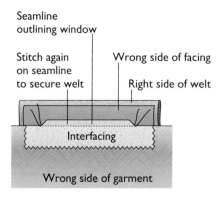

Diagram 7

9. Repeat step 7 to stitch the other side of the pocket.

10. For extra strength, you can edgestitch through all layers around the pocket opening. For instructions, see "How to Edgestitch" on page 6. Begin with the garment right side up and stitch around the pocket $\frac{1}{16}$ inch from the opening, as shown in **Diagram 8.** If you don't edgestitch around the pocket, be sure to follow the instructions in steps 7 and 8 to stitch the ends of the welt in place.

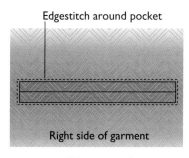

Diagram 8

11. Prepare and sew the pocket sack and complete the pocket.

Men's jackets always have one or more pockets on the inside, but even though they would be very useful, they are rarely found in women's designs. By following these steps, you can easily add a pocket to your next jacket lining.

Generally, the pocket is placed about 1 inch below the waist and 3 inches from the center front. The opening is at least $4\frac{1}{2}$ inches wide and the pocket is $4\frac{1}{2}$ to $5\frac{1}{2}$ inches deep. The pocket can be a single or double-welt design with or without a button. When only one pocket is used, it is generally located on the left-hand side.

The following instructions are for a double-welt pocket that is 5 inches wide.

TOOLS & SUPPLIES

- ◆ Lining for the pocket sack
- ◆ $1\frac{1}{2}$-inch-wide strip of lightweight fusible interfacing
- ◆ Edgestitch or wide straight-stitch foot

PREPARE THE LINING

1. With right sides together, stitch the jacket's front facing and lining. Press the seam toward the lining.
2. With the right side up, chalk-mark the pocket location on the facing/lining section so it is on the crossgrain about 1 inch below the waist and 3 inches from the center front, as shown in **Lining Diagram 1.**

Duplicate the convenience of menswear by adding a pocket to a jacket lining.

How to *Sew* a *Pocket* on a *Lined Jacket*

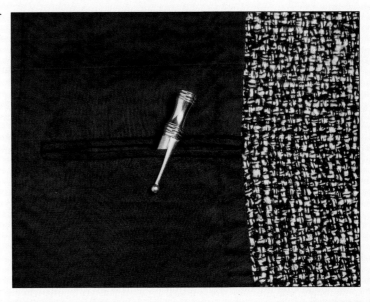

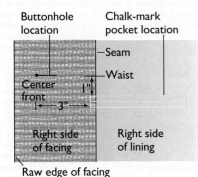

Lining Diagram 1

3. Turn the facing/lining section wrong side up. Cut the 1½-inch-wide interfacing strip 1 inch longer than the pocket opening, and center it over the marked line. Fuse the interfacing in place.

MAKE THE POCKET

1. Make the welt opening using your favorite method.

2. With the facing/lining section right side up, edgestitch around the opening. For instructions see "How to Edgestitch" on page 6.

3. Cut two pocket sacks that are 1 inch wider than the pocket opening and 6 inches long.

4. Turn the facing/lining section wrong side up. With the wrong side up, place one pocket sack over the opening. Align and pin the raw edges of the pocket sack to the top welt, as shown in **Lining Diagram 2**.

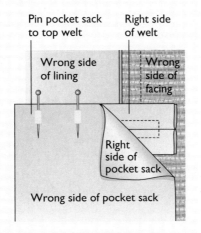

Lining Diagram 2

5. Turn the facing/lining section right side up. Fold the facing and lining back to expose the seamline at the top of the opening. Then stitch again on the seamline to secure the top of the underpocket, as shown in **Lining Diagram 3**.

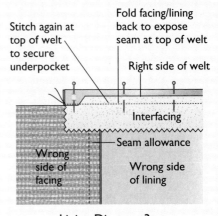

Lining Diagram 3

6. Repeat steps 4 and 5 to set the remaining pocket sack to the bottom welt.

7. Smooth the pocket sacks toward the hem and pin them together.

8. Stitch the sides and bottom of the pocket, rounding the corners at the bottom.

9. Trim away the excess fabric on the pocket sacks.

10. Check the pocket length to be sure the sack does not extend below the hem lining. If it does, restitch the pocket to make it shallower and trim as needed.

How to *Make* a *Porthole Flap*

Used on a classic Chanel suit, this easy pocket design features a pair of oval-shaped porthole pockets with flaps to cover them. The porthole pocket is simply a faced opening without welts. On the Chanel suit, the flap was hand sewn to the right side of the jacket. One advantage of this design is that you can use the flaps to hide a pair of less-than-perfectly stitched pockets.

TOOLS & SUPPLIES
♦ Pattern paper
♦ Lining for the flaps
♦ Lightweight sew-in interfacing
♦ Chalk wheel

MAKE THE POCKET

1. Mark the pocket openings as indicated on the pattern.
2. Make the pockets using the method of your choice. To make the porthole pocket, use the Windowpane Method described on page 60, but do not add the welts.

MAKE THE FLAP PATTERN

1. Draw the shape of the finished flap on the pattern paper. Generally it is ½ to 1 inch wider than the pocket opening and 2¼ to 2½ inches deep.
2. Add ⅜-inch seam allowances to all edges. Cut out the pattern.

■ SEWING SECRET: *To prevent the seam allowances from showing at the ends of the flap, mark and clip the top corners of the flap, as shown in* **Flap Diagram 1.**

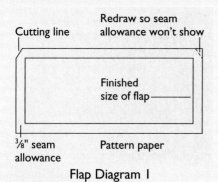

Cutting line

Redraw so seam allowance won't show

Finished size of flap

⅜" seam allowance

Pattern paper

Flap Diagram 1

CUT OUT AND INTERFACE THE FLAP

1. For each flap, cut one flap from the garment fabric, one from the lining, and one from a lightweight interfacing. Clip-mark the centers on the long edges of each piece.

■ SEWING SECRET: *Pocket flaps are usually cut on the same grain as the garment section. But they can also be cut on the bias or on the crossgrain. You can also use pocket flaps as a design element by cutting them from a different colored or textured fabric.*

2. Trim the lining flap ⅛ inch on the sides and bottom. Do not trim the top—that edge that will be sewn to the garment.
3. With the flap wrong side up, place the interfacing on top. Baste them together 3/16 inch from the edges.

MAKE THE FLAP

1. With the right sides together, place the lining on top of the flap. Match and pin the centers of the two pieces. Align and pin the edges together at the ends, making the flap curl toward the lining.
2. Stitch a ¼-inch seam on the sides

and bottom of the flap, stretching the lining to fit the flap, as shown in **Flap Diagram 2.**

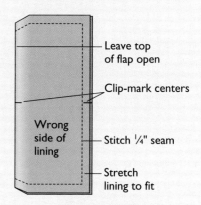

Leave top of flap open

Clip-mark centers

Wrong side of lining

Stitch ¼" seam

Stretch lining to fit

Flap Diagram 2

■ SEWING SECRET: *The seam is stitched only ¼ inch wide, even though the seam allowances were ⅜ inch. The ⅛-inch difference is absorbed by the fabric thickness when the flap is turned right side out.*

3. Grade the seam allowance as needed so the flap will turn smoothly.

■ SEWING SECRET: *To tame the seam allowances at the corners, fold one seam flat. Then fold the other seam flat against the first one. Sew the seam allowances together with a few catchstitches, as shown in* **Flap Diagram 3.** *This will prevent them from shifting and creating a lump when the corner is turned right side out.*

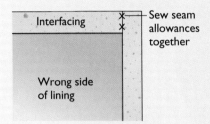

Flap Diagram 3

4. Turn the flap right side out.
5. With the flap lining side up, arrange the seam at the edge so you can see it. Press.
6. Make the remaining flaps, and check to be sure all appear to be the same size.

SEW THE FLAPS ON THE GARMENT

1. Fold the top of the flap under ¼ inch and pin, as shown in **Flap Diagram 4.** If the lining bubbles under the flap, remove the pins, smooth the lining, and repin. Trim away any excess lining at the raw edge.
2. Pin the flaps in place on the garment, and check to be sure they are spaced evenly.
3. Pin-mark a line on the garment at the top and sides of the flap to mark the flap location. Remove the flap, chalk-mark a line ¼ inch below the pinned line, and then remove the pins from the garment.
4. Remove the pins from the flap, and with right sides together, place the flap on the garment, aligning the raw edge

of the flap with the chalked line. Pin the flap in place, as shown in **Flap Diagram 5,** and machine stitch ¼ inch from the raw edges of the flap.
5. Stitch the remaining flaps and check to be sure they appear even.
6. At the ends of the flaps, pull the threads to the wrong side. Give them a sharp tug and knot them securely.
7. With the garment right side up, trim the flap seam to ⅛ inch. Fold

the flap in place and press, using a press cloth.
8. Carefully fold the flap back just below the seam allowance, and hand stitch the flap lining to the garment, as shown in **Flap Diagram 6.**

■ SEWING SECRET: *Be careful when hand sewing so that you don't catch the right side of the pocket flap in your stitches.*

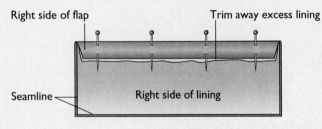

Flap Diagram 4

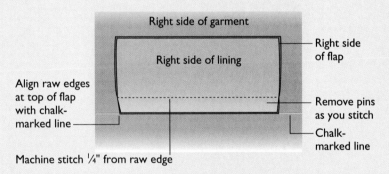

Flap Diagram 5

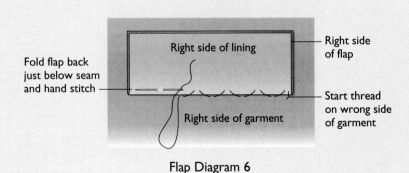

Flap Diagram 6

Inseam Pocket with Invisible Zipper at Seam

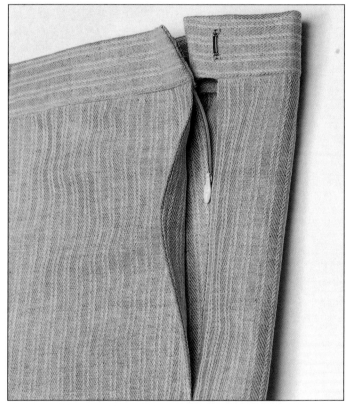

DESIGNER DETAIL

Giorgio Armani

One of Italy's foremost designers of men's and women's ready-to-wear fashions, Giorgio Armani is known for his soft, unstructured tailoring, his sumptuous Italian fabrics, and his use of neutral colors. Armani's supple, uncontrived shapes are easy to wear and enhance the wearer's natural elegance.

Give your slacks a polished look by placing the zipper at an inseam pocket.

Used by Italian designer Giorgio Armani on an elegant pair of wool pants, this ingenious closure combines the easy-to-apply invisible zipper with the familiar inseam pocket.

You can duplicate this high-fashion pocket and closure on almost any pants design. But this sophisticated detail is especially attractive on dressy pants that are made in beautiful natural fiber fabrics, such as fine wools and linens.

Tools & Supplies

♦ Lining material
♦ 2 strips of lightweight fusible interfacing ⅝ inch wide and 9 inches long
♦ 9-inch invisible zipper
♦ Chalk wheel or air erasable pen
♦ Invisible zipper foot

Plan the Design and Adjust the Pattern

1. Draw a sketch of the design you'd like to make. Select a pants pattern that has pockets at the side seams, and press the pattern pieces with a dry iron.

2. If the front and back patterns have extensions at the pocket opening, trim the extensions off the garment sections and add them to the pocket sections.

Cut Out and Mark the Pockets

1. For each pocket, cut the under-pocket from the pants fabric and the upper pocket from the lining.

2. Transfer any matchpoints and construction marks to the pocket sacks, pants front, and pants back.

3. Set the upper pockets aside and clip-mark the bottom of the pocket opening on the seam allowances.

4. Turn the pants fronts over so the wrong sides are up. Starting about 1 inch below each pocket opening, place one ⅝ × 9-inch interfacing strip on the pocket opening seam allowance, and fuse it in place.

Prepare and Set an Invisible Zipper

1. To mark the opening, begin with the left pants back right side up. Chalk-mark the seamlines at the waist and on the opening, as shown in **Diagram 1**.

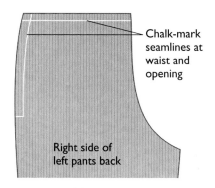

Chalk-mark seamlines at waist and opening

Right side of left pants back

Diagram 1

2. Chalk-mark the seamlines on the left underpocket.

3. To prepare the zipper, set the iron for a medium setting. A hot iron will melt the zipper coils and zipper tape. Open the zipper, and press the zipper tape flat.

4. Key the zipper, following the instructions on page 96.

5. Select the appropriate adaptor shank for your machine, and attach the invisible zipper foot, as shown in **Diagram 2**. Slide the foot left or right as needed until the needle is centered above the foot.

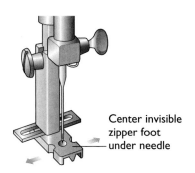

Center invisible zipper foot under needle

Diagram 2

6. With the left pants back right side up, open the zipper and place it face down on the seam allowance. Key the stitched lines on the zipper to the chalk-marked seamline at the waist. Align the stitching line on the coil with the chalk-marked seamline on the pants back, as shown in **Diagram 3**.

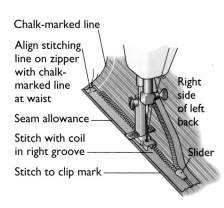

Chalk-marked line

Align stitching line on zipper with chalk-marked line at waist

Seam allowance

Stitch with coil in right groove

Stitch to clip mark

Right side of left back

Slider

Diagram 3

7. Baste as needed so the zipper won't shift during stitching. Remove any pins.

8. Lower the zipper foot so the zipper teeth are in the groove to your right. Stitch down the zipper tape, stopping at the clip-mark at the bottom of the pocket opening, as shown in **Diagram 3**.

9. To position the zipper on the underpocket, close the zipper and place it face down on the right side of the underpocket. Place one pin at the top. Check to be sure the top stops are aligned. Open the zipper and align the stitching line on the coil with the chalk-marked seamline on the under-pocket. Baste the zipper as needed and remove any pins.

10. Lower the zipper foot so the zipper teeth are in the left groove. Stitch down the zipper, as shown in **Diagram 4**, stopping at the clip-mark at the bottom of the pocket opening.

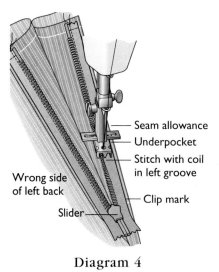

Seam allowance

Underpocket

Stitch with coil in left groove

Clip mark

Wrong side of left back

Slider

Diagram 4

11. Remove the invisible zipper foot from the machine and attach a straight-stitch foot or an all-purpose zigzag foot.

Set the Upper Pocket

1. With the right sides together, place the upper pocket on top of the left pants front, as shown in **Diagram 5.** Match and pin the edges. Stitch the seam as indicated on the pattern.

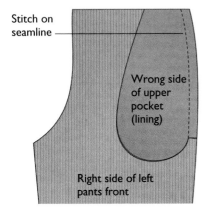

Stitch on seamline

Wrong side of upper pocket (lining)

Right side of left pants front

Diagram 5

2. Fold the seam toward the pocket, and with the right sides up, understitch the seam.

3. With the front wrong side up, press the pocket opening.

Stitch the Side Seam

1. Open the zipper, and with the pants front and underpocket right sides up, place the pants on top of the underpocket, as shown in **Diagram 6.** Match the edges at the waist. On a design like this with a closed inseam pocket, lap the pocket opening over the zipper a scant $\frac{1}{16}$ inch. Pin the pocket opening to the underpocket, placing the pins about $\frac{1}{2}$ inch away.

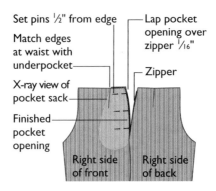

Set pins $\frac{1}{2}$" from edge

Match edges at waist with underpocket

X-ray view of pocket sack

Finished pocket opening

Lap pocket opening over zipper $\frac{1}{16}$"

Zipper

Right side of front

Right side of back

Diagram 6

2. To stitch the side seam below the zipper, change to a zipper foot.

3. Close the zipper. With the right sides together, hold the end of the zipper to the right and stitch the side seam, beginning about $\frac{1}{8}$ inch above the clip-mark and stopping about 2 inches below the bottom of the zipper placket, as shown in **Diagram 7.**

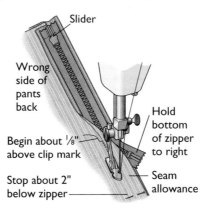

Slider

Wrong side of pants back

Begin about $\frac{1}{8}$" above clip mark

Stop about 2" below zipper

Hold bottom of zipper to right

Seam allowance

Diagram 7

4. Change to a straight-stitch foot or an all-purpose zigzag foot and stitch the rest of the seam.

■ SEWING SECRET: For a smooth finish just below the zipper, stitch the ends of the zipper tape to the seam allowances after the seam is pressed, as shown in **Diagram 8.**

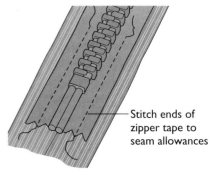

Stitch ends of zipper tape to seam allowances

Diagram 8

Assemble the Pants

1. Stitch the remaining vertical seams. Finish the edges, and press.

2. Stitch the crotch, finish the edges, and press.

3. Turn the pants wrong side out, and close the zipper. Place the pants flat on a table with the front on top. Fold the pocket toward the center front.

■ SEWING SECRET: To be sure the pocket sacks fit smoothly, smooth the underpocket over the upper pocket before pinning the two edges together. If the raw edges don't match, don't force them.

4. Stitch the pocket sacks together with a $\frac{1}{2}$-inch seam allowance. Trim and finish the raw edges as desired.

5. Finish the raw edges of the pocket.

Finish the Pants

1. Finish the pocket on the right side of the pants.

2. Apply the waistband, and finish the hems.

Inseam Pocket with Faux Flap

db

D E S I G N E R   D E T A I L

Geoffrey Beene

Always in style, never in fashion, Geoffrey Beene is known for his imaginative use of color and unusual fabric combinations. One of America's foremost designers, he focuses on beautiful, proportioned lines and supple architectural silhouettes that flatter the figure and maximize the wearer's natural elegance.

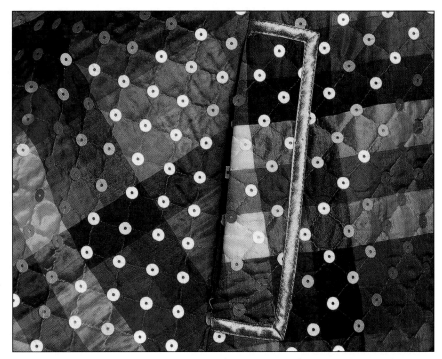

A pocket with a flap trimmed in gold? It's simply an illusion.

Used by Geoffrey Beene on a marvelous, multicolor, quilted evening coat, this imaginative design looks like a pocket with a flap. However, it is just an illusion created by topstitching bias trim to the coat.

You can duplicate this fabulous detail on almost any garment that has inseam pockets, but the faux pocket flap is most attractive when the trim is a contrasting color. Gold and silver trims can transform an ordinary design into a show-stopper.

Tools & Supplies

◆ Cardboard

◆ 30 inches of 1¼-inch-wide bias strip

◆ 2 strips of lightweight fusible interfacing, ⅝ inch wide and 7 inches long

◆ Chalk wheel

◆ Edgestitch or wide straight-stitch foot

Plan the Design

1. Draw a sketch of the design you'd like to make, and select a pattern that closely matches your design.

2. Press the pattern pieces.

3. Make a cardboard template for the faux pocket flap that is 2⅝ inches wide and 6¾ inches long. This length is ½ inch longer than the pocket opening.

4. Pin the pocket flap template on the pattern front so the top of the flap is ¼ inch above the top of the pocket opening. Align one long edge of the pocket flap template with the cutting line on the pattern, as shown in **Diagram 1.**

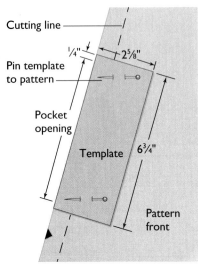

Diagram 1

5. "Try on" the front pattern to check the flap size and placement. At this stage, it is easy to move the flap or to make it larger or smaller.

■ SEWING SECRET: One method I use for trying on a pattern is to pin the shoulder and underarm seams of the front pattern to a blouse with a front opening. Then I put on the blouse.

Make the Bias Trim

1. Cut the 30-inch bias strip in half crosswise. For instructions on "How to Cut and Join Bias Strips," see page 5.

2. Press the bias, stretching it slightly.

3. With wrong sides together, fold the bias strips in half lengthwise. Press the folded edge as shown in

Diagram 2A. With wrong sides together, fold one raw edge in to meet the foldline (as shown in **2B),** on both strips. Press again. Turn each strip over and trim the remaining raw edge to a generous ⅛ inch, as shown in **2C.**

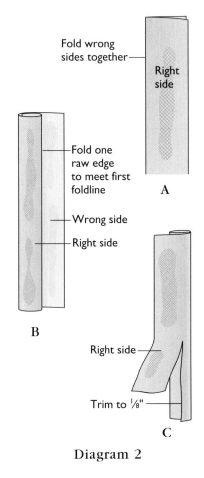

Diagram 2

Cut Out and Prepare the Garment

1. Cut out the garment.

2. On the front and back pieces, clip-mark the top and bottom of the pocket openings in the seam allowances.

3. With the right side up, place the flap template on each garment front and mark around it with the chalk wheel.

4. With the front wrong side up, fuse one of the strips of interfacing to the seam allowance, beginning 1 inch above the pocket opening.

Make the Flap

1. With the front and bias trim right sides up, align and pin the lower edge of the bias to the chalked line. At the corner, fold and pin the bias to make a miter, as shown in **Diagram 3.** Continue until three sides of the flap are outlined.

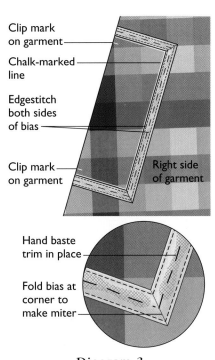

Diagram 3

2. Hand baste the bias in place.

3. Edgestitch both sides of the trim at 12 spi (2.0 mm), as shown in **Diagram 3.** (For instructions, see "How to Edgestitch" on page 6.)

4. Repeat steps 1 through 3 to make the other flap.

5. Sew the pocket and complete the garment.

Collars and Lapels

In this section you will discover ways to use visually striking collars and lapels to transform your favorite patterns into fabulous garments.

An elegant tie collar lends sophistication to any blouse or dress design.

Tie Collar

Used by many designers, including Adolfo, Bill Blass, Chanel, Valentino, and Yves Saint Laurent, the tie collar is one of the easiest collars to sew. It is also one of the most flattering to wear, and it is a striking accent to wear with a suit or jacket.

The tie collar can be applied to almost any round or oval neckline, but its most common use is on a jewel neckline at the base of the neck. The tie can be cut on any grain, but it is usually cut on the lengthwise grain or crossgrain to save fabric, except when a bias cut will enhance the design.

The tie collar is most often made from the same fabric as the blouse, but it can be made of a contrasting fabric or even ribbon. Most tie collars are not interfaced so the tie will drape and tie attractively.

The directions for this technique are based on a classic red-and-black print blouse that was designed by Adolfo. The blouse has a jewel neckline, and the tie collar and the cuffs are both cut from lustrous black silk charmeuse. The finished tie collar is 2 inches wide and 70½ inches long. The button/buttonhole closure at the center front is finished with an extended interfaced facing.

Tools & Supplies

♦ See-through ruler
♦ Pattern paper

DESIGNER DETAIL

Adolfo

A native of Cuba, Adolfo began his fashion career as a millinery designer in Paris and New York. Greatly influenced by the legendary Coco Chanel, Adolfo frequently features popular Chanel details on his suits, such as elaborate braid trims, gilded buttons, chain weights, and tie collars.

Plan the Design and Prepare the Pattern

1. Draw a sketch of the design you'd like to make, and select a blouse pattern with a jewel neckline.

2. If your pattern doesn't have a button/buttonhole closure at the center front, see "Adding Buttons and Buttonholes" on page 235 for details. (For instructions on how to add an extended interfaced facing, see "Facing as Trim" on page 27.)

3. Draft the collar pattern following the instructions in "How to Draft a Tie Collar Pattern," below.

4. All stitching is 12 stitches per inch (2.0 mm).

How to Draft a Tie Collar Pattern

The tie collar pattern is a simple rectangle. It can be designed with or without a seam at the center back, and it can be cut on the lengthwise grain, crossgrain, or bias. It can be as narrow as 1 inch or as wide as 4 inches. The tie ends can be blunt, pointed, or even rounded. And even though most ties are doubled and seamed, a tie can be a single layer with hemmed edges.

These instructions are for a 2-inch-wide tie with blunt ends. Since it is a simple rectangle, the ¼-inch seam allowances are added before the pattern is drafted.

TOOLS & SUPPLIES
♦ Pattern paper

1. On a piece of pattern paper, draw a rectangle 4½ inches wide and 71 inches long.

2. Mark the center back with a notch 35 inches from one end, as shown. Mark the foldlines with a notch at the midpoints on the ends of the tie. Also mark the grainline. For this design, the collar is cut on

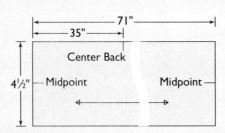

the straight grain with the grainline parallel to the long edges. The tie collar can also be cut on the crossgrain or bias, if desired.

3. If the tie requires a seam at the center back, see "Adding a Seam" on page 201 for instructions.

Cut Out the Garment

1. Cut out the blouse fronts and back with ⅝-inch seam allowances at the neckline.

2. Cut out the tie. Clip-mark the notch at the center back and set the tie aside.

Prepare the Neckline

1. Staystitch the blouse neckline and trim the seam allowances at the neck to ¼ inch.

2. With right sides together, join the shoulders with ⅝-inch seams. Press the seam allowances open or as directed by the pattern guide. Finish the edges.

3. Mark the foldlines for the interfacing and the front edge with clip marks at the top on the neckline and at the bottom on the hem edge. Clip-mark the neckline at the center back.

4. With the blouse wrong side up, fold the self-fabric interfacing to the wrong side at the first set of clip marks, as shown in **Diagram 1.** Press the folded edge.

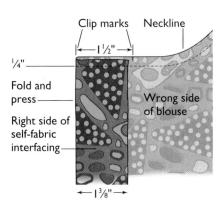

Diagram 1

5. With the blouse right side up, fold the facing using the clip marks as a guide so that the facing and the front are right sides together and the self-fabric interfacing is on top, as shown in **Diagram 2.**

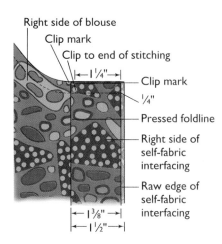

Diagram 2

6. Stitch a ¼-inch seam at the neckline, as shown in **Diagram 2,** stopping 1¼ inches from the edge. Backtack. Clip the neckline edge to the end of the stitching.

7. Turn the front edge facing right side out, and press the foldline at the front edge, as shown in **Diagram 3.**

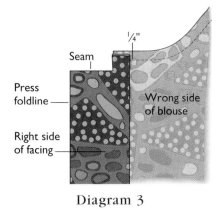

Diagram 3

8. Repeat steps 3 through 7 to stitch the left front.

Attach the Tie Collar

1. With wrong sides together, place the blouse on top of the collar. Match and pin the center back clip marks. Match and pin the raw edges, clipping the neckline only if needed. Check to be sure both sides of the neckline are the same length. Measure each side from the center back to the front, and repin if needed.

2. Stitch the neckline with a ¼-inch seam, as shown in **Diagram 4.**

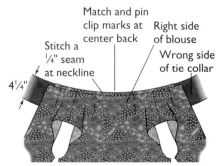

Diagram 4

3. With right sides together, fold the collar lengthwise. Pin the raw edges together. Stitch the tie, beginning at the center front with a ¼-inch seam allowance. Stitch off the end. Begin again without cutting the threads, and stitch across the end, as shown in **Diagram 5.** Repeat to stitch the other tie end.

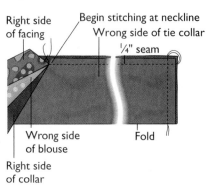

Diagram 5

4. Press the tie ends flat.

5. Tame the seam allowances as described in step 3 of "Make the Flap" on page 70.

6. Turn the collar right side out. Carefully press the seamed edges so the seamlines are flat and right on the edge of the tie.

7. To finish the collar, begin with the blouse right side up. Turn under the raw edge ¼ inch so the folded edge is aligned with the seamline. Pin the collar to the neckline with the pin heads set toward the blouse.

8. With the blouse toward the right, edgestitch the collar in place, as shown in **Diagram 6**. (For instructions, see "How to Edgestitch" on page 6.)

How to *Tie* a *Perfect* *Bow Tie*

If you find it difficult to tie a pretty bow like the one pictured on page 71, you will be delighted to find that these instructions will end your frustrations. The ties have been shortened in these illustrations for clarity.

1. Hold one end of a tie in each hand.

2. Cross the tie ends right over left.

3. Loop the right tie (A) around the left tie (B), as shown in **Bow Diagram 1**.

5. Bring the upper tie (A) down and around the loop (B), as shown in **Bow Diagram 3**.

Bow Diagram 3

6. Then pull the upper tie (A) through the loop it forms around the lower tie loop (B), as shown in the diagram above.

7. Grasp both loops and pull them horizontally to tighten the knot, as shown in **Bow Diagram 4**.

Bow Diagram 1

4. Make a loop with the lower tie (B), as shown in **Bow Diagram 2**.

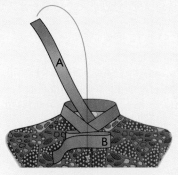

Bow Diagram 2

Bow Diagram 4

8. Adjust the bow as needed.

Edgestitch tie collar in place

Right side of blouse

Diagram 6

■ SEWING SECRET: To prevent the presser foot from pushing the collar forward, many professionals use the points of their scissors or a large T-pin to ease the collar up to the needle.

9. At the ends of the neckline, pull the threads to the wrong side and give them a sharp tug. Secure them with a tailor's knot. See "How to Fasten Threads" on page 35 for instructions.

Remove this fashion-able turtleneck collar and you'll have a jewel neckline.

Detachable Turtleneck

This versatile detachable turtle-neck collar was used on a simple private label design from high-fashion retailer Amen Wardy. The collar is attached with small buttons and buttonholes.

Tools & Supplies

♦ Tape measure

♦ See-through ruler

♦ Pattern paper

♦ Underlining for collar

♦ Lightweight fusible inter-facing for facings

♦ Lightweight, woven, sew-in interfacing for garment

♦ Invisible zipper

♦ Seven ⅜-inch buttons

♦ 2 hooks and eyes

db
DESIGNER DETAIL

Private Label

Private label is a fashion line made especially for a particular store. Sometimes it carries a label such as Saks Fifth Avenue's SFA, but fre-quently it has a store label. Generally these designs reflect current fashion trends, but not high fashion, and since they are designed for value-conscious customers, they are frequently a good source for design ideas.

Plan the Design and Prepare the Pattern

1. Draw a sketch of the design you'd like to make, and select a pattern with a jewel neckline and back opening. If your pattern doesn't have a back opening, see "Adding a Seam" on page 201 for instructions. If your garment front is not cut on the fold, see "Eliminating a Seam" on page 204 for instructions.

2. On the front and back pattern pieces, draw the stitching lines at the neck edge.

3. As shown in **Diagram 1**, tape the pattern pieces to a piece of pattern paper and redraw the front neckline so it is ¼ inch lower at the center front. Redraw

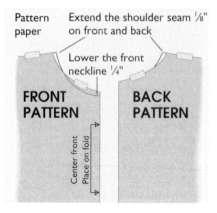

Pattern paper Extend the shoulder seam ⅛"
on front and back

Lower the front neckline ¼"

FRONT PATTERN **BACK PATTERN**

Center front
Place on fold

Diagram 1

both the front and back necklines so they are ⅛ inch higher at the shoulder.

4. Measure the length of the neckline.

◼ SEWING SECRET: To measure a curved line accurately, stand the tape measure or see-through ruler on its edge and shape it to fit the line. Measure the front neckline beginning at the fold and ending at the shoulder seam. Measure the back neckline from the shoulder seam to the center back.

5. Draft the collar pattern, using the directions in "How to Make a Turtleneck Collar Pattern," below.

Cut Out and Sew the Collar

1. Use the turtleneck collar pattern to cut one collar from the fashion fabric and one underlining from a very lightweight material, such as organza or China silk. Trim all edges of the underlining to 1/16 inch. All stitching is 12 spi (2.0 mm).

2. To apply the underlining, place it on the wrong side of the collar. Match and pin the raw edges together. With the underlining on top, stitch a scant ¼ inch from the edges. At the ends, stitch off

How to *Make* a *Turtleneck Collar Pattern*

The detachable turtleneck collar in the photograph on page 75 has a double fold. Since the collar is cut on the bias, the neckline of the collar pattern is 1 inch shorter than the garment neckline to allow for the stretch of the bias.

1. On the front and back pattern pieces, measure the stitching lines at the neck edge. Note the measurement at the shoulder seam.
2. Fold a piece of pattern paper in half vertically.
3. Square a line from the fold. (For instructions, see "Square a Line from a Line" on page 161.) On the squared line, begin at A—the center front—and measure and mark B at the shoulder seam ¼ inch shorter than the front neck measurement, as shown. Measure and mark C at the center back

¼ inch shorter than the back neck measurement.
4. Draw a parallel line 9 inches away to define the total finished width of the turtleneck collar. Draw the foldline midway between the two parallel lines. Then connect the ends of the parallel lines, as shown in the diagram, and add ¼-inch seam allowances to all the edges.
5. Mark the grainline for cutting on the bias, using the instructions in "How to Cut and Join Bias Strips" on page 5.

TOOLS & SUPPLIES
♦ Tape measure
♦ Pattern paper

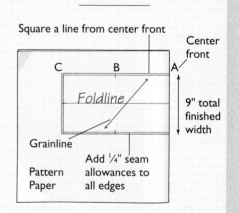

Square a line from center front

Center front

C B A

Foldline

9" total finished width

Grainline

Pattern Paper Add ¼" seam allowances to all edges

A B = front neck minus ¼"
B C = back neck minus ¼"

of the fabric and start stitching again on the adjacent side.

3. With right sides together, fold the collar in half lengthwise at the notches. Pin the edges together, and stitch a ¼-inch seam at one end, beginning at the folded edge and stopping about 1 inch from the center front, as shown in **Diagram 2**. Repeat to sew the other end.

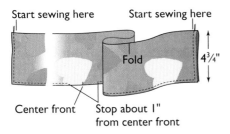

Start sewing here Start sewing here
Fold 4¾"
Center front Stop about 1" from center front

Diagram 2

4. Tame the seam allowances at the corners with a catchstitch, as described in step 3 of "Make the Flap" on page 64.

5. Turn the collar right side out through the opening.

6. Fold the seam allowances into the collar and press all of the edges carefully.

7. Edgestitch the opening closed, as shown in **Diagram 3**.

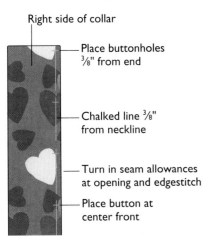

Right side of collar

Place buttonholes ⅜" from end

Chalked line ⅜" from neckline

Turn in seam allowances at opening and edgestitch

Place button at center front

Diagram 3

8. Chalk-mark a line ⅜ inch from the neckline seam. Mark the locations for seven buttonholes on the chalked line, beginning and ending ⅜ inch from the ends and spacing them evenly, as shown in **Diagram 3**.

9. Stitch the buttonholes and set the collar aside.

Cut Out and Sew the Neckline Facings

1. Block-fuse a lightweight fusible interfacing to the fabric that is being used for the front and back neck facings. (For directions on "How to Block-Fuse," see page 86.) Then cut out the front and back neck facings.

2. Serge the unnotched edges of the facings.

3. With the facing right sides together, stitch ⅝-inch seams at the shoulders. Trim the seam allowances to ¼ inch and trim the ends at an angle.

4. Press the seams open and set the facings aside.

Prepare the Garment Neckline

1. With right sides together and raw edges even, stitch ⅝-inch seams at the shoulders. Trim the ends of the seam allowances at an angle.

2. Press the seams open and finish the edges.

3. Staystitch the neckline.

SEWING SECRET: Interface the garment neckline when you staystitch. Generally, the garment is not interfaced when the facings are; however, for this design, the interfacing helps prevent the neckline seam and buttons from peeking out. To make the interfacing, cut a bias strip from a lightweight woven, sew-in interfacing, such as cotton batiste or muslin, that is 1½ inches wide and as long as your neckline (including the back seam allowances). Place the interfacing on the wrong side of the garment beginning at the center back, and pin it to the neckline.

With the garment on top, ease the interfacing to the neckline as you staystitch just inside the seamline. It doesn't matter if the raw edges don't match. Turn the garment wrong side up and clip the edge of the interfacing as needed so it will lie flat, as shown in **Diagram 4**.

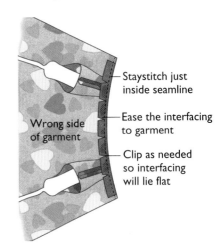

Wrong side of garment

Staystitch just inside seamline

Ease the interfacing to garment

Clip as needed so interfacing will lie flat

Diagram 4

4. Set an invisible zipper at the opening. (See "Prepare and Set an Invisible Zipper" on page 67 for instructions.)

Set the Facing

1. With right sides together, place the facing on top of the garment. Match the seams and pin the raw edges together.

2. As shown in **Diagram 5**, fold the ends of the facing in place, using the directions for "How to Sew a Facing Finish for a Slot Zipper" on page 113.

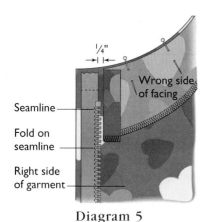

Seamline

Fold on seamline

Right side of garment

¼"

Wrong side of facing

Diagram 5

3. Stitch a ⅝-inch seam at the neckline, as shown in **Diagram 6**.

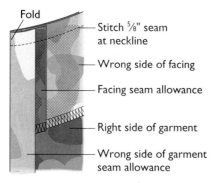

Fold

Stitch ⅝" seam at neckline

Wrong side of facing

Facing seam allowance

Right side of garment

Wrong side of garment seam allowance

Diagram 6

4. Grade the seam allowances and turn the facing right side out.

■ SEWING SECRET: To grade the seam allowances, trim them so that they are uneven in width.

Trim the seam allowance on the bias interfacing to ¼ inch, then trim the seam allowance on the garment so it is slightly narrower. Them trim the seam allowance on the facing so it is the narrowest.

5. With right sides up, understitch. For instructions, see "How to Understitch" on page 22.

6. With the facing side up, roll the seamline toward the facing and press the neck edge.

Finish the Neckline

1. Chalk-mark a line on the facing ⅜ inch below the neckline as a guide for setting the buttons, as shown in **Diagram 7**.

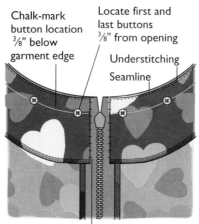

Chalk-mark button location ⅜" below garment edge

Locate first and last buttons ⅜" from opening

Understitching Seamline

Slipstitch edges of facing to wrong side of zipper tape

Diagram 7

2. Mark the button locations on the chalked line, using the buttonholes on the collar as guides.

3. With the facing right side up, sew the buttons in place, as shown in **Diagram 7**.

Sew the Hooks and Eyes on the Collar

1. With the garment wrong side up, sew a hook on the left back at the neckline just above the zipper. Sew the corresponding eye on the right back.

2. Slipstitch the ends of the facing to the wrong side of the zipper tape, as shown in **Diagram 7**.

3. Fold the collar lengthwise as it will be worn so the top layer is ½ inch longer than the under-layer. At the ends, sew a stitch or two through both layers about ¼ inch below the top of the collar so the collar will maintain its folded position.

4. Turn the collar to the neck side, and sew a hook to one side of the collar ¼ inch below the folded edge, as shown in **Diagram 8**. Sew the corresponding eye to the other side. Sew a second hook and eye about 1 inch below the first one.

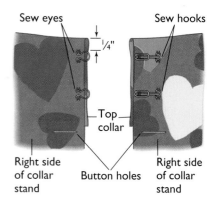

Sew eyes

Sew hooks

¼"

Top collar

Right side of collar stand

Button holes

Right side of collar stand

Diagram 8

5. Complete the garment.

Double Flounce Collar

Diane Fries's signature dresses typically feature double flounce collars finished with bias bindings at the neck. This collar can be used on most neckline shapes, but it is especially attractive on jewel, round, oval, and V-shaped necklines. You can duplicate this feminine look by following these instructions.

Tools & Supplies

♦ Tape measure
♦ Pattern paper

Add a double flounce collar in two different but coordinating prints for a romantic and feminine look.

Plan the Design and Prepare the Pattern

1. Draw a sketch of the design you'd like to make, and select a blouse pattern with a V-neck. If your pattern has a different neckline, see "Basic V-Neck" on page 225 for directions.

2. On the front and back patterns, trim away any seam allowances at the neck edge, since that edge will be finished with a binding.

3. Draft the patterns for the flounce collar, using the directions for "How to Make a Flounce Collar Pattern" on page 80.

4. There are no seam allowances at the neckline. The seams joining the flounces are ¼ inch, and the stitch length is 12 spi (2.0 mm), unless otherwise noted.

Prepare the Neckline

1. Use the front and back blouse pattern pieces to cut the bodice. Use the front and back flounce pattern pieces to cut the collar sections.

2. Cut the bias strips for the binding. See "How to Cut and Join Bias Strips" on page 5 for instructions. For a finished binding ¼ inch wide, cut the bias strips 2½ inches wide. To determine the length of the binding strip, measure the length of the neckline and add 5 to 6 inches.

3. With right sides together, join the front and back at the shoulders with ⅝-inch seams and trim the ends of the seam allowances on a diagonal. Press the seams open or press as directed by the pattern guide. Finish the edges of the seam allowances.

4. Staystitch the neckline a scant ¼ inch from the edge or, if the binding will be a different width, slightly narrower than the finished binding.

Make the Collar

1. With right sides together, join the lower front flounces at the center front with a ¼-inch seam. Repeat to join the upper front flounces.

How to *Make a Flounce Collar Pattern*

A flounce is a circular-cut ruffle. Most flounces have little or no gathers at the edge joining the garment, but they can be cut with added fullness and gathered.

The principles for making this flounce collar pattern can be adapted for making flared skirts, sleeves, and palazzo and bell-bottom pants.

TOOLS & SUPPLIES

♦ Tape measure
♦ Pattern paper

PREPARE THE DESIGN

1. If you don't have a picture of the design, make a sketch.
2. Examine the sketch to determine where you want to place the seams on the flounce. On a V-neck, there are generally three seams: one at the center front (the bottom of the V), and one at each shoulder seam.

MEASURE THE NECKLINE

1. Mark the stitching lines—the width of the binding—at the neck on the front and back pattern pieces.
2. On the front pattern piece, measure the marked stitching line, beginning at the center front and ending at the shoulder seam.
3. On the back pattern piece, measure the marked stitching line, beginning at the shoulder seam and

ending at the fold. Multiply that number by two.

DRAFT AND MAKE THE FRONT FLOUNCE PATTERNS

1. On pattern paper, draw a rectangle equal to the finished length of the blouse neckline from the center front to the shoulder seam and the finished width of the narrowest flounce plus a ½-inch hem allowance, as shown in **Flounce Diagram 1**. For this design, the lower flounce is 2⅝ inches

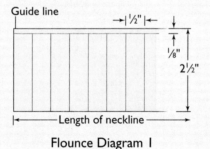

Guide line $\rightarrow$ |½"| $\leftarrow$

⅛"

2½"

|← Length of neckline →|

Flounce Diagram 1

wide and the upper flounce is 2 inches wide.

2. Draw a guide line ⅛ inch from one long edge. Mark the slash lines on the pattern every ½ inch, beginning at the other long edge and stopping at the guideline, as shown in **Flounce Diagram 1.** Cut along each slash line, starting at the bottom of the pattern and ending at the guide line.
3. Place the flounce pattern on another piece of pattern paper. Spread each slash open ¼ inch and tape them to the paper, as shown in **Flounce Diagram 2** on the opposite page. For more fluting at the edge, spread the slashes a greater amount. Redraw the hemline curve.
4. Add ¼-inch seam allowances at the center front and shoulder seams, as shown in **Diagram 2**. Do not add a seam allowance at the neck because

2. With right sides together, join the front and back lower flounces with a ¼-inch seam. Trim the seam allowances to ⅛ inch, and serge or zigzag the edges together. Press the seam allowances to one side. Repeat to join the lower flounces.

3. Use a serger or a zigzag stitch to hem the collar with a narrow satin-stitched hem, beginning and ending at the left shoulder. At the

end, pull the threads to the wrong side and secure them with a tailor's knot. (See page 35 for instructions on "How to Fasten Threads.") Repeat this step to hem the upper flounce. Press the hems.

■ SEWING SECRET: To make a narrow satin-stitched hem using a zigzag stitch, begin with the collar right side up. Machine stitch ½ inch from the edge. Fold

the hem under on the stitched line, and edgestitch close to the folded edge of the hem. Then trim close to the edgestitching, as shown in **Diagram 1.** (For instructions,

Trim as close as possible to edgestitching

Fold under on stitched line and edgestitch

Right side of flounce

Diagram 1

the edge will be finished with a binding.

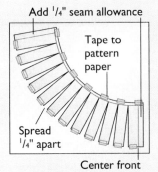

Flounce Diagram 2

5. Mark the grainline parallel to the center front.

6. Cut out the pattern and label it "Upper Front Flounce—Cut 2."

7. To make the lower flounce pattern, trace the upper flounce pattern and add ⅝-inch to the hem edge, as shown in **Flounce Diagram 3**. Mark the grainline, and label the pattern "Lower Front Flounce—Cut 2."

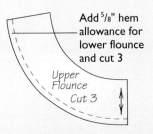

Flounce Diagram 3

8. Cut out the lower flounce pattern.

MAKE THE BACK FLOUNCE PATTERNS

1. On a piece of pattern paper, draw a rectangle the finished length of the back neckline, as calculated in step 3 of "Measure the Neckline," and 2½ inches wide (the finished width of the narrowest flounce plus a hem).

2. Follow steps 2 and 3 of "Draft and Make the Front Flounce Patterns." Trace the upper back flounce pattern, and mark it for placement on the fold at the center back. Label the pattern "Upper Back Flounce—Cut 1."

3. Add ¼-inch seam allowances at the shoulder seams. Do not add a seam allowance at the neckline because that edge will be finished with a binding.

4. Mark the grainline parallel to the center back.

5. Cut out the pattern and label it "Upper Back Flounce—Cut 1."

6. To make the lower back flounce pattern, trace the upper back flounce pattern and add ⅝ inch at the hem edge.

7. Cut out the pattern and label it "Lower Back Flounce—Cut 1."

see "How to Trim Closely" on page 19.)

Thread the sewing machine with machine embroidery thread (preferably size 30). Set the stitch length for 24 spi (0.5 mm) and the stitch width for 2.0 mm.

With the right side up, center the edge of the collar hem under the needle. Hold the ends of the threads and begin to stitch, allowing the needle to stitch off

the collar when it swings to the right, as shown in **Diagram 2**.

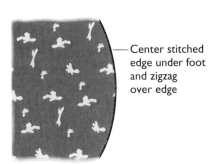

Center stitched edge under foot and zigzag over edge

Diagram 2

Attach the Collar

1. Rethread the machine with regular sewing thread and reset the machine for a straight stitch at 12 spi (2.0 mm).

2. With the right sides up, place the smaller flounce on top of the larger flounce. Match the seamlines and pin the raw edges together.

3. With right sides up, place the collar on top of the bodice neckline. Match the shoulder seamlines and hand baste the collar in place. Machine stitch a scant ¼ inch from the edges.

4. Bind the neckline using the directions for "French Binding" on page 45.

■ SEWING SECRET: Since the binding on the inside of the garment will not be visible, I stitch in the ditch by hand with a tiny running stitch. Sewing by hand allows me to control the bias, and it prevents twists and ripples on the finished binding.

5. At the bottom of the V, fold the bodice in half with right sides together and stitch a small dart on the binding by hand or machine, as shown in **Diagram 3**.

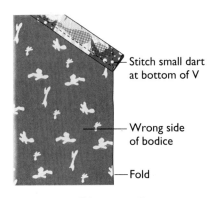

Stitch small dart at bottom of V

Wrong side of bodice

Fold

Diagram 3

6. Complete the garment.

Use the embroidery functions on your sewing machine to create a one-of-a-kind fancy lapel.

Fancy Lapels

The fancy lapel is another of those fabulous details that belies the notion that high fashion must be difficult or time consuming. It can be used on a variety of designs from collarless blouses and jackets to traditional blazers or double-breasted styles.

The two lapels are the same on most designs, but they can be wide or narrow. And, if you can't decide which you prefer, you can follow the lead of English designer Vivienne Westwood and create a design with two entirely different lapels.

In these instructions, the fancy lapel is applied to a simple blouse with a front opening.

Tools & Supplies

♦ Pattern paper
♦ See-through ruler
♦ Stiletto tracing wheel
♦ Fusible interfacing

Design the Lapel

1. Sketch the design and select a blouse pattern with a front opening. Don't worry if it has a collar.

2. Trace the blouse front pattern onto a piece of pattern paper to make a working pattern. Indicate the cutting lines, center front, notches, and grainline on the

traced pattern. Do not cut out the new pattern.

3. On the line marking the front seamline of the working pattern, label a point 2 to 3 inches above the bustline A, as shown in **Diagram 1.** On a jacket or coat, it can be located much lower.

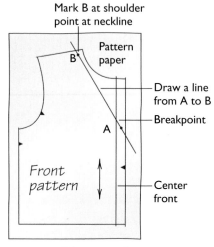

Diagram 1

4. Mark B on the shoulder at the neckline, as shown in **Diagram 1.**

5. Draw a line from A, which is the breakpoint, to B, as shown. The lapel breakpoint is located on the front edge at the beginning of the roll line.

6. Fold the pattern to the underside on line AB, as shown in **Diagram 2.**

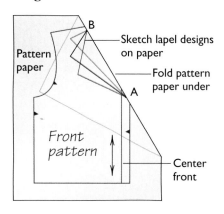

Diagram 2

7. Draw the lapel shape—the seamline—on the pattern as shown in **Diagram 2.** You can see a few of the many possibilities. Experiment with a variety of shapes and straight and curved lines until you find a lapel shape that you like.

Make the Front Pattern

1. Add ⅝-inch seam allowances to the new lapel, as shown in **Diagram 3.**

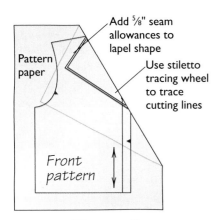

Diagram 3

2. Trace the cutting lines of the lapel with a stiletto tracing wheel to transfer them to the layer of paper underneath.

3. Open the pattern flat and examine the traced lines. Redraw the lines as needed so they meet the cutting lines at the shoulder and front edge smoothly, as shown in **Diagram 4.**

■ SEWING SECRET: A professional patternmaker will trace the working pattern to make a clean pattern, but I'm always so anxious to cut and sew that I frequently skip this step.

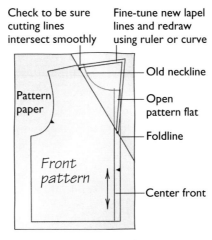

Diagram 4

Make the Front Facing Pattern

1. Place the original facing pattern on top of the front pattern, and align the center fronts and shoulder seams. Use the stiletto tracing wheel to trace the inside edge of the facing, as shown in **Diagram 5.**

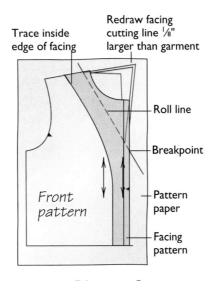

Diagram 5

2. Redraw the cutting line on the facing ⅛ inch larger than the garment section, as shown in **Diagram 5.** That little bit of fullness will keep the lapel points

from curling up and the lapel will roll smoothly when the blouse is worn.

3. Pin the working pattern to a piece of pattern paper. Use the stiletto tracing wheel to trace the cutting lines, any notches, and the grainline on the front facing pattern, as shown in **Diagram 6.**

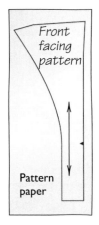

Diagram 6

4. Cut out the working pattern and the facing pattern.

Cut Out the Garment

1. From the fashion fabric, cut out the fronts, back, back facing, and sleeves.

2. Block-fuse the interfacing to the wrong side of the fashion fabric, and cut out the front facings. (For instructions, see "How to Block Fuse" on page 86.)

Prepare the Garment

1. All seam allowances are ⅝ inch, and the stitch length is 12 spi (2.0 mm).

2. With right sides together, join the fronts and back at the shoulders. Repeat to join the front and back facings.

3. Press the seams open. Trim as needed, and finish the edges.

Stitch the Facing

1. With right sides together, place the facing on top of the garment. Match the shoulder seams and notches. Pin the edges together.

■ SEWING SECRET: To avoid pleats on the facing and to prevent the lapel from curling up, begin pinning at the center back and pin toward the front. Pin the edges evenly, stopping about 3 inches from the lapel points. Place a pin at each point. Then pin the front edges, beginning at the hem.

At the lapel points, the facing will bubble slightly because it is longer than the garment edge. Stretch the front and ease the facing to the blouse. Use a short basting stitch to baste for 2 inches on each side of the points, as shown in **Diagram 7**.

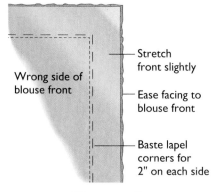

Stretch front slightly

Wrong side of blouse front

Ease facing to blouse front

Baste lapel corners for 2" on each side

Diagram 7

2. As shown in **Diagram 7**, stitch the neckline and front edges. Begin stitching at the center back for the right and left sides. Since the lapel points are basted, it doesn't matter that the blouse will not always be on top when stitching. Remove the basting stitches.

3. Press the seams open, and grade the seams.

■ SEWING SECRET: It's important to grade the seam allowances when you want to eliminate bulk. This is done by trimming the seam allowances to different widths. In this technique, trim the seam allowance that will be closest to the body to less than ¼ inch. Then trim the seam allowance toward the facing side—the lapel on this blouse design—to ¼ inch so it provides a buffer for the raw edges beneath it, as shown in **Diagram 8**.

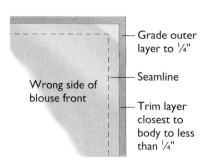

Grade outer layer to ¼"

Seamline

Wrong side of blouse front

Trim layer closest to body to less than ¼"

Diagram 8

On inward curves, clip the seam allowances as needed so the edge will lie flat, as shown in **Diagram 9A**. On outward curves, cut small triangles out of the seam allowances to reduce bulk, as shown in **9B**.

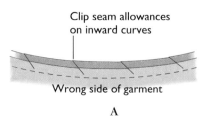

Clip seam allowances on inward curves

Wrong side of garment

A

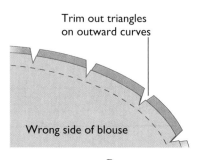

Trim out triangles on outward curves

Wrong side of blouse

B

Diagram 9

4. To ensure a sharp lapel point, tame the seam allowances with a couple of catchstitches as described in "Make the Flap" in step 3 on page 64 so the seam allowances will lie flat and turn smoothly.

5. Turn the facings right side out.

6. With the blouse side up, roll the seamline toward the blouse and press the edge.

■ SEWING SECRET: To avoid a pressing imprint, use a press cloth. If the design is made of wool, cover the garment first with a wool press cloth and then with a muslin cloth. When you remove the wool press cloth, the static electricity will give the fabric depth.

7. Topstitch or understitch the edge of the seam. (For instructions, see "How to Understitch" on page 22.)

8. Finish the garment.

Notched Collar

Ellen Tracy

The Ellen Tracy house is known for its fashionable career wardrobes. Designed by Linda Allard, they are favorites of value-conscious executives who appreciate fine fabrics and quality construction.

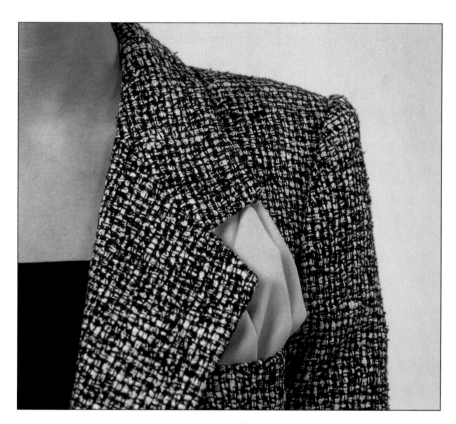

Use this designer method to make perfect notched collars.

The traditional notched collar can be challenging even for experienced tailors. But with these directions from a former employee at Ellen Tracy, success is almost guaranteed.

Tools & Supplies

♦ Fusible knit or weft-insertion interfacing in an appropriate weight

Prepare the Jacket Sections

1. Select a pattern with a notched collar.

2. All seams are ⅝ inch and all stitching is 12 spi (2.0 mm) unless indicated otherwise.

3. Block-fuse the interfacing to the wrong side of the fabric from which you will cut the jacket fronts, front facings, collar, and undercollar. (For instructions, see "How to Block-Fuse" on page 86.)

4. From the interfaced fabric, cut out the fronts, front facings, collar, and undercollar.

5. Cut out the rest of the jacket sections from the remaining fabric.

Prepare the Collar

1. With the undercollar right sides together, match and pin the seam at the center back and stitch, as shown in **Diagram 1**.

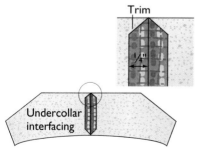

Diagram 1

How to *Block-Fuse*

Widely used in the fashion industry, block-fusing is the technique of bonding a large piece of interfacing to the fabric before the garment sections are cut. Follow these simple steps to block-fuse at home.

1. Cover the pressing surface with paper towels.
2. Place the fabric wrong side up on the paper towels.
3. Place the interfacing on top of the fabric with the fusible side against the fabric.
4. Following the manufacturer's instructions, fuse the interfacing.

2. Press the seam open and trim it to ¼ inch, as shown in **Diagram 1** on page 85.

3. With right sides together, match and pin the edges of the collar and undercollar and stitch, as shown in **Diagram 2**.

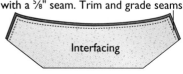

Stitch upper collar and undercollar with a ⅝" seam. Trim and grade seams.

Interfacing

Diagram 2

4. Press the seam allowances open, and trim and grade them.

5. Tame the seam allowances at the points with a couple of catchstitches (see "Make the Flap" step 3 on page 64) and turn the collar right side out.

6. With the undercollar side up, roll the seamline toward the facing and press the collar.

7. Set the collar aside.

Prepare the Jacket

1. Tape the lapel roll lines on the jacket fronts. (See "How to Tape a

Roll Line" on the opposite page.)

2. With right sides together, join the jacket fronts and backs at the shoulders. Repeat this step to join the front and back facings.

3. Press the seam allowances open, and trim as needed. If the jacket will not be lined, finish the edges of the shoulder seam allowances.

Attach the Collar

1. With right sides up, place the collar on top of the jacket. Match the notches and pin the edges together. Be sure the ends of the collar match the marked circles on the jacket. Stitch a seam, as shown in **Diagram 3**. Begin and end ¼ inch from the ends with a spottack.

Stitch seam stopping ¼" from end of collar and spottack

Wrong side of undercollar

Raw edges

Interfacing

Match ends of collar to circle

Right side of upper collar

Right side of jacket front

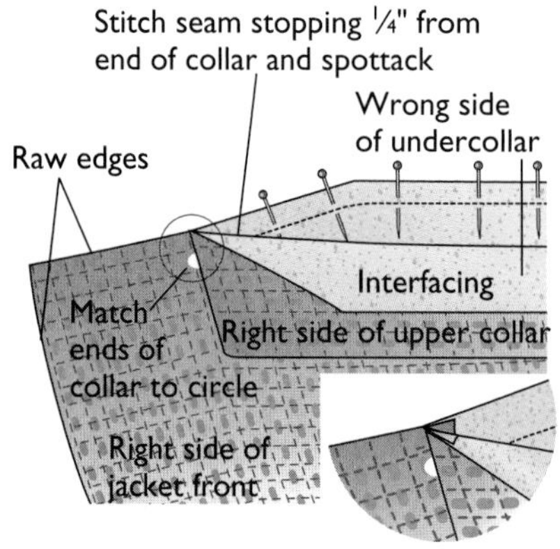

Diagram 3

2. With right sides together, place the jacket on top of the facing with the collar in between the two layers.

3. Match the edges of the facing and the upper collar. Match the notches and pin the edges together. Check to be sure the ends of the collar match the marked circles on the jacket and stitch, as shown in **Diagram 4**, beginning and ending ¼ inch from the ends with a spottack.

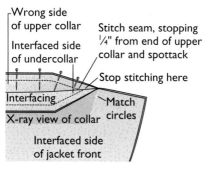

Wrong side of upper collar

Interfaced side of undercollar

Stitch seam, stopping ¼" from end of upper collar and spottack

Stop stitching here

Interfacing

Match circles

X-ray view of collar

Interfaced side of jacket front

Diagram 4

■ SEWING SECRET: Check to be sure the upper collar of the jacket is wide enough to cover the undercollar. With wrong sides together, place the facing on top of the jacket. Align the seams you have just sewn, and fold the collar into the position it will have when the jacket is worn. If the edge of the collar curls up or the seamline shows, the upper collar is too short. To correct it, restitch the collar/facing seam with a narrower seam and rip out the original stitching.

4. With right sides together, sandwich the collar between the jacket and facing. At the front edge, match the notches and pin the edges together. At the lapel

How to *Tape* a *Roll Line*

You can stabilize the roll line on jacket lapels by adding a stay, in this case a strip of interfacing, during the construction process.

1. Interface the jacket fronts.

2. With the interfacing side up on the right jacket front, mark the roll line with a pencil.

3. Place the stay—the strip of interfacing—on the roll line so that the edge toward center front is aligned with the line, as shown.

4. Pin the ends of the tape to the seamlines at the neckline and front edges.

5. Unpin one end of the tape and repin so the tape is ½ inch shorter, as shown.

6. Adjust the fullness under the tape, and trim any excess tape. Then sew or fuse the tape to the interfacing following the manufacturer's instructions.

7. Repeat steps 2 through 6 to tape a roll line on the left jacket front.

TOOLS & SUPPLIES

♦ 2 strips of lightweight fusible interfacing ¼ to ⅜ inch wide

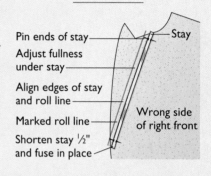

Pin ends of stay
Stay
Adjust fullness under stay
Align edges of stay and roll line
Marked roll line
Shorten stay ½" and fuse in place
Wrong side of right front

---

points, ease the facing to the jacket and baste.

■ SEWING SECRET: Turn the seam right side out. If the facing is too tight or there is a dimple next to the notch, rebaste, easing more of the facing to the jacket.

5. Stitch the jacket front and facing together. At the ends of the collar, stitch onto the collar ¼ inch, as shown in **Diagram 5,** and spot-tack at the ends of the stitching.

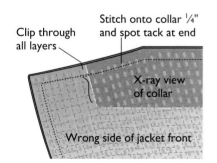

Clip through all layers
Stitch onto collar ¼" and spot tack at end
X-ray view of collar
Wrong side of jacket front

Diagram 5

6. At the spottacks, clip through all the layers to the seamline, as shown in **Diagram 5.**

Finish the Collar and the Jacket

1. Press the collar and facing seams open. Grade the seams as needed.

2. Tame the seam allowances with a couple of catchstitches at the lapel points. For instructions, on how to tame seam allowances, see step 3 of "Make the Flap" on page 64.

3. Turn the lapels right side out, and with the jacket side up, press the edges of the lapels.

4. With the jacket right side out, reach between the jacket and

facing. Grasp the neckline seam allowances of the facing and the jacket and pull them out.

5. Stitch the neckline seam allowances together by hand or machine, as shown in **Diagram 6.**

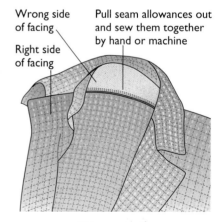

Wrong side of facing
Pull seam allowances out and sew them together by hand or machine
Right side of facing

Diagram 6

6. Complete the jacket.

Plackets and Fasteners

More than just a device to ease dressing, plackets and fasteners run the gamut from inconspicuous zippers to decorative plackets.

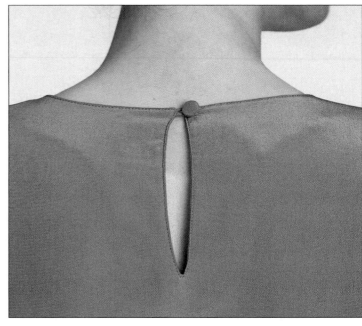

Dress up your keyhole neckline with a classy button and button loop.

Keyhole Opening

This keyhole opening is simply a faced neckline with a slashed placket. It is frequently used on better-quality blouses because it is easy to finish, and since it is a flat, bulk-free finish, it can be used at either the center front or center back of the blouse. It requires less fabric than a zipper or a button/buttonhole closure, and suitable fasteners—a hook and eye or button and button loop—are readily available and less expensive than zippers and multiple buttons.

In these instructions, the placket replaces a button/buttonhole closure on the blouse front. The jewel neckline is fastened with a hook and eye at the neckline, but it can be fastened with a button and button loop. For dressier designs and longer openings, the opening can be located at the center back, as shown in the photo.

Tools & Supplies

♦ Pattern paper

♦ Chalk wheel

♦ Air-erasable pen

♦ Edgestitch or wide straight-stitch foot (optional)

♦ Lightweight fusible interfacing

Prepare the Pattern

1. Sketch the design, and select a blouse pattern with a jewel neckline and a button/buttonhole closure at the center front. Press the pattern pieces with a dry iron.

2. If your pattern doesn't have a neck facing, see "Making a Neckline Facing" on page 210.

3. Trim the end of the facing pattern so that the pattern ends at the center front.

4. Draft the placket pattern following the directions in "How to Draft a Keyhole Placket Facing," below.

5. Trim the seam allowances on all the pattern pieces at the neckline so they are ¼ inch wide.

How to Draft a Keyhole Placket Facing

To draft a front facing pattern, begin with a commercial pattern that has a button/buttonhole closure at the center front. This pattern can be adapted for designs with a fold at the center front or to add a keyhole opening at the center back. It can also be used when adding a keyhole opening to a design with a collar or a bias binding neckline.

1. Review the directions for "Making a Neckline Facing" on page 210.
2. On the pattern front, find the center front and draw the slash line for the placket on it. Begin at the neckline seamline and extend the slash line 5 inches, as shown in **Keyhole Diagram 1.** When placing the placket at the center back, draw the slash line 4 to 5 inches long.

3. Draw the finished edge of the facing 1½ inches from the slash line. Round the corners at the bottom, as shown in **Diagram 1,** and trace the cutting line at the neckline.
4. To finish the pattern, fold a piece of pattern paper vertically. Align the fold with the center front on the front pattern and trace the facing pattern. Then remove the pattern paper, as shown in **Keyhole Diagram 2.**

5. Mark the grainline, the slash, and the end of the opening on the facing pattern.
6. Cut out the facing pattern and open it. Mark the pattern "Cut 1," as shown in **Keyhole Diagram 3.**

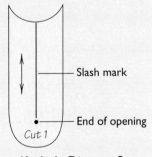

Keyhole Diagram 3

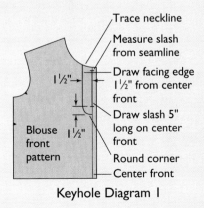

Keyhole Diagram 1

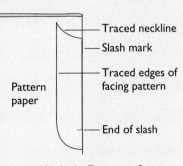

Keyhole Diagram 2

Cut Out the Garment

1. The seam allowances for this technique are ¼ inch at the neckline and at the slash. All other seam allowances are ⅝ inch unless otherwise stated. At the keyhole the facing width is 1¼ inches.

2. Cut out the blouse front and blouse back with folds at the centers.

3. On the blouse front, make a 1-inch clip mark at the center front neckline edge.

4. Mark the end of the slash with a chalk mark or air-erasable marking pen.

5. Before cutting the front and back facings from the fashion fabric, block-fuse a very light-weight interfacing to the wrong side of the fabric following the instructions in "How to Block-Fuse" on page 86. Then cut the front and back facings from the interfaced fabric.

6. With the front facing wrong side up, chalk-mark the slash at the opening.

7. Slash the opening, stopping ¼ inch from the bottom, as shown in **Diagram 1**.

8. Use a temporary marking pen to mark the stitching line at the bottom of the opening, as shown in **Diagram 1**. Notice that the stitching line does not have a point at the bottom of the opening.

■ SEWING SECRET: Always test any fabric marking tool on a scrap of the fashion fabric you are using and remove the marks before marking the garment pieces. Follow the manufacturer's instructions for removing your test mark.

Assemble the Garment and Facing

1. All stitching for this technique is 12 spi (2.0 mm) unless otherwise noted.

2. With the blouse front and back right sides together, stitch the shoulder seams.

3. Press the shoulder seams open or as directed by the pattern guide.

■ SEWING SECRET: Remember to use a press cloth between the fashion fabric and the iron. You may want to purchase a press cloth at your favorite fabric and notions store or by mail order (see "Resources" on page 243), or you can make your own from a scrap of silk organza or a piece of muslin. Be sure to wash the muslin first to remove any sizing that may have been applied to the surface of the fabric.

4. Serge or finish the edges of the shoulder seam allowances.

5. With the front and back neckline facings right sides together, stitch the shoulder seams, and press them open.

6. Serge or finish the outer edges of the facings.

7. Staystitch the neckline of the blouse a scant ¼ inch from the edge.

Stitch the Keyhole and Neckline Facings

1. With right sides together, place the keyhole and neckline facings on top of the blouse, as shown in **Diagram 2**.

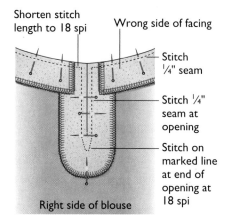

Shorten stitch length to 18 spi

Wrong side of facing

Stitch ¼" seam

Stitch ¼" seam at opening

Stitch on marked line at end of opening at 18 spi

Right side of blouse

Diagram 2

2. Match the seams and notches, and align the facing and blouse at the ends of the slash.

3. Pin the edges of the facings and the blouse together around the neckline and around the slash, as shown in **Diagram 2**.

■ SEWING SECRET: At the keyhole opening, set the pins so the heads are toward the slash so they will be easy to remove as you sew.

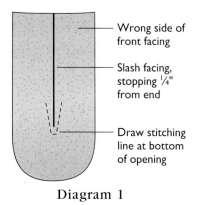

Wrong side of front facing

Slash facing, stopping ¼" from end

Draw stitching line at bottom of opening

Diagram 1

4. Before continuing, fold the front vertically. Match the shoulder seams and raw edges at the underarm. The fold and slash should be aligned on the center front. If they are not, correct the alignment and repin.

5. To stitch the neckline, set the stitch length for 15 spi (1.5 mm) and stitch a ¼-inch seam around the neckline, stopping ½ inch from the clip mark at the center front. Shorten the stitch length to 18 spi (1.0 mm) and stitch 1 inch, as shown in **Diagram 2**. Reset the stitch length to 15 spi (1.5 mm) and continue stitching the neckline.

6. To stitch the keyhole placket, begin ¼ inch from the clip mark at center front. Stitch toward the bottom, stopping 1 inch from the end of the slash, as shown in **Diagram 2**.

■ SEWING SECRET: To secure the threads at the beginning and end of the slash, shorten the stitch length to 18 spi (1.0 mm). Stitch about ½ inch, then reset the stitch length for regular stitching.

7. Shorten the stitch length and stitch to the end of the placket—¼ inch beyond the end of the slash, following the marked stitching line, as shown in **Diagram 2**. Make one or two stitches horizontally across the

bottom of the slash mark and then stitch up the other side for 1 inch. Reset the stitch length to 15 spi (1.5 mm) and finish stitching the placket.

Finish the Keyhole Opening and Neckline

1. Slash the keyhole opening. At the bottom, clip to the stitches so the opening can be turned neatly.

2. Understitch the neckline and opening.

3. At the top of the keyhole opening, tame the seam allowances, following the instructions in step 3 of "Make the Flap" on page 64.

4. Turn the keyhole and neckline facings to the wrong side.

5. With the facing side up, press the neckline and the keyhole opening, as shown in **Diagram 3**.

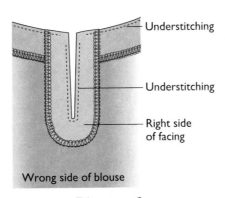

Diagram 3

6. Edgestitch and/or topstitch around the blouse neckline and placket, if desired, following the instructions in "How to Edgestitch," on page 6.

7. Sew a hook and eye in place at the top of the opening at the neckline.

■ SEWING SECRET: When I'm stitching a blouse design that doesn't have a collar, I like to use a button loop closure with a small ball button at the top of the neckline opening, as shown in **Diagram 4**. Sometimes I use several button loops to break the monotony of an otherwise plain blouse design. When you are using button loops on your blouses, position and pin the loop or loops onto the facing before stitching the neckline facing in place.

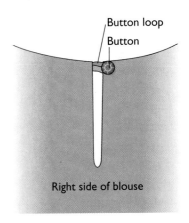

Diagram 4

7. Complete the blouse.

This binding technique is equally attractive when used with printed or solid color fabrics.

Bound Neckline Placket

Used by many designers instead of a faced placket, the bound neckline placket can be inconspicuous with a self-fabric binding, or it can be decorative with a contrast binding.

When Zandra Rhodes uses bound neckline plackets on her famous silk-screened silk chiffon designs, some bindings are made from the silk chiffon in a matching color but without the silkscreen print, while others are made from satin in a contrasting color. However, Diane Fries and Adolfo favor self-fabric bindings.

This finish also makes a nice binding for sleeve plackets on lightweight silk or polyester blouses.

If you think this binding looks like a French binding on a slash, you're right.

Tools & Supplies

♦ Safety pin
♦ Chalk wheel

Cut Out the Garment and Make the Binding

1. Cut out the garment with a fold at the center back.

2. Mark the center back at the neck edge with a short clip. This is the top of the opening. Use a safety pin to pin-mark the end of the opening.

■ SEWING SECRET: At Zandra Rhodes, the machinists (the English name for sewing machine operators) use small brass safety pins to mark the silk chiffon because they won't fall out as easily as straight pins.

3. Cut the binding strip on the true bias 2½ inches wide and twice the opening length plus 3 inches. (See "How to Cut and Join Bias Strips" on page 5.)

4. With wrong sides together, fold the bias binding strip in half lengthwise.

5. Press the folded edge of the strip, stretching as you press.

6. Trim the folded strip to a width of ¾ inch and set it aside.

Prepare the Garment Opening

1. With the chalk wheel, draw a line to connect the clip mark at the top of the opening and the pin at the bottom. Remove the pin.

2. Staystitch around the opening. With the right side up, begin 3/16 inch to the left of the marked line. Stitch to the bottom of the slash mark and up the other side, stitching a small V at the bottom.

3. Cut the center of the opening. At the bottom of the slash mark, cut precisely to the stitching line but not through it, as shown in **Diagram 1.**

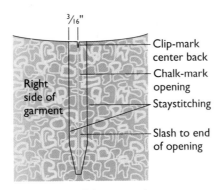

Diagram 1

Bind the Opening

1. With the garment wrong side up, place it on top of the binding. Align the raw edges and pin, stopping about 2 inches from the bottom of the slash, as shown in **Diagram 2.**

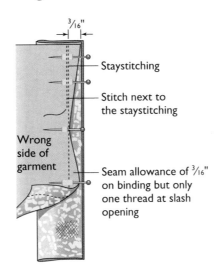

Diagram 2

2. Pin the bottom of the slash, arranging it as shown in **Diagram 2,** so there is a 3/16-inch seam allowance on the binding but only one

thread at the end of the slash opening. Pin the binding to the remaining side of the opening.

3. Set the machine for 12 spi (2.0 mm) and stitch the binding to the garment. Begin at the top of the opening one thread to the left of the staystitching, as shown in **Diagram 2,** and stitch to the other side of the top of the opening. Check to be sure both sides of the opening are the same length. If they are not, unpick the stitches as needed and restitch.

4. Wrap the folded edge of the bias around the raw edges of the opening. The bias should overlap the stitching from step 3 by ⅛ inch.

■ SEWING SECRET: If the binding overlaps the stitching line less than ⅛ inch, trim the raw edges to 1/16 inch.

5. Press the folded edge lightly, and pin the bias in place close to the binding. Set the pins on the left side of the binding with the heads toward the bottom of the opening. On the right side, set the pins so the heads are toward the top of the opening, as shown in **Diagram 3.**

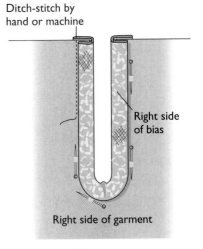

Diagram 3

6. Ditch-stitch by hand or machine to secure the binding permanently, as shown in **Diagram 3** on page 93. (See step 6 of "Sew the Binding to the Garment" on page 48.)

7. To shape the bottom of the opening attractively, fold the garment with right sides together.

Beginning at the garment edge at the bottom of the opening, stitch a small dart in the binding, as shown in **Diagram 4A,** which will smooth the right side of the binding at the bottom of the opening, as shown in **4B.**

8. Complete the garment.

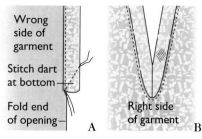

Wrong side of garment

Stitch dart at bottom

Fold end of opening

Right side of garment

A   B

Diagram 4

How to *Sew* a *Bound Placket* with a *Zipper*

When a longer placket is required, Zandra Rhodes frequently uses the bound zipper placket on her signature Works of Art Collection. The placket is made by sewing a zipper behind a bound opening.

The most obvious advantage of the bound zipper placket is that it eliminates the need to match the fabric pattern below the zipper opening. It is also more attractive than a traditional zipper placket on fabrics such as cut velvets, metallics, pleated and embroidered fabrics, many brocades, and, of course, silk-screened silk chiffons, which appear uneven at folded edges as a result of the printing process.

Hide a zipper behind a bound opening.

PREPARE THE PATTERN AND MAKE THE BINDING

1. If the pattern has a seam at the center back for an opening, trim away the seam allowance. Mark the pattern "Place on fold." Mark the end of the opening on the foldline.

2. Cut a binding strip on the true bias 1½ inches wide and twice the opening length plus 3 inches. See "How to Cut and Join Bias Strips" on page 5.

3. Press the bias, stretching the strip as you press. Trim the strip to a width of 1 inch and set it aside.

BIND THE OPENING AND SET THE ZIPPER

1. Cut out the garment and mark the opening.

2. Bind the opening using the direc-

tions in "Bound Neckline Placket" on page 92.

3. Key the zipper and the garment at the neckline seamlines. (See "How to Key a Zipper" on page 96 for instructions.)

4. Open the zipper. With the garment and zipper wrong sides up, place the zipper on top of the binding with the edges of the zipper coil aligned with the edge of the binding, as shown in **Zipper Diagram 1.**

5. Hand-baste the zipper in place next to the binding seam and ditch-stitch the zipper by hand or machine to secure it permanently, as shown in **Zipper Diagram 2.**

6. Remove the basting stitches and finish the garment.

Right side of binding   Align edge of coil with edge of binding

Wrong side of garment

Wrong side of zipper

Zipper Diagram 1

Baste next to binding seam   Ditch-stitch by hand or machine

Right side of garment

Zipper Diagram 2

How to *Sew Ribbon Trim* on the *Back* of a *Zipper*

Ribbon trim on the back of the zipper is only one of several special details Zandra Rhodes uses on her Works of Art Collection. In addition to adding a decorative detail that only the wearer will see, the trim also covers the raw edges when the zipper is shortened.

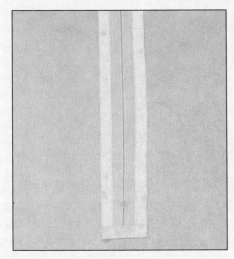

Cover the raw edges of a zipper with soft satin ribbon.

APPLY THE RIBBON TRIM TO THE ZIPPER TAPE

1. Shorten the nylon coil zipper as needed, following the directions in "How to Shorten a Zipper" on page 96.

2. With wrong sides together, place a piece of ribbon the length of the zipper on top of each side of the zipper tape. Align the edges of the ribbons with the woven guidelines on the zipper tape, as shown in **Ribbon Diagram 1.**

3. Edgestitch along the side of the ribbon closest to the zipper coil at 12 spi (2.0 mm), as shown in **Ribbon Diagram 1,** making sure not to catch the garment fabric in the stitching. For instructions on edgestitching, see "How to Edgestitch" on page 6.

4. Repeat step 2 to edgestitch the other length of ribbon, as shown in **Ribbon Diagram 1.**

APPLY THE RIBBON TRIM TO THE BOTTOM OF THE ZIPPER

1. With wrong sides together, place the 3-inch length of satin ribbon on top of the bottom of the zipper, so the ribbon covers the raw edges of the bottom of the zipper tape. Extend the ribbon ends about 1/4 inch on either side of the vertical ribbons. Edgestitch the side of the ribbon that is closest to the zipper opening, as shown in **Ribbon Diagram 2.**

2. At the bottom of the zipper, turn the short ends of the ribbon to the wrong side of the seam allowance and hand sew the ribbon ends permanently, as shown in **Ribbon Diagram 3.**

3. Set the zipper using the method you prefer.

TOOLS & SUPPLIES

♦ Nylon coil zipper
♦ 1/4-inch-wide satin ribbon, two pieces the length of the zipper, plus one 3-inch piece
♦ Edgestitch or wide straight-stitch foot

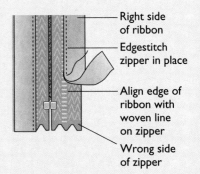

Right side of ribbon
Edgestitch zipper in place
Align edge of ribbon with woven line on zipper
Wrong side of zipper

Ribbon Diagram 1

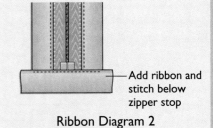

Add ribbon and stitch below zipper stop

Ribbon Diagram 2

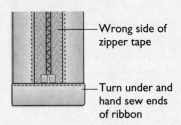

Wrong side of zipper tape
Turn under and hand sew ends of ribbon

Ribbon Diagram 3

How to *Shorten* a *Zipper*

For most small businesses and alteration workrooms, it is more economical to buy zippers in only three sizes: 9 inches, 14 inches, and 22 inches. Then, when a different size is required, the zipper is simply shortened to the desired length. This is the method professionals use to shorten nylon coil zippers.

Many mail-order catalogs sell zippers that can be cut to any length desired. Extra zipper pulls are also available. (See "Resources" on page 243 for sources.)

To shorten zippers at home, follow these four simple steps.

1. Close the zipper. Beginning at the top stop, measure and mark the desired zipper length.
2. Hand sew a bartack across the zipper at the marked length.
3. Cut off the zipper about 1 inch below the bartack.
4. Stitch a piece of ribbon or binding at the bottom of the zipper.

How to *Key* a *Zipper*

Key the top of the zipper and garment before setting the zipper to create easy-to-use matchpoints for setting the zipper.

1. To key the zipper, close the zipper and stitch across the zipper tapes $1/4$ inch above the top stop, as shown in **Key Diagram 1**. Then clip the stitching between the zipper tapes.

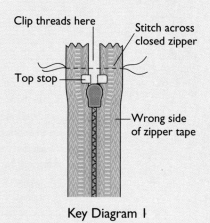

Clip threads here

Stitch across closed zipper

Top stop

Wrong side of zipper tape

Key Diagram 1

■ **SEWING SECRET:** *When keying a zipper that will be finished with a waistband instead of a facing, stitch only $1/8$ inch above the top stop since you don't have to leave room at the top of the zipper for a hook and eye.*

2. To key the garment, staystitch across the neckline just inside the seamline, as shown in **Key Diagram 2**. Before continuing, check to be sure both sides of the opening are the same length between the stitching and the end of the garment. Clip the threads between the sides of the garment.

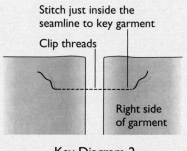

Stitch just inside the seamline to key garment

Clip threads

Right side of garment

Key Diagram 2

3. Align the stitching on the zipper to the stitching on the garment when you set the zipper.

■ **SEWING SECRET:** *Keying the zipper and the garment ensures that plackets at necklines and waistbands are finished the same length.*

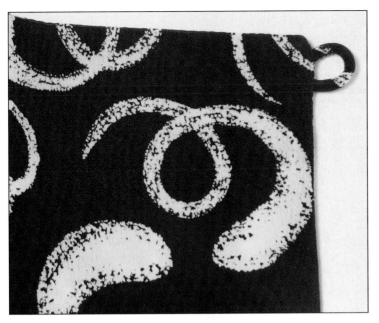

Traditional button loops add a touch of glamour to any garment.

DESIGNER DETAIL

Galanos

James Galanos, America's premier designer, is known for extraordinary workmanship and inventive designs that transcend trends. According to Galanos clients who sometimes wear his designs for a decade or more, his clothes are so exquisitely finished that they could be worn with the wrong side out.

Button Loops

Used by most designers at one time or another, button loops have been used in very imaginative locations on a variety of unusual designs on jackets, blouses, and dresses. At the same time, button loops have served as functional closures at the tops of keyhole openings, on turtleneck collars, and on sleeve cuffs.

Particularly attractive when used with ball buttons, button loops are located at garment edges. They are suitable for closures that meet at the opening as well as for closures that lap.

The size of the button loop depends on factors such as the weight, bulk, and texture of the fabric, as well as the size of the button.

Tools & Supplies

♦ Pattern paper
♦ One or more buttons
♦ Cord, purchased trim, or custom-made fabric tubing
♦ Fusible interfacing
♦ Pattern weights (optional)

Plan the Design

1. Sketch the design.
2. Select a collarless jacket pattern.

Prepare the Pattern

1. On a piece of pattern paper, draw a vertical line. Align the center front on the pattern with the line. Tape the pattern in place or use pattern weights.

2. Trace the cutting edges of the front pattern, excluding all of the details on the facing, as shown in **Diagram 1.**

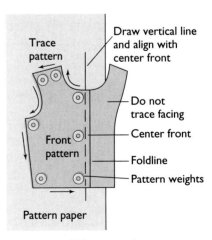

Diagram 1

3. Mark the button/button loop locations on the front edge.

■ SEWING SECRET: To determine the placement of button loops, pin the pattern front to your dress form or a T-shirt dummy. (For directions on making a T-shirt dummy, see the Sewing Secret under step 1 of "Sew the Pockets to the Jacket" on page 56.) Then experiment with different placements of the buttons—evenly spaced or arranged in groups of three or five—and different size buttons. Use cord, purchased trim, and custom-made fabric tubing in contrasting and self-fabrics to experiment with different loop materials, sizes, and arrangements.

4. Add ¼-inch seam allowances to the front edges of the jacket front pattern. Trim all seam allowances at the neckline to ¼ inch.

5. To make the front and back facings, review the directions for "Making a Neckline Facing" on page 210 for details and then draft the facings.

Cut Out the Jacket

1. The seam widths are ¼ inch at the neckline and front edge. All other seams are ⅝ inch unless otherwise stated.

2. Block-fuse the interfacing to the fabric for the jacket fronts and facings. (For instructions, see "How to Block-Fuse" on page 86.) Then cut the jacket fronts and facings.

3. Clip-mark the button loop locations with the clip at the top of the loop, as shown in

Diagram 2A. When you plan to have a space between the top and bottom of the loop, make 2 clips, as shown in **2B.** Otherwise, make only one clip.

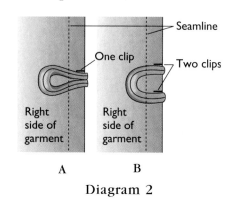

Diagram 2

4. Cut out the remaining jacket sections.

5. For custom-made button loops, cut enough bias strips to make the button loops. (For instructions on "How to Cut and Join Bias Strips," see page 5.)

■ SEWING SECRET: Before cutting all the bias strips, I cut only enough to make a few samples. If the strips are not wide enough, I don't have strips I can't use.

Stitch the Button Loops

1. Make the button loops using your favorite method. If you want skinny loops, use my favorite method, which is described in "How to Make Self-Filled Tubing" on the opposite page.

2. With the left front right side up, pin the loops in place using the clip marks as a guide. Trim away the excess loop.

3. Machine baste the loops in place a scant ¼ inch from the edge.

Assemble the Jacket and Facings

1. With the jacket front and back right sides together, join the shoulders with ⅝-inch seams. Press them open or as directed by the pattern guide. Finish the edges for an unlined jacket.

2. Repeat step 1 to join the neckline facings.

3. Staystitch the jacket neckline a scant ¼ inch from the edge.

■ SEWING SECRET: Staystitching is used to prevent the neck edge from stretching. If you handle your work carefully and baste and rip only occasionally, you can eliminate staystitching.

Set the Facing

1. With right sides together, place the facings on top of the jacket. Match the seams and notches. Pin the edges together at the neckline and front edge, as shown in **Diagram 3.** Hand baste if needed.

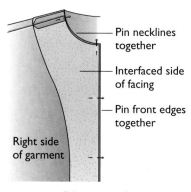

Diagram 3

2. Stitch a ¼-inch seam. Tame the corners, and turn the jacket right side out. Understitch or topstitch if desired.

3. Finish the jacket.

How to *Make Self-Filled Tubing*

This method for making self-filled tubing can be used for making button loops, spaghetti straps, Chinese ball buttons, and tie belts. The tubing is stitched, trimmed, and turned so that the seam allowances make the tubing firm and round. The finished tubing will be much smaller than tubing made by other methods. It is also softer than tubing that is made with cord. Keep in mind that the finished size of self-filled tubing depends on the texture and weight of the fabric you use.

TOOLS & SUPPLIES
- Bias strips
- Tapestry needle
- Topstitching thread or buttonhole twist
- Pressing board

CUT AND SEW THE TUBE

1. Cut a 1-inch-wide bias strip. When making button loops, I find it easier to work with strips 4 to 6 inches long, but you may prefer one long strip.
2. Set the machine for a very short stitch length (20 spi or 1.0 mm).

■ SEWING SECRET: *To prevent the machine stitches from breaking when I turn the tube right side out, I use a very short stitch, which makes a more elastic seam, and I stretch the strip as much as possible when stitching it.*

3. With right sides together, fold the strip in half lengthwise. Beginning at one end, hold the threads and stitch a small funnel, as shown.

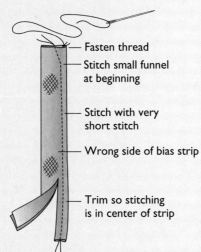

Fasten thread

Stitch small funnel at beginning

Stitch with very short stitch

Wrong side of bias strip

Trim so stitching is in center of strip

■ SEWING SECRET: *Stitching a small funnel at the end makes it easier to begin turning the tubing right side out. I often put a funnel at both ends just in case I have a section at the center that has been stitched too narrow and has to be cut off. Then I can start to turn the tube from the other end.*

4. Stop stitching about ⅛ inch from the folded edge with the needle down. Stretch the strip and notice how much the bias narrows. Release the strip and watch it return to its original width. Stitch the remainder of the tubing, as shown.

FINISH THE TUBE

1. Trim the seam so the trimmed edge is slightly narrower than the tube and so the stitching is almost in the center of the strip, as shown.
2. Thread a small tapestry needle with about 8 inches of topstitching thread or buttonhole twist. Knot the ends together, and secure the knot in the folded edge of the funnel, as shown.
3. Take a backstitch over the edge, and insert the needle into the tube.
4. Let the needle drop through the tube and then pull the needle to turn the tube right side out. If the tube turns too easily, it is too fat. Discard the tube and stitch another.
5. Wet the tube, and squeeze it dry in a towel.
6. Pin one end of the self-filled tube to the pressing board. Straighten the tube so the seam is straight. Stretch the tube as much as possible, and pin the other end to the pressing board. Leave the tube pinned on the board to dry.

■ SEWING SECRET: *To prevent the stitches from breaking when you turn the tube right side out, use a very short stitch, which makes a more elastic seam, and stretch the strip as much as possible when stitching it.*

How to *Sew Novelty Button Loops*

Novelty button loops come in many shapes and sizes. Some, such as these Zandra Rhodes loops, are fancy, decorative loops, while others, such as ribbon loops at the tops of zippers and keyhole openings, are simply functional.

I learned to make these attractive novelty loops from Dru, one of the machinists at Zandra Rhodes, when I visited that design house several years ago. At Zandra Rhodes, the tubing, or rouleau as it's called in England, is made of silk chiffon or silk satin, but it can be made of any lightweight fabric.

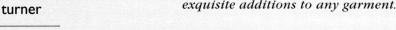

TOOLS & SUPPLIES
♦ Tube turner

These novelty button loops are exquisite additions to any garment.

MAKE THE ROULEAU

1. Cut a chiffon strip 2 inches wide on the bias.

2. With right sides together, fold the strip in half lengthwise. Place it under the presser foot with the fold to your right.

3. Align the folded edge with the outside edge of the presser foot and stitch, as shown in **Loops Diagram 1,** stretching the fabric slightly as you sew. Dru called this (and any other seam stitched using the edge of the foot as a guide), a "foot seam." The width of her foot seam was ³⁄₁₆ inch, or 5 mm; yours may be slightly narrower or wider.

4. Trim the seam allowances to ³⁄₁₆ inch.

5. Use a loop or tube turner to turn the rouleau right side out, or follow the instructions in steps 2 through 4 of "Finish the Tube" on page 99.

MAKE THE LOOP

1. Begin with a piece of rouleau about 5 inches long. Make a flat knot at one end, as shown in **Loops Diagram 2.**

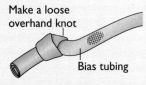

Make a loose overhand knot

Bias tubing

Loops Diagram 2

2. Make the loop by tucking the other end of the rouleau into the knot, as shown in **Loops Diagram 3.**

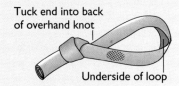

Tuck end into back of overhand knot

Underside of loop

Loops Diagram 3

3. Using a needle and thread, tack the loop just above the knot and trim the end of the rouleau, leaving about ¼ inch to be folded over the back of the knot, as shown in **Loops Diagram 4.**

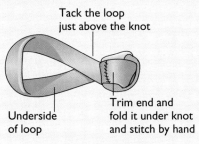

Tack the loop just above the knot

Underside of loop

Trim end and fold it under knot and stitch by hand

Loops Diagram 4

4. Fold the end of the rouleau to the wrong side and use small whip-stitches to secure it, as shown in **Loops Diagram 4.**

5. Repeat steps 1 through 5 to make all the loops.

6. Position the loops on the garment and hand sew them in place permanently.

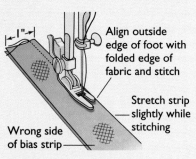

Align outside edge of foot with folded edge of fabric and stitch

Stretch strip slightly while stitching

Wrong side of bias strip

Loops Diagram 1

This adaptation of a Valentino technique hides the buttons and buttonholes with a fly front placket.

DESIGNER DETAIL

Valentino

A favorite of Elizabeth Taylor and Sophia Loren, Valentino is known for his sophisticated suits and over-the-top evening wear. Located near the Spanish Steps in Rome, his couture house is one of the few not situated in Paris.

Fly or Concealed Front Placket

Sometimes called a concealed placket, the fly placket hides the button/buttonhole closure. It is especially attractive when you are matching print patterns, stripes, or plaids. It is also the perfect solution when it's difficult to find buttons to match your fabric.

There are many variations of the fly placket. This particular version was adapted from a Valentino blouse, and it is my favorite. It can be used at the center front, on an asymmetrical closure, or on the back. It can be used with two-piece shirt collars, tie collars, or collarless designs. These directions focus on the collarless neckline.

The fronts are cut with ex-tended plackets, but the patterns are plotted independently, and the fronts are cut separately because the right front has the fly placket and the left does not. The finished fly width on the right front is 1¼ inches.

Tools & Supplies

♦ Pattern paper
♦ Edgestitch or wide straight-stitch foot (optional)
♦ Six or seven ½-inch buttons
♦ Lightweight fusible interfacing
♦ Pattern weights (optional)

Plan the Design

1. Sketch the design.

2. Select a blouse pattern with or without a button/buttonhole closure.

Plot the Front Patterns

1. On the pattern front, find the center front. Measure and draw the lap ⅝ inch away and parallel to the center front, as shown in **Diagram 1** on page 102. This is the front edge for both fronts.

2. Trim the neckline seam allowances to ¼ inch wide.

3. On a piece of pattern paper, draw a vertical line. Align the front edge of the pattern with the line, tape the pattern to the paper or use pattern weights, as shown in **Diagram 1** on page 102, and trace the cutting edges of the front pattern.

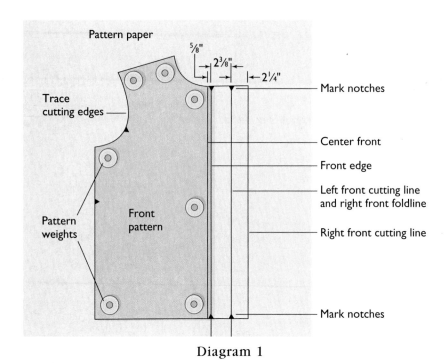

Pattern paper

Trace
cutting edges

Pattern
weights

Front
pattern

⅝"

2⅜"

←2¼"→

Mark notches

Center front

Front edge

Left front cutting line
and right front foldline

Right front cutting line

Mark notches

Diagram 1

4. Measure and draw a line 2⅜ inches to the right of and parallel to the front edge, as shown in **Diagram 1.** This is the cutting line for the left front and a foldline for the right front.

5. Draw the cutting line for the right front 2¼ inches away, as shown in **Diagram 1.**

6. Mark the foldlines at the top and bottom with notches.

Prepare the Back and Facing Patterns

1. If your pattern doesn't have a neck facing, see "Making a Neckline Facing" on page 210 for details.

2. Trim the seam allowances at the neckline on the back and facing patterns to ¼ inch.

3. On the facing patterns, reduce the finished width to 1 inch. On the front facing pattern, extend it

⅝ inch beyond the center front to the front edge.

Cut Out the Garment

1. The seam allowances are ¼ inch at the neckline. All other seams are ⅝ inch unless otherwise stated.

2. Cut out the blouse front, blouse back, and neckline facing.

3. On the right blouse front, clip-mark at the notches marking the front edge and foldline. On the left front, clip-mark at the notches marking the front edge.

4. Before cutting the neckline facings, block-fuse a very lightweight interfacing to the wrong side of the fabric following the instructions in "How to Block-Fuse" on page 86. Then cut the neckline facings from the interfaced fabric.

Prepare the Right Front

1. With right sides together, fold the right front edge at the first set of notches and press. Pin the raw edges at the neck edge together. Set the machine for a stitch length of 12 spi (2.0 mm), and stitch a ¼-inch seam, as shown in **Diagram 2.** Backtack at the end.

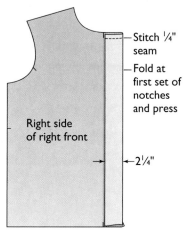

Stitch ¼"
seam

Fold at
first set of
notches
and press

Right side
of right front

←2¼"

Diagram 2

2. Clip from the neckline edge to the end of the seamline and turn the seam right side out.

3. With the right front wrong side up, press the seam at the neckline edge. Then press the fold at the front edge, as shown in **Diagram 3.**

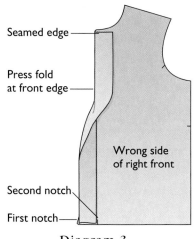

Seamed edge

Press fold
at front edge

Wrong side
of right front

Second notch

First notch

Diagram 3

■ SEWING SECRET: When sewing silks and fabrics that will be marred by pins, use very small needles instead of pins.

4. Using the second set of notches as a guide, fold the right front again to the wrong side, as shown in **Diagram 3,** and press.

Prepare the Left Front

1. With the left front wrong side up, fold the front edge wrong sides together at the notches, as shown in **Diagram 4,** and press.

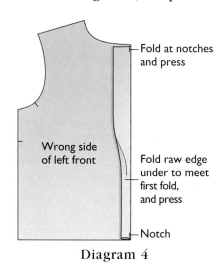

Diagram 4

2. Fold the raw edge in to meet the foldline at the front edge, and press, as shown in **Diagram 4.**

Assemble the Garment

1. With the front and back right sides together, join the shoulders with ⅝-inch seams. Press them open or as directed by the pattern guide. Trim the ends and finish the edges.

■ SEWING SECRET: Always stitch shoulder seams from the neckline, where accuracy is most critical, to the armscye.

2. Repeat step 1 to join the neckline facings.

3. Serge the outer edges of the facing.

4. At the front edge of the left blouse front, or underlap, fold and pin the facing to the right side of the left front, as shown in **Diagram 5.**

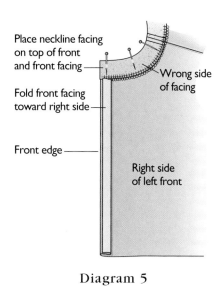

Diagram 5

5. Then, with right sides together, place the facings on top of the blouse, as shown in **Diagram 5.** Match the seams and notches at the neck edge, and pin the edges together at the neckline.

6. With the right front right side up, open the facing flat at the end of the overlap.

7. Pin the facing and the front together at the neckline, as shown in **Diagram 6.**

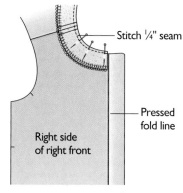

Diagram 6

8. Stitch the blouse neckline with a ¼-inch seam, as shown in **Diagram 6.**

9. Understitch the neckline, and clip as needed.

10. Fold the facing to the wrong side, and press with the facing side up.

Finish the Placket

1. With the right front right side up, open the facing flat and stitch the buttonholes ⅝ inch from the edge. (On the finished blouse, this will be the underlay.) Begin about 1 inch below the neck edge and space the buttonholes 3¼ inches apart, as shown in **Diagram 7.**

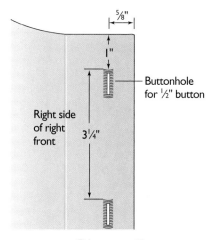

Diagram 7

■ SEWING SECRET: When the fly placket is used in haute couture, the buttonholes are embroidered by hand. If you are learning to make hand-embroidered buttonholes, this is a good opportunity to practice your stitching because the buttonholes will be concealed on the finished garment.

2. Fold the facing and underlay to the wrong side, as shown in **Diagram 8.**

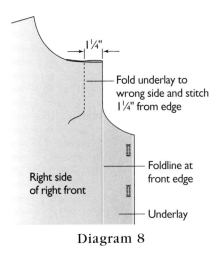

Diagram 8

3. With the front right side up, stitch through all layers 1¼ inches from the folded edge, as shown in **Diagram 8,** basting if needed to prevent the layers from shifting.

4. With the wrong side up, press the front facing and underlay flat, then press the underlay toward the finished edge, as shown in **Diagram 9.**

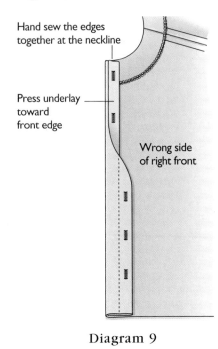

Diagram 9

5. At the neckline, hand sew the underlay and facing to the blouse front with a slipstitch, as shown in **Diagram 9.** To prevent the stitches from showing on the right side of the blouse, do not pull the stitches tight.

■ SEWING SECRET: To prevent the fly placket from gaping and exposing the buttons, Valentino places a short (¼-inch) thread chain between each button location to join the underlay and the facing. For instructions on how to sew a thread chain, see "How to Tame a Free-Hanging Lining" on page 151.

Finish the Underlap and the Neckline of the Blouse

1. Place the left blouse front wrong side up.

2. Pin the underlap and the neckline facing in place.

3. Edgestitch the folded edge of the underlap flat against the blouse front, as shown in **Diagram 10,** following the instructions in "How to Edgestitch" on page 6.

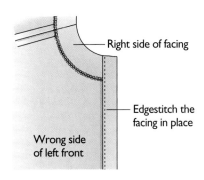

Diagram 10

4. Sew the buttons in place on the underlap.

5. With the right side of the blouse up, edgestitch the neckline if desired.

6. Complete the garment.

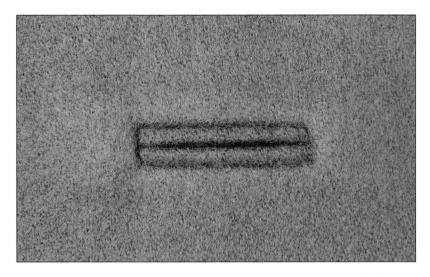

Use the strip method to duplicate the bound buttonholes found on expensive ready-to-wear.

Bound Buttonholes

Called the strip method, this technique for making bound buttonholes is used on very expensive ready-to-wear designs by David Hayes and Bill Blass. I learned it from Adeline Giuntini, who was a tailor in Berkeley, California, for many years. But you can make bound buttonholes using a variety of methods, including the windowpane opening method described on page 60. Simply choose the method that is easiest for you.

In recent fashion collections, bound buttonholes frequently have been used as a decorative trim in one or more contrasting colors. When this is done, they are many times made wider and longer so they will stand out against the background fabric. These exquisite buttonholes are ¼ inch wide and 1⅜ inches long.

Tools & Supplies

♦ Fusible interfacing
♦ Two fabric strips 1 inch longer than the finished buttonhole and at least 2 inches wide
♦ Chalk wheel

Select and Prepare the Pattern

1. Draw a sketch of your design.

2. Select a jacket pattern.

3. Plan the size and location of the buttonholes. If your pattern doesn't have a button/buttonhole closure, see "Adding Buttons and Buttonholes" on page 235.

Prepare the Jacket Front

1. Use the pattern front to cut the jacket fronts and front interfacings. (For directions, see "Interfacing a Jacket" on page 136.) Set aside some fabric scraps to use for the buttonhole strips.

2. Begin with the jacket front wrong side up. Place the interfacing on the wrong side of the front, and fuse it in place.

3. Mark the buttonhole locations

on the right front with hand basting stitches. (For directions, see "Tips for Making Bound Buttonholes" on page 108.)

Make the Buttonhole Strips

1. For each buttonhole, you will need two fabric strips that are 1 inch longer than the finished buttonhole and at least 2 inches wide.

■ SEWING SECRET: I press and stitch the strips, then cut them out. The folded edge of a larger piece of fabric is easier to press straight without wiggles and waves, and you are less likely to burn your fingers.

2. Begin by trimming one edge of a fabric scrap on the desired grain. Generally I trim on the lengthwise grain so that the welts will retain their shape without interfacing.

3. With wrong sides together, fold the strip of fabric 1 inch from the trimmed edge. Press the folded edge, as shown in **Diagram 1.**

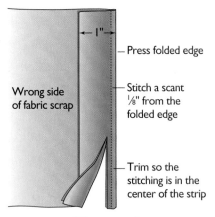

Wrong side of fabric scrap

← 1" →
— Press folded edge

— Stitch a scant ⅛" from the folded edge

— Trim so the stitching is in the center of the strip

Diagram 1

4. Machine stitch a guideline through both layers a scant ⅛ inch from the fold, as shown in

Diagram 1. (The distance between the folded edge and the stitching equals the finished width of one welt or half the finished width of the buttonhole.)

5. Trim the strip so the stitching, or guideline, is in the center of the strip, as shown in **Diagram 1.**

6. Make enough strips for all the buttonholes, but do not cut them into short lengths.

Stitch the Strips to the Jacket

1. With the front right side up, place one strip on top of the jacket. Align the raw edges of the strip with the basting that marks the buttonhole opening. Chalk-mark the ends of the buttonhole precisely. Stitch on the guideline between the chalk marks. Trim the end of the welt so it is only ½ inch longer than the stitching, as shown in **Diagram 2.**

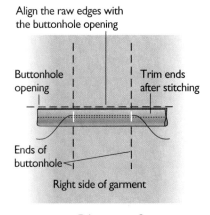

Align the raw edges with the buttonhole opening

Buttonhole opening

Trim ends after stitching

Ends of buttonhole

Right side of garment

Diagram 2

2. Repeat step 1 to stitch the remaining welt to the buttonhole, butting the raw edges of the welts together, as shown in **Diagram 3.** Check to be sure the stitching lines are parallel and the same length.

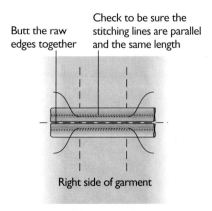

Butt the raw edges together

Check to be sure the stitching lines are parallel and the same length

Right side of garment

Diagram 3

3. Stitch the welts to the remaining buttonholes, following steps 1 and 2. Pull all threads to the interfacing side and knot.

Cut and Turn the Buttonholes

1. With the interfacing side up, clip the buttonhole between the stitched lines. At the corners, hold the welts out of the way; clip exactly to the ends of the stitching without cutting the stitched line, as shown in **Diagram 4.**

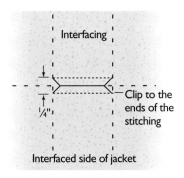

Interfacing

¼"

Clip to the ends of the stitching

Interfaced side of jacket

Diagram 4

2. With the jacket right side up, push the welts through to the wrong side. Straighten the welts and baste them together with a diagonal basting, as shown in **Diagram 5** on the opposite page.

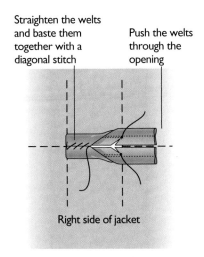

Straighten the welts and baste them together with a diagonal stitch

Push the welts through the opening

Right side of jacket

Diagram 5

Finish the Ends of the Buttonholes

1. With the jacket right side up, fold the edge back to expose the triangle and welts at the end of the buttonhole. Give the welts a sharp tug, and stitch across the end, as shown in **Diagram 6**, using a short stitch and swinging in slightly to catch the corners. Repeat to stitch the other end and the remaining buttonholes.

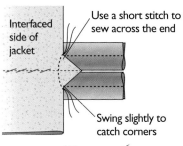

Interfaced side of jacket

Use a short stitch to sew across the end

Swing slightly to catch corners

Diagram 6

2. Trim the ends of the welts so they won't overlap the front/facing seam. Remove the basting stitches.

3. Finish the jacket.

How to *Stitch* a *Facing Finish* for a *Bound Buttonhole*

1. With the jacket wrong side up, smooth the facing from the front edge toward the side seam and pin at the raw edges.

2. Turn the jacket over with the right side up, and hand baste around each buttonhole, as shown in **Facing Diagram 1**.

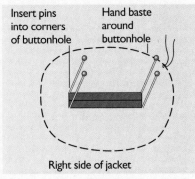

Insert pins into corners of buttonhole

Hand baste around buttonhole

Right side of jacket

Facing Diagram 1

3. With the right side up, insert a straight pin into each corner of the buttonhole. To mark the corners accurately, set the pins straight into the corners perpendicular to the fabric, as shown in **Facing Diagram 1**.

4. Turn the jacket over so the facing side is up. Cut the facing at the center of the buttonhole, stopping ¼ inch from each end, as shown in **Facing Diagram 2**.

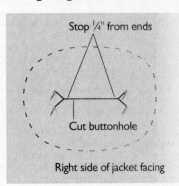

Stop ¼" from ends

Cut buttonhole

Right side of jacket facing

Facing Diagram 2

5. Beginning at the center of one long edge, turn under the raw edge. Use a small-size needle and small stitches to sew the folded edge to the back of the buttonhole, as

shown in **Facing Diagram 3**. To finish the facing, continue sewing around the buttonhole.

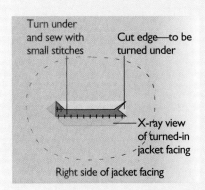

Turn under and sew with small stitches

Cut edge—to be turned under

X-ray view of turned-in jacket facing

Right side of jacket facing

Facing Diagram 3

■ **SEWING SECRET:** *Instead of sewing the facing once with tiny stitches, I sew around it twice with slightly longer stitches to reinforce it.*

6. To press the jacket, place it facing side up on a softly padded surface. Cover with a press cloth, and steam press it lightly.

Tips for Making Bound Buttonholes

These hints ensure success when stitching bound buttonholes.

♦ Always make a sample buttonhole from an interfaced fabric scrap. I make at least one sample and sometimes several. By making a sample, you will be able to determine if the fabric has any special characteristics that need to be considered before the buttonhole is made on the garment; to choose the buttonhole construction method that is most appropriate for the fabric; and to be sure the buttonhole will be neither too small nor too large for the size button you have chosen.

♦ To determine the size of the buttonhole, use a scrap of paper to measure the button width, as shown in **Bound Diagram 1.**

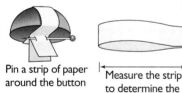

Pin a strip of paper around the button

Measure the strip to determine the buttonhole size

Bound Diagram 1

Then cut a slash in a fabric scrap equal to the button width. Place the button at one end of the slash. You should be able to see about ⅜ inch (9 mm) of the slash. To avoid making buttonholes that are too short, add at least ⅛ inch to the size of your button.

When the buttonhole is decorative, not functional, the aesthetics of the buttonhole are particularly im-portant. If it looks too long or too short, make additional slashes until you find a size that you like.

♦ If the fabric is limp or the welts are cut on the bias, interface or cord the welts so they will hold their shape.

♦ Change to a straight-stitch foot so you can see the beginnings and ends of the buttonholes easily.

♦ Set the machine for a short stitch length or 18 spi (1.0 mm), so if you are one stitch off, it is less likely to show. Begin and end the stitching precisely at the ends of the buttonhole, leaving long thread ends.

♦ Mark the buttonhole location on the right side of the interfaced jacket front with hand basting, which is easy to remove. The basting stitches mark the right side and the interfacing side at the same time, and they hold the layers together if you are using a sew-in interfacing.

When basting, use a very fine needle and white thread. Baste through the garment fabric and the interfacing to mark the center of the opening and the lines that mark the ends of the buttonhole, as shown in **Bound Diagram 2.**

♦ To be sure all bound buttonholes are identical in shape, examine them before cutting. Turn the front of the garment so the interfacing side is up, and examine the stitched lines. The buttonholes should be evenly spaced, exactly the same length and width, and on the grain-

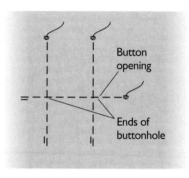

Button opening

Ends of buttonhole

Bound Diagram 2

line. They should begin and end the same distance from the edge.

If a stitched line is too long, use a small needle to unpick the stitches until the stitching line is the correct length. If a stitched line is too short, insert the thread end into a needle and take a stitch or two by hand to make it longer.

When necessary, unpick any buttonholes that cannot be corrected and restitch them.

♦ Before knotting the threads at the end of the stitching line, pull both threads to the interfacing side. Give them a sharp tug and then knot them.

♦ To clip the corners of the buttonholes, hold the welts out of the way. Position the points of the scissors exactly where the clip is to be and then close the scissors. (See **Diagram 2** on page 61.)

♦ When making several bound buttonholes on a garment, begin at the hem and work toward the neckline, so your most perfect buttonholes will be the first that are seen.

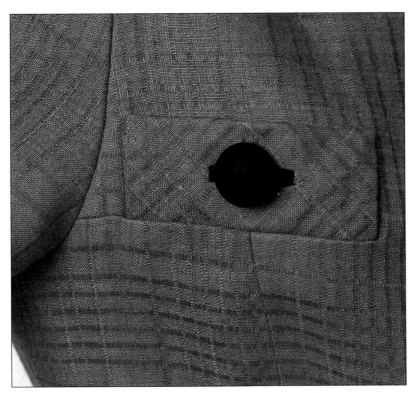

A blind bound buttonhole is used in ready-to-wear to accommodate gorgeous decorative buttons.

Blind Bound Buttonholes

Add instant glamour to your favorite special occasion fabrics with the simple addition of a jeweled or decorative button. Particularly attractive when used with bound buttonholes, decorative buttons are often used on expensive ready-to-wear and haute couture designs. Unfortunately, these beautiful fasteners will damage most special occasion fabrics when the buttonhole is used, and many of them will require such a large opening that it would be unattractive when fastened.

Designers avoid this problem by using a blind buttonhole.

When used on special occasion fabrics, the buttonholes are bound with two narrow welts at the opening. The blind buttonhole provides the elegance you want, but it doesn't actually button. In fact, the facing doesn't even have an opening at the back of the buttonhole. Instead, a functional fastener is sewn on the facing side of the overlap to close the garment inconspicuously.

Although many designers use snaps to fasten their jackets, I prefer Victor Costa's button/buttonhole closure, because it allows the jacket to move with the body more gracefully.

Tools & Supplies

♦ Decorative button
♦ Flat button ⅝ to ⅞ inch (15 to 22 mm) wide in a matching color or transparent

Select and Prepare the Pattern

1. Draw a sketch of your design.

2. Select a jacket pattern.

■ SEWING SECRET: Blind bound buttonholes are also attractive when used on coat-dresses.

Make the Bound Buttonholes

1. Make the bound buttonholes using your favorite method, or you can use the strip method described on page 105.

■ SEWING SECRET: Blind bound buttonholes can be made from the same fashion fabric as the garment, or you can use a contrasting color (as shown in the photo on page 109) or contrasting fabric, such as synthetic suede or satin.

2. Press the buttonhole.

■ SEWING SECRET: Always make a test buttonhole on a scrap of fabric before stitching the buttonhole in the garment section.

3. Stitch the facings.

4. Stitch a line of basting in an oval around each buttonhole. Do not cut and finish the facings at the buttonhole.

Make the Underlap Buttonhole

1. To mark the buttonhole on the underlap, stack the two jacket fronts with the facing sides to-

gether and the right side of the jacket on top.

2. Insert a straight pin into the end of the bound buttonhole toward the center front, as shown in **Diagram 1**, and mark the exit point on the right side of the left front, which is the underlap.

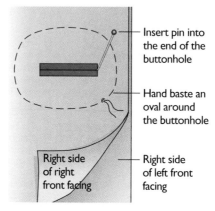

Insert pin into the end of the buttonhole

Hand baste an oval around the buttonhole

Right side of right front facing

Right side of left front facing

Diagram 1

3. Measure the flat button and add ⅛ inch.

4. Mark the buttonhole this length.

5. Set the machine to stitch a keyhole buttonhole on the underlap. Stitch the buttonhole.

■ SEWING SECRET: When possible, stitch a keyhole instead of a straight buttonhole. Women's tailored jackets frequently feature keyhole buttonholes. With this buttonhole, the button sets in the

rounded end of the keyhole opening, and the garment moves with the body. Keyhole buttonholes can be made by hand or by machine.

6. Cut the buttonhole opening, trimming the excess fabric from the keyhole.

Stitch the Buttons

1. With the right front right side up, place the decorative button in the buttonhole at the end toward the center front of the jacket.

2. Using a hand-sewing needle and thread, sew the button neatly to the facing, hiding the thread knots under the button.

3. Turn the front so the facing side is up.

4. Mark the location for the facing button directly under the decorative button.

5. Sew the facing button to the facing.

■ SEWING SECRET: To be sure the facing button will not create ripples and pulls in your facing, make the threads on the shank as long as the fabric layers are thick.

Easy Slot Zipper

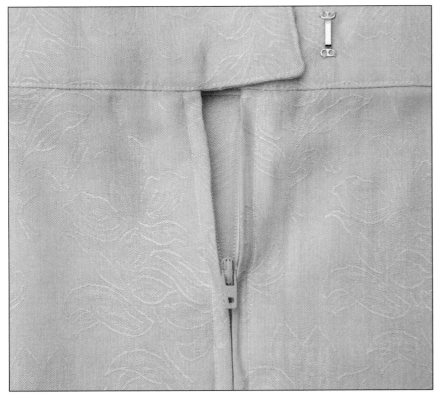

Slot zippers are commonly found not only in ready-to-wear, but also in haute couture.

The slot zipper is the most common zipper application for ready-made garments and haute couture. Since it is stitched with two narrow welts instead of one wide welt, its symmetry is more pleasing to the eye. It lies flat and is more slimming, and fabric patterns are easier to match.

Unfortunately, most home sewers don't like the slot zipper because it often gaps when sewn using the traditional home sewing method. The foolproof method described here is an adaptation of a couture technique.

Tools & Supplies

♦ Nylon coil zipper
♦ Paper-backed fusible web
♦ Zipper foot
♦ Fusible interfacing

Prepare the Opening

1. With right sides together, begin at the bottom of the opening with a backtack and stitch a ⅝-inch seam to the hem.

■ SEWING SECRET: Always begin stitching at the point where matching is most important.

2. Chalk-mark the seamline on both sides of the opening.

3. Cut two ⅝-inch-wide strips of fusible interfacing the length of the zipper, plus 2 inches. With the wrong side up, fuse the interfacing strips, also called stays, to the seam allowances, as shown in **Diagram 1**. Then press the seam allowances to the wrong side.

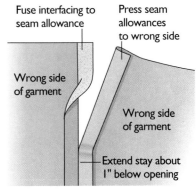

Fuse interfacing to seam allowance

Press seam allowances to wrong side

Wrong side of garment

Wrong side of garment

Extend stay about 1" below opening

Diagram 1

4. Key the edges of the garment sections at the opening, following the instructions in "How to Key a Zipper" on page 96.

5. If the design has a facing, complete the facing at the opening as described in "How to Sew a Facing Finish for a Slot Zipper" on page 113.

Prepare the Zipper

1. Make a self-basting zipper. Cut narrow strips of paper-backed fusible web. Apply the strips to the right sides of the zipper tape, as shown in **Diagram 2** on page 112.

Tips for Perfect Zippers

♦ To avoid having skirts look home-made, use only zippers that are 8 inches long or shorter, unless you are extremely tall.

♦ When possible, set the zipper before assembling the garment, while the sections are still flat.

♦ Finish the seam allowances before beginning to set the zipper.

♦ Chalk-mark the seamline.

♦ Do not baste the zipper opening closed before setting the zipper, but instead carefully press the seam allowances under.

♦ Steam press the zipper to remove any creases or wrinkles. Nylon and polyester zipper tapes don't require preshrinking.

♦ Always use a stay at the opening. For most garments, I simply apply a ⅝-inch-wide strip of fusible inter-facing to the wrong side of the seam allowances. Or, you could sew a row of staystitching just inside the seamline.

♦ Ease the fabric to the zipper tape. The minimum amount of ease is ⅛ inch of fabric to 12 inches of zipper. Stretchy and loosely woven fabrics and openings that are on the bias or off-grain require even more ease.

♦ Always key the ends of the zipper and garment, following the instructions in "How to Key a Zipper" on page 96.

♦ Experiment with self-basting zippers if you don't like to baste. For instructions on how to make a self-basting zipper, see the Sewing Secret under step 1 of "Prepare the Zipper" on page 111.

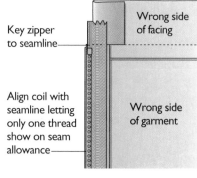

Key zipper to seamline

Align coil with seamline letting only one thread show on seam allowance

Wrong side of facing

Wrong side of garment

Diagram 3

2. Fuse the zipper in place.

3. Close the zipper. The edges should form a small peak where they meet at the center. If they don't, the zipper coil will show when the garment is worn.

4. Check the alignment of any stripes or patterns.

5. If you are sewing a better garment, hand baste the zipper in.

6. If the garment has already been assembled, try it on carefully.

Stitch the Zipper

1. Open the zipper. With the right side up, begin at the top of the zipper and stitch a scant ¼ inch from the edge of the opening, as shown in **Diagram 4,** using the guides on the needle plate as an aid for stitching a straight line. Stop stitching about 2 inches from the bottom of the zipper.

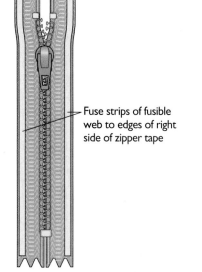

Fuse strips of fusible web to edges of right side of zipper tape

Diagram 2

2. Key the ends of the zipper, following the instructions in "How to Key a Zipper" on page 96.

3. Open the zipper.

Set the Zipper

1. With the garment wrong side up, place one side of the zipper face down on the seam allowance. Key the stitched line at the top of the zipper with the stitched line on the garment edge, and align the edges of the zipper coil with the pressed edge of the garment opening, as shown in **Diagram 3.**

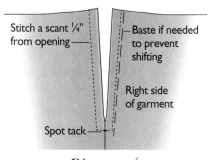

Stitch a scant ¼" from opening

Baste if needed to prevent shifting

Right side of garment

Spot tack

Diagram 4

2. Raise the foot, and close the zipper.

3. Stitch to the end of the zipper. At the end of the zipper, pivot and stitch to the seamline, and then spottack, as shown in **Diagram 4.**

■ SEWING SECRET: If you prefer a hand-picked zipper,

wax a single strand of sewing thread and then press it with a warm iron. Using the waxed thread, sew the zipper in place with a very, very short running stitch, which will move with the body more attractively than a backstitch.

4. Repeat steps 1 through 3 to

stitch the other side of the zipper.

5. Pull the threads to the wrong side and clip.

■ SEWING SECRET: I frequently machine stitch the garment opening before setting the zipper, and then sew in the zipper by hand.

How to *Sew* a *Facing Finish* for a *Slot Zipper*

Neat and flat, this industry technique is commonly used for finishing facings for slot and invisible zippers. It can also be adapted for a lapped zipper application.

This versatile finish can be used at front and back openings and can be applied before or after the garment and facings are assembled. When used for a slot or lapped zipper, it must be sewn before the zipper is set, but when used for an invisible zipper, it can be sewn afterward.

PREPARE THE FACINGS

1. Using your favorite method, finish the unnotched edges of the facings.
2. Trim ¼ inch off the facing ends at the opening.
3. At the opening end, as shown in **Facing Diagram 1,** turn up and pin the ⅝-inch seam allowance on the facing.

STITCH THE FACINGS

1. The seam widths at the placket are ⅝ inch. At the neckline, they are ¼ inch.
2. With right sides together, place the facing on top of the corresponding back section. Match the notches and pin the edges together so the back section extends ⅞ inch beyond the end of the facing, as shown in **Facing Diagram 1.**
3. At the opening, fold and pin the seam allowance (⅝ inch) so right sides are together and the facing is in between, as shown in **Facing Diagram 2.**

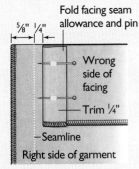

Facing Diagram 1

4. Set the machine for 12 spi (2.0 mm) and stitch a ¼-inch seam at the neckline, as shown in **Facing Diagram 2.** If the zipper is set into the garment sections before the shoulder seams are joined, stitch only about 4 inches from the opening so the neckline edges will be free when you stitch the shoulder seam.
5. Grade and clip the seam only if needed.
6. Turn the seam right side out, as shown in **Facing Diagram 3.**
7. Repeat steps 1 through 6 to sew the other facing. Press.
8. Set the zipper.
9. Assemble the garment and attach the facings. Understitch the neckline.

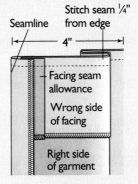

Facing Diagram 2

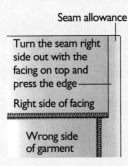

Facing Diagram 3

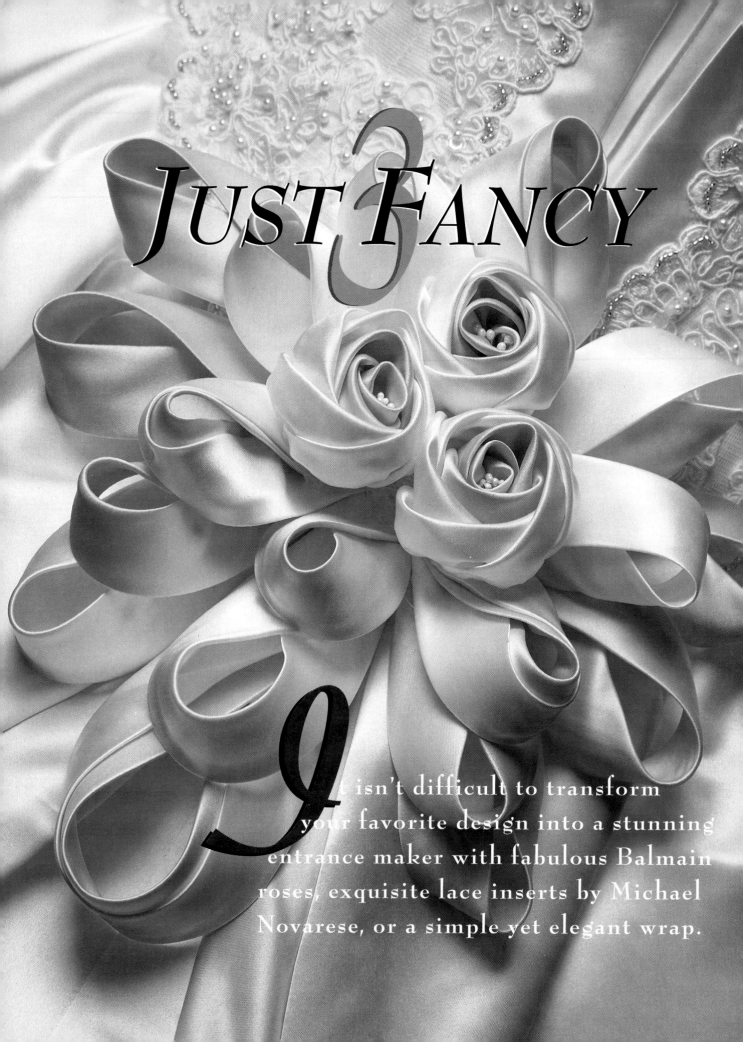

JUST FANCY

It isn't difficult to transform your favorite design into a stunning entrance maker with fabulous Balmain roses, exquisite lace inserts by Michael Novarese, or a simple yet elegant wrap.

Trims

These elegant trims can make a plain design provocative, a simple line sophisticated. Dress up your next holiday design with one of these exciting yet easy-to-sew embellishment techniques.

Lush fabric roses are a glamorous addition to evening wear.

Roses

I first saw this beautiful rose on a magnificent evening coat at the Parisian couture house of Balmain. Created in such fabrics as satin and velvet, the roses varied in size from large to extra large. Since then, I've seen them made of many different fabrics and used on a variety of designs from couture fashions to wedding gowns to prom dresses.

The following instructions are for a medium-size, full rose. You can make them larger or smaller by varying the width and the length of the fabric strips, and you can make tight buds or full, open flowers. Use one rose or a cluster of them on your next special occasion design.

Tools & Supplies

♦ 7-inch strip of 45-inch-wide fabric

♦ Topstitching or other heavy-duty thread for gathering

♦ Lightweight fusible interfacing (optional)

Prepare the Fabric Strip

1. For each rose, cut one strip of fabric on the crossgrain 7 inches wide and 36 inches long. Cut one 2-inch fabric square to cover the bottom of the rose.

■ SEWING SECRET: To save time, you can use a rotary cutter, cutting mat, and see-through ruler to cut the strip and square from the fabric.

2. With wrong sides together and raw edges even, fold the strip in half lengthwise (so that the strip is still 36 inches long, but now appears 3½ inches wide), and pin the edges together.

3. Trim one short end of the strip to a point, starting about 8 inches from the end, as shown in **Diagram 1**, and then pin the edges together.

4. At the end of the strip that was not trimmed, fold the corner upward until the raw edges on the end of the strip are even with the raw edges on the long edge, as shown in **Diagram 1**. Pin the edges together.

5. Stitch the raw edges at the folded corner together with a row of gathering stitches ¼ inch from the raw edges, as shown in **Diagram 1**.

■ SEWING SECRET: To gather fabric easily, don't try to gather large sections with one set of long gathering threads. Instead, divide each section into smaller sections. To do this, lengthen the stitch length on the machine to 8 spi (3.5 mm). Loosen the upper tension and fill the bobbin with topstitching thread or other heavy-duty thread that won't break when you pull the thread to adjust the gathers. Stitch the row of gathering

stitches in short segments 8 to 10 inches long, so you can pull up the gathers easily.

Make the Rose

1. Pull up the gathering stitches at the narrow end of the strip and roll the strip like a newspaper to make the center of the rose.

■ SEWING SECRET: If the threads lock when you pull the gathering thread, you're pulling the wrong thread or both of the threads. Pull only the bobbin thread for easy gathering.

2. Hand sew the rose together on the row of gathering stitches as you roll the strip, as shown in **Diagram 2**.

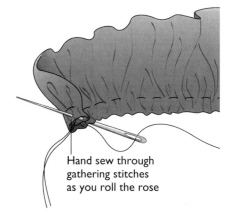

Hand sew through gathering stitches as you roll the rose

Diagram 2

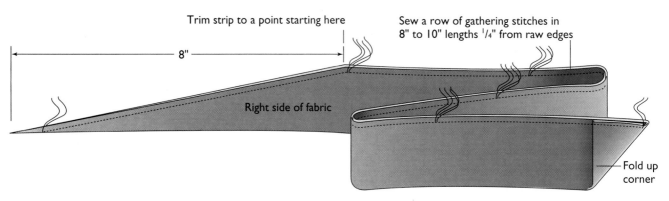

Trim strip to a point starting here

Sew a row of gathering stitches in 8" to 10" lengths ¼" from raw edges

8"

Right side of fabric

Fold up corner

Diagram 1

■ SEWING SECRET: If your thread constantly twists and snarls when you are hand sewing, use only a single strand of thread that is no more than 20 inches long.

3. If you want a tight rosebud, pull the gathering stitches only slightly. For a rose that is open, pull the gathering stitches tightly.

4. Continue gathering, rolling, and stitching the fabric strip until the rose is completed, as shown in the photo on page 115.

5. Carefully trim away any gathering threads and frayed edges on the bottom of the rose.

6. Flatten the bottom of the rose, and then hand sew back and forth across the bottom to tame the raw edges.

Finish the Bottom of the Rose

1. If you are not sewing the rose directly to the garment, finish the bottom of the rose with a small fabric circle. To do this, cut a circle from the 2-inch square of fabric that is large enough to cover the raw edges at the bottom of the rose plus a ¼-inch hem.

2. With the bottom of the rose up, cover the raw edges of fabric with the circle.

3. Turn under the raw edge of the circle as you slipstitch it in place, as shown in **Diagram 3.**

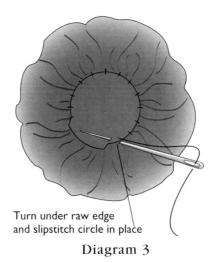

Turn under raw edge
and slipstitch circle in place

Diagram 3

■ SEWING SECRET: Before stitching the fabric circle to the bottom of the rose, cut a circle from lightweight fusible interfacing that is the finished size of the small fabric circle. Then fuse the circle of interfacing to the wrong side of the fabric circle. This will make it easier to turn under the raw edge of the fabric circle as you slipstitch it in place on the bottom of the rose.

db

DESIGNER DETAIL

Pierre Balmain

*Born in St. Jean de Maurienne, France, Pierre Balmain studied architecture for a time. He worked for British designer Edward Molyneux and then Lucien Lelong. It was during his tenure with Lelong that he met Christian Dior. One of the leading couturiers in Paris after World War II, Balmain began selling ready-to-wear in the United States in 1951.
He specialized in exquisite evening designs and quiet, elegant day wear. Today, Balmain's Haute Couture Collection is designed by Oscar de la Renta, who also creates high-end ready-to-wear under his own name.*

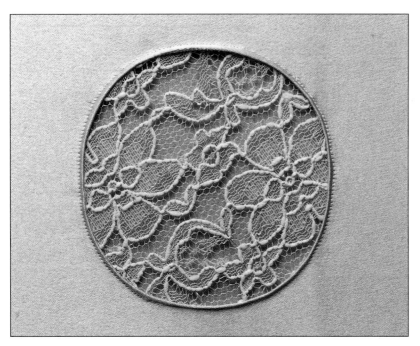

Lace inserts add a feminine touch to any after-five design.

Lace Inserts

Michael Novarese's lace inserts are not only breathtakingly elegant, they are also very easy to sew. Lace inserts are particularly attractive when used in sophisticated after-five designs and wedding party attire.

Novarese's basic design is a simple but exquisite four-ply silk dress. The inserts are plain faced openings placed over squares of lace that are then edgestitched to secure the lace permanently.

I saw the same technique used on an Anne Klein skimmer, but instead of lace, the inserts were a clear plastic and the garment fabric was black synthetic leather. The effect was unique and quite stunning.

Tools & Supplies

- ♦ Pattern paper or light-weight interfacing
- ♦ Lid from a one-pound coffee can
- ♦ Lightweight lining fabric or organza
- ♦ Lace
- ♦ Chalk wheel

Plan the Design

1. Draw a sketch of the design.

■ SEWING SECRET: Since I don't draw well, I used to trace the fashion figures on pattern envelopes. Now I use the fashion figure on page 238.

2. Select a pattern with a similar silhouette.

3. Separate the pattern pieces into three stacks: the pieces that won't be used, the pieces that will have inserts, and the remaining pieces. Return the first stack to the pattern envelope and press the rest with a dry iron.

4. Trim away the excess tissue from your pattern.

■ SEWING SECRET: When planning an asymmetrical design, cut duplicate pattern pieces so you can plan both sides of the design easily, using old interfacing or tissue paper from old patterns.

5. Count the number of inserts on your design.

6. On the interfacing or paper, draw a 4½-inch circle for each insert. Cut out the circles. Mark the center of each circle with a pin hole.

■ SEWING SECRET: The plastic lid on a one-pound coffee can is a nice-size circle, and it makes a handy template.

7. Pin the circles to the paper pattern. Pin-baste the pattern together and try it on, as shown in **Diagram 1.** Examine the design. Rearrange the circles as desired until you like the effect.

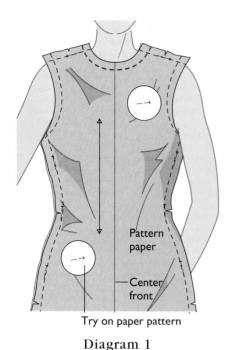

Try on paper pattern

Diagram 1

Prepare the Pattern

1. Remove the pins from the pattern pieces except for those on the circles.

2. Mark the center of each circle on the pattern.

■ SEWING SECRET: Use a large sewing machine needle to mark the centers of the circles on the pattern. Insert the point of the needle into the pattern, and pull it through to the other side. The needle will leave a large, visible hole. To avoid confusing a spot on the paper with a circle loca-

tion, draw a circle around the needle hole.

Cut Out the Garment

1. Cut out the garment, and on the wrong side of the appropriate sections, mark the center of each circle with a pencil.

2. For each insert, cut one 6-inch circle from the lace, and cut one 7-inch square of facing from the lightweight lining fabric.

Set the Lace Insert

1. With the garment wrong side up, center the circle template on one of the pencil marks. Chalk-mark a line around the template.

2. With the garment right side up, center the facing over the center of the chalk mark. Pin it in place so the pins are inside the circle.

3. Set the machine stitch length to 18 spi (1.0 mm).

■ SEWING SECRET: When stitching curves and circles, I use a short stitch length to get a smooth, rounded line. For smaller circles, I use a very short stitch length.

4. Turn the garment section wrong side up. Check to be sure the facing is flat and not rumpled. Then stitch around the circle on the marked line, as shown in **Diagram 2.** When you return to where you started stitching, overlap the stitches about ¼ inch.

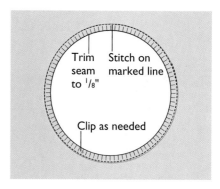

Trim seam to ⅛" Stitch on marked line

Clip as needed

Diagram 2

5. Cut out the center of the circle and trim the seam to ⅛ inch. Clip the seam as needed so the circle will be a smooth curve when the facing is turned to the wrong side, as shown in **Diagram 2.**

6. Turn the facing to the wrong side. With the facing side up, press the opening.

7. With the garment right side up, center and pin the circle of lace under the opening.

8. Edgestitch through all the layers around the circle, as shown in **Diagram 3.** Cover with a press cloth and press.

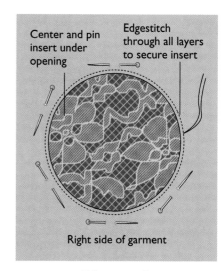

Center and pin insert under opening   Edgestitch through all layers to secure insert

Right side of garment

Diagram 3

9. Repeat steps 1 through 8 for all of the lace inserts.

Wraps and Shawls

Whether worn with day or evening wear, shawls are always fashionable.

This exquisite cocoon wrap is extremely comfortable and is easy to sew.

Cocoon Wrap

The design for this versatile wrap came from the Neiman Marcus accessories department. The original version was fabricated from wool double knit, but I've made them from silks and polyesters for light summer wraps, metallics for cocktail wear, and acrylic knits for everyday wear.

This wrap is simple to stitch—make it this afternoon and wear it tonight.

Tools & Supplies

♦ 1⅛ yards of 54-inch-wide wool double knit
♦ Thread in a matching or contrasting color

Cut Out the Wrap

1. Trim away the selvages from the fabric and trim the crosswise fabric edges so they are straight.

■ SEWING SECRET: Use a rotary cutter to trim quickly and easily. You'll get fewer zigs and zags on the edges of the fabric.

2. Check to be sure the two lengthwise edges are exactly the same length.

Assemble the Wrap

1. With right sides together, fold the fabric in half on the crosswise grain.

2. To mark the armhole openings, measure 9 inches from the folded edge. Place a pin at this point on both sides of the fabric.

3. Set the machine for 12 spi (2.0 mm) and stitch a 1-inch seam, beginning with a backtack at the pin and ending with a backtack at the raw edges, as shown in **Diagram 1**.

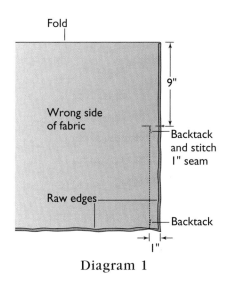

Fold

9"

Wrong side of fabric

Backtack and stitch 1" seam

Raw edges

Backtack

1"

Diagram 1

4. Press one seam open. At the armhole, press the 1-inch seam allowances to the wrong side, as shown in **Diagram 2**, and pin the seam allowances in place. Repeat this step for the other armhole.

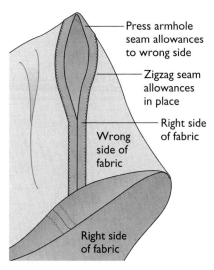

Press armhole seam allowances to wrong side

Zigzag seam allowances in place

Right side of fabric

Wrong side of fabric

Right side of fabric

Diagram 2

5. Set the machine for a zigzag stitch. Beginning at the hemline, center the raw edge of one side seam allowance under the presser foot, and stitch it in place, as shown in **Diagram 2**. Continue stitching around the armhole and back to the hemline.

6. Repeat steps 4 and 5 to secure the seam allowances at the other armhole.

7. With the wrong side of the wrap up, fold and press a 1-inch hem along the bottom. Pin the hem in place.

8. Center the raw edge of the hem under the presser foot, and zigzag it in place.

9. Press the finished wrap and turn it right side out.

■ SEWING SECRET: For a smoother fit over the shoulders, make an inverted pleat at the center back. Pin-mark the center back at the neckline and then pin-mark a point on each side of the center back 2 inches away. Bring the two outer pins together, as shown in **Diagram 3A**, then with right sides together, stitch a seam 1 inch long next to the pins, as shown in **3B**. Pin the pleat in place and stitch a triangle, as shown in **3C**, to secure it.

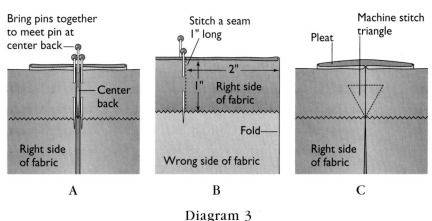

Bring pins together to meet pin at center back

Center back

Right side of fabric

A

Stitch a seam 1" long

2"

1"

Right side of fabric

Fold

Wrong side of fabric

B

Machine stitch triangle

Pleat

Right side of fabric

C

Diagram 3

A captivating Yves Saint Laurent design inspired this lovely ruffled shawl. The shawl can be combined with any garment for a touch of elegance during the day or during the evening.

Ruffled Shawl

Inspired by Yves Saint Laurent's offset ruffle, this ruffled shawl will add pizzazz to any wardrobe. This seasonless accessory can be made in any lightweight fabric to match or accent a favorite dress.

Tools & Supplies

♦ 1¾ yards of 45-inch-wide fabric

♦ Topstitching thread

Cut Out the Shawl

1. Cut one 45-inch square from the fabric. Find the midpoint on each edge of the square, and mark it with a small clip.

2. On the crossgrain, cut four strips 45 inches wide and 4½ inches long.

Make the Ruffle

1. With right sides together, match and pin the ends of the strips to make one long strip. Set the machine for 12 spi (2.0 mm) and stitch the ends of the strips together with ¼-inch seams. Press the seams open.

2. With right sides together, fold the strip lengthwise. Stitch a ¼-inch seam at each end and turn the ends right side out.

3. Beginning at one end of the strip, rub the seam between your thumb and forefinger to move the seam ½ inch to the left, as shown in **Diagram 1**.

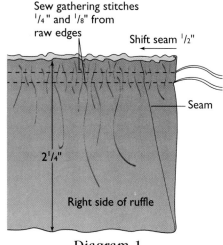

Sew gathering stitches ¹/₄" and ¹/₈" from raw edges

Shift seam ¹/₂"

Seam

2¹/₄"

Right side of ruffle

Diagram 1

Pin the two layers together. Then pin the remaining raw edges together so that the folded edge of the strip twists slightly.

4. Wind the topstitching thread onto a bobbin, and place that bobbin into the machine.

5. Set the machine for 8 spi (3.5 mm) and thread the needle with all-purpose sewing thread.

6. Sew a row of gathering stitches ¼ inch from the raw edges of the ruffle. Stitch a second row of gathering stitches about ⅛ inch from the raw edges, as shown in **Diagram 1**. For easy gathering, follow the instructions in the Sewing Secret under step 4 of "Prepare the Fabric Strip" on page 116.

Sew the Ruffle to the Shawl

1. As shown in **Diagram 2**, place the shawl right side up. With the raw edges even, place the ruffle on top of the shawl so the heavy bobbin thread is on top.

2. Match and pin one end of the ruffle to one corner of the shawl, as shown in **Diagram 2**.

3. Pin the first seam on the ruffle to the midpoint on one edge of the shawl, as shown in **Diagram 2**. Then pin the middle seam on the ruffle to the next corner of the shawl.

4. In the same manner, pin the rest of the ruffle to the adjacent edge, as shown in **Diagram 2**, and pull up the heavy bobbin threads to gather the ruffle.

5. Arrange the gathers on the ruffle evenly, adding additional pins if needed.

6. Stitch the ruffle to the shawl with a ¼-inch seam.

■ SEWING SECRET: When sewing a gathered section of fabric to an ungathered section, place the fabric under the presser foot with the ungathered section on top so you can adjust the gathers easily before stitching.

Finish the Shawl

1. With right sides together, fold the shawl to make a triangle. Match the clip marks and pin the raw edges together.

2. Turn the shawl over so you can use the ruffle stitching line as a guide. Beginning with a backtack at one corner, stitch to the next corner, pivot, and continue stitching to the clip mark on the adjacent side, as shown in **Diagram 3**. Backtack.

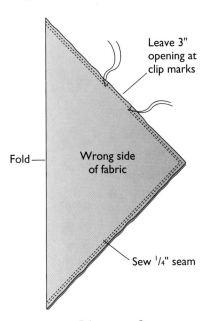

Leave 3" opening at clip marks

Fold—

Wrong side of fabric

Sew ¼" seam

Diagram 3

3. Begin stitching with a backtack about 3 inches away from where you stopped stitching. Stitch to the corner and then backtack.

4. Turn the shawl right side out. Turn the raw edge under and press lightly.

5. To close the opening, edgestitch on the shawl close to the seam. For instructions on edgestitching, see "How to Edgestitch" on page 6.

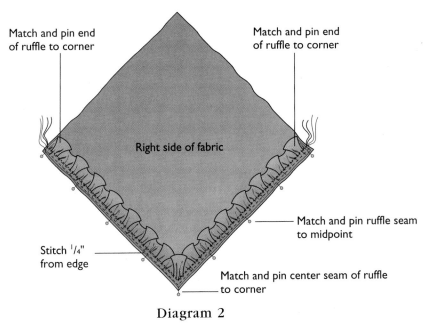

Match and pin end of ruffle to corner

Match and pin end of ruffle to corner

Right side of fabric

Stitch ¼" from edge

Match and pin ruffle seam to midpoint

Match and pin center seam of ruffle to corner

Diagram 2

Wrap yourself in luxury for an evening on the town.

Evening Wrap

This lovely wrap was inspired by an evening float designed by Charles Kleibacker in shocking pink silk gauze. Even though the shape is the same as a traditional ethnic ruana, you will be quick to agree that this heavenly creation is a masterpiece of elegance with little resemblance to its humble origin.

This evening wrap is particularly lovely when made from chiffon, crepe de chine, georgette, voile, or charmeuse, and it's a marvelous design for practicing your hand sewing skills.

Tools & Supplies

♦ 2 yards of soft, lightweight fabric 45 to 48 inches wide
♦ Chalk wheel

Cut and Mark the Wrap

1. From the fabric, cut a rectangle 44 inches wide and 72 inches long.

2. Chalk mark the midpoint at the center of one short end.

3. Beginning at the chalk mark, draw a line 43 inches long toward the center of the fabric, as shown below. The most accurate method for marking this line is to pull a thread along the lengthwise grain.

4. Cut on the marked line.

5. Finish all edges of the wrap with a hand-rolled hem.

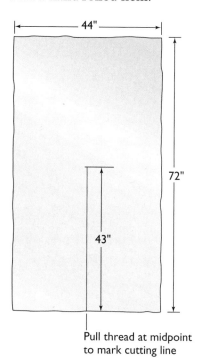

Pull thread at midpoint to mark cutting line

Charles Kleibacker

New York couturier Charles Kleibacker is known for his elegant bias-cut designs. Fluid and flattering, his designs were a favorite of many American women, including former First Lady Pat Nixon. He closed his business in 1984 to become designer-in-residence and curator of the Historic Costume Collection at Ohio State University.

How to *Hand Roll* a *Hem*

For a first-class and expensive-looking finish, stitch a hand-rolled hem on your finest garments. Although stitching a hand-rolled hem takes time, it adds a beautiful touch to fine, lightweight fabrics.

By following these simple instructions, you'll be able to stitch a perfect hand-rolled hem every time.

TOOLS & SUPPLIES
♦ Small-size hand sewing needle
♦ Machine embroidery thread or silk thread

PREPARE THE HEMLINE

1. Machine stitch ⅛ inch below the finished hemline of your garment. On the evening wrap design on the opposite page, that is ¼ inch from the raw edge.
2. Along the raw edge of the garment, trim the fabric close to the stitched line for 6 to 8 inches.

STITCH THE HEM

1. Thread the small-size hand sewing needle with the machine embroidery thread or silk thread.
2. Using your thumb and forefinger, gently roll the edge of the hem to the wrong side, enclosing the stitched line, as shown in **Rolled Hem Diagram 1**.

■ **SEWING SECRET:** *To get a tiny roll, which will give*

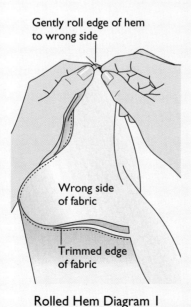

Gently roll edge of hem to wrong side

Wrong side of fabric

Trimmed edge of fabric

Rolled Hem Diagram 1

your garment a more professional look, wet your thumb and forefinger with a little saliva before starting the roll.

3. Hold the rolled edge over your forefinger, and hem it with a small slipstitch, as shown in **Rolled Hem Diagram 2**.
4. Continue trimming and stitching in 6- to 8-inch sections until the hem is completed.

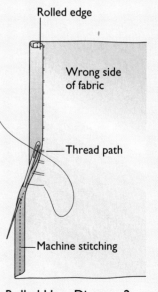

Rolled edge

Wrong side of fabric

Thread path

Machine stitching

Rolled Hem Diagram 2

BEHIND THE SEAMS

Many of my favorite high-fashion secrets are hidden on the inside of the garment. Designed to achieve professional results, they are easy-to-sew construction details that will improve the looks, comfort, and fit of your designs.

Inner Secrets

Invisible when the garment is worn, the interfacings, linings, and stays are key ingredients of high-quality fashions. Learn to use them effectively to control the drape of the fabric, to establish and preserve the shape of your designs, and to improve the fit and comfort of your garments.

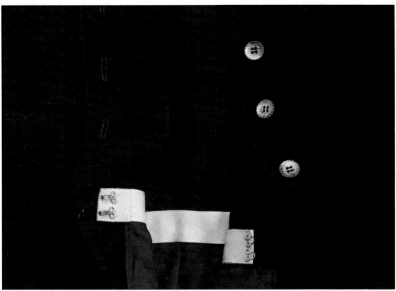

This easy-to-sew grosgrain ribbon stay will ensure your dress sits at the waistline properly.

Waist Stay

A waist stay is used to anchor the garment at the waistline and prevent the zipper or garment opening from gaping under stress. The waist stay can help to improve the fit of a garment, and when a person loses or gains weight, frequently the waist stay can be adjusted without altering the garment.

Follow these instructions to make a simple stay from grosgrain ribbon.

Tools & Supplies

- ♦ 1-inch-wide grosgrain ribbon
- ♦ 2 large hooks and eyes

Make the Waist Stay

1. Cut the grosgrain ribbon 4 inches longer than your waist measurement.

■ SEWING SECRET: Always make the waist stay before making the garment so you can use the stay as an anchor when fitting the skirt or bodice separately.

2. Pin the length of ribbon around your waist and sit down. If it is too snug, adjust the pins until it is comfortable. Mark the length of the stay and remove it.

■ SEWING SECRET: When creating designs with a fitted waistline, Galanos uses ¾-inch-wide elastic instead of grosgrain ribbon for a more comfortable stay.

3. Fold under the raw edges at both ends of the ribbon 1 inch. Then turn those folded edges under 1 inch, creating a double hem. Edgestitch close to the first fold on both ends, as shown in **Diagram 1.** (For instructions on edgestitching, see "How to Edgestitch" on page 6.)

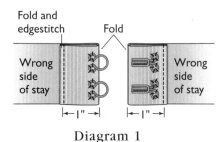

Diagram 1

4. As shown in **Diagram 1,** sew the two large hooks securely to the overlap.

5. Sew the corresponding eyes to the underlap, as shown in **Diagram 1.**

■ SEWING SECRET: To keep your hand sewing needles sharp and free from rust, occasionally insert them into a strawberry emery cushion.

If you don't have a strawberry emery cushion in your sewing box, insert your needles into a steel wool pad. These pads are available at most supermarkets, and at hardware and discount stores.

You can make your own needle cushion by simply covering the steel wool pad with a firmly woven fabric.

Sew the Stay in Place

1. Assemble the garment.

■ SEWING SECRET: Cut and sew the garment waist at least 1 inch larger than the waist stay. Then, if the waistline becomes a little snug at a later date, the waist stay can be let out 1 inch without altering the vertical seams of the garment.

2. Measure and mark each end of the stay 1¾ inches from the end. Divide and mark the rest of the stay into quarters.

3. With the garment wrong side up, measure 2 inches from the opening. Mark this distance on the waist seam. Divide and mark the rest of the waist seam into quarters.

Tips for Sewing Waistlines

Improve the fit and feel of the waistlines on all your skirts and pants by following these simple construction tips.

READY

♦ If you don't have enough fabric to cut a self-fabric waistband, use grosgrain ribbon to make the waistband, face the waistband, or face the waistline edge.

♦ Make a ribbon guide to use for marking waistbands easily. To make the guide, cut a piece of 1-inch-wide ribbon several inches longer than your waist measurement. Pin it around your waist and sit down. Repin it if needed so the band will be comfortable when sitting. Mark the ribbon at the center front, center back, and the side seams.

♦ If you expect to take in or let out the waistline of slacks at a later date, it will be easier to do if the waistband has a seam at the center back, as on men's trousers. To adjust the pattern, see "Adding a Seam" on page 201. Stitch the waistband on the right and left sections before stitching the center back seam.

♦ To create a longer-waisted look when you are short-waisted, finish the waist edge of skirts and pants with facings instead of waistbands.

♦ For skirts and pants that fit attractively, cut the garments so the waist seamline is 2 inches longer than the corresponding seamline on the waistband. Ease the garment to the waistband when you stitch.

SET

♦ To make a waistband that won't stretch out of shape, cut it on the lengthwise grain of the fabric.

♦ To eliminate finishing the unnotched edge on a waistband, cut it on the selvage.

♦ If the size of your waist varies from day to day, make the waistband to fit your largest waist measurement; interface the waistband with a piece of elastic that will make the band fit your smallest measurement.

♦ If your dirndl skirts are too bulky at the waistline, add six to eight small darts before you gather to remove some of the fullness.

♦ To make a more comfortable elastic waistband, substitute two or more strips of narrow elastic for one wide

strip. Make a separate tunnel for each.

SEW

♦ Sew grosgrain ribbon to the inside of your waistband to hold blouses in place.

♦ To prevent elastic casings in pull-on skirts and pants from rolling, ditch-stitch at each vertical seamline after you insert the elastic and adjust the gathers. For instructions on ditch-stitching, see step 6 of "Sew the Binding to the Garment" on page 48.

♦ When sewing pull-on skirts and pants, sew a small loop of colored ribbon at the center back so it will be easy to identify when dressing.

♦ When fitting a skirt before the waistband is sewn, pin or baste the seamline at the waist edge to your ribbon guide or a seam binding stay so it will set at the waist properly.

♦ When the skirt has horizontal wrinkles just below the waistband, it is generally because the skirt is too tight around the hips. Release the side seams until the skirt fits smoothly.

■ SEWING SECRET: The waist stay is sewn into the finished garment so the unsewn ends are shorter than the garment waistline. This eliminates stress on the zipper or placket opening, which will give your garment a more attractive finish.

4. Center the waist stay over the seamline. Align the marked

points on the stay and the seam, and pin them together.

5. Ease the garment to the stay and, as shown in **Diagram 2**, hand sew it to the seam permanently with a short running stitch. Begin and end the short running stitches 2 inches from the opening so the ends of the stay remain free.

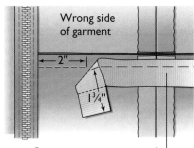

Center stay over seam and hand sew to seam allowances

Diagram 2

Ribbon Secrets

When you think of ribbons you might imagine a pretty, decorative trim on the outside of a garment. But when used inside a garment as hanger loops and lingerie guards, ribbons are not only practical, but they are also an inner secret that you will enjoy every time you wear the garment. Ribbons are much more attractive than the functional tubings and tapes they replace, and they can be stitched in a fraction of the time.

HANGER LOOPS

Hanger loops are particularly useful for fabrics that are easily marred by clip hangers or for designs you want to hang from the waist. They can be used on skirts and pants with waistbands or elastic casings.

TOOLS & SUPPLIES

♦ ⅝ yard of ¼-inch-wide double-satin ribbon

MAKE THE LOOP

1. For each loop, cut a piece of ribbon 11 inches long.
2. Fold the loops in half, and pin the ends together.

■ **SEWING SECRET:** *Although it's nice when the ribbon matches the fabric, it is more practical to purchase neutral-color ribbons in quantity so you will have the materials on hand.*
3. With the garment wrong side up, pin one ribbon loop at each side seam with the ends extending ½ inch over the seamlines at the waist. Hand baste the loops in place, as shown in **Ribbon Diagram 1.**

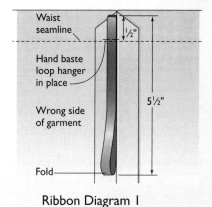

Waist seamline
½"
Hand baste loop hanger in place
Wrong side of garment
5½"
Fold

Ribbon Diagram 1

■ **SEWING SECRET:** *On pleated trousers, use three loops: one at the top of each of the front pleats and one at the center back. This will hold the pleats in the position they will be in when the trousers are worn.*
4. Attach the waistband or finish the casing to secure the hanger loops permanently.

LINGERIE GUARDS

Lingerie guards are set at shoulder seams and other strategic locations to prevent unattractive lingerie straps from peeking out from underneath a garment. They are particularly effective on designs with scoop necks and cut-away armholes. But since they also prevent straps from falling off the shoulders, they are practical for any design. Lingerie guards can be made of seam binding, lining fabric tubes, ribbons, or thread chains.

TOOLS & SUPPLIES

♦ ¼ yard of ¼-inch-wide double-satin ribbon
♦ Small snaps

MAKE THE LINGERIE GUARDS

1. To make a pair of lingerie guards, cut a piece of ribbon 9 inches long.
2. At one end and with the wrong side of the ribbon up, fold the raw end up ¼ inch.
3. Cover that raw end of the ribbon with the ball of the snap and sew it in place, as shown in **Ribbon Diagram 2.**

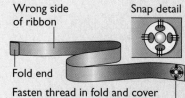

Wrong side of ribbon
Snap detail
Fold end
Fasten thread in fold and cover raw edge of ribbon with ball of snap

Ribbon Diagram 2

4. Snap the socket in place.

5. Repeat steps 2 through 4 to finish the socket end.

6. Set the strap aside until you're ready to sew it into the garment.

ATTACH THE LINGERIE GUARDS

1. Cut the strap created in "Make the Lingerie Guards" on the opposite page.

2. With the garment wrong side up, examine the shoulder seam to determine the location for the lingerie guard. On a wide shoulder, the strap is centered on the seam so it will be over the bra or slip straps. On designs with scooped necklines it is closer to the neckline, and on designs with cut-away armholes it is closer to the armscye.

3. Mark the location for the snap socket near the neckline. Then sew it in place, as shown in **Ribbon Diagram 3**.

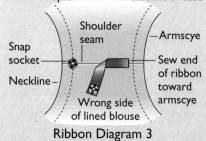

Allow strap to have small amount of ease

Shoulder seam — Armscye

Snap socket

Neckline —

Sew end of ribbon toward armscye

Wrong side of lined blouse

Ribbon Diagram 3

■ **SEWING SECRET:** *When sewing lingerie guards on a garment with a wide shoulder, leave about $\frac{1}{4}$ inch ease on the strap to avoid creating an unattractive dip on the shoulder seam of the garment. On a narrow shoulder, allow only a little ease so the strap won't show at the edges.*

4. Snap the guard in place and turn under the raw edge at the end. Pin

and then sew the raw edge to the shoulder seam, as shown in **Ribbon Diagram 3**.

LOOPS FOR STRAPLESS DESIGNS

Hanging a strapless dress can be a challenge, but these simple ribbon loops make it easy.

TOOLS & SUPPLIES

♦ $\frac{3}{4}$ yard of $\frac{1}{4}$-inch-wide double-satin ribbon

ATTACH THE BACK LOOPS

1. For each hanger loop, cut a piece of ribbon 13 inches long.

2. Fold the loop in half and pin the ends together.

3. With the garment back wrong side up and the loop toward the waistline, position the ribbon on the back 2 to 3 inches from the side seams and $\frac{1}{2}$ to 2 inches below the finished edge of the dress. Hand sew the ribbon in place about $\frac{1}{2}$ inch from the ends.

4. Fold the ribbon toward the garment edge, and with a small stitch, hand sew it permanently for $\frac{1}{2}$ inch on each side, as shown in **Ribbon Diagram 4**.

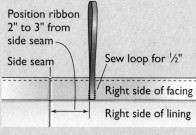

Position ribbon 2" to 3" from side seam

Side seam

Sew loop for $\frac{1}{2}$"

Right side of facing

Right side of lining

Ribbon Diagram 4

5. Measure the distance from the center back to the loop. Measure and mark an equal distance on the other side of the back for the remaining loop.

6. Make the other back loop, following steps 2 through 4.

SEW THE FRONT THREAD CHAINS

1. Using the measurement between the center back and a back loop as a guide, measure and pin-mark the locations of the front thread chains about 1 inch below the top of the garment.

2. As shown in **Ribbon Diagram 5**, beginning about $\frac{3}{8}$ inch from the pin, make a $\frac{3}{4}$-inch thread chain, following the directions in "How to Tame a Free-Hanging Skirt Lining" on page 151.

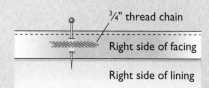

$\frac{3}{4}$" thread chain

Right side of facing

Right side of lining

Ribbon Diagram 5

3. To hang the dress, thread the ribbon loops through the thread chains from bottom to top, as shown in **Ribbon Diagram 6**; then hang the ribbons on a hanger.

■ **SEWING SECRET:** *To prevent straps from falling off a fabric-covered hanger, sew a small button with a shank 4 to 5 inches from each end of the hanger, as shown in **Ribbon Diagram 6**.*

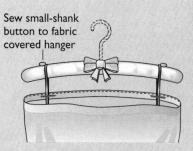

Sew small-shank button to fabric covered hanger

Ribbon Diagram 6

A blouse stay not only protects the garment from body oils, but it can also be used to help control pleats and gathers.

Blouse Stays

Blouse stays are used in the shoulder area to protect the blouse from perspiration and body oils and to control any fullness. They are rarely used on ready-made garments because they require additional fabric, which would make the blouse very expensive.

Blouse stays look like facings, but they are applied to the wrong side of the garment section like an underlining. Some stays duplicate the garment section, but many are cut smaller to control pleats or gathers. Stays are particularly useful when used at the shoulder to control fullness that has been added to accommodate a large bust. Stays can extend to the middle of the armscye to the underarm or to the top of the slip.

Tools & Supplies

♦ Pattern paper
♦ Lightweight fabric to match your flesh color, or self-fabric

Plot and Make the Stay Patterns

1. To plot the stay pattern for a garment section that has a dart or no fullness at the shoulder, draw the bottom of the stay on the original pattern piece, as shown in **Diagram 1A** on the opposite page. On the front and back pattern pieces, measure 1 inch down from the bottom of the armscye, and draw a horizontal line to indicate the cutting line for the bottom of the stay.

■ SEWING SECRET: To make a pattern for a garment section that has easing, gathers, pleats, or tucks at the shoulders, pin out the fullness in the shoulder area so the pinned shoulder length equals the finished shoulder length of the corresponding section, as shown in **Diagram 1B.**

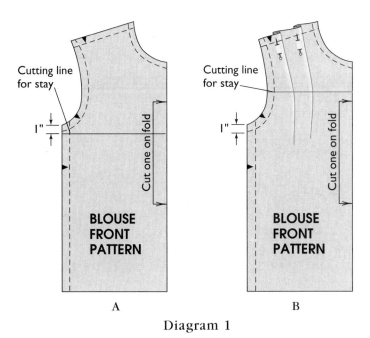

Diagram 1

2. On a piece of pattern paper, trace the cutting lines for the front and back stays.

3. Trace the stitching lines for any darts, and mark the grain, notches, and any foldlines.

4. Cut out the front and back stay patterns, as shown in **Diagrams 2A** and **2B.**

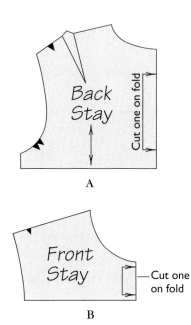

Diagram 2

Make the Front and Back Stays

1. Cut the stays from self-fabric or from lightweight flesh-color material such as organza, georgette, China silk, crepe de chine, or Sewin' Sheer.

■ SEWING SECRET: Flesh-color fabric stays are less noticeable under prints than self-fabric. When selecting flesh-color fabrics, remember that on most skin tones, shades of light to medium or dark brown appear more flesh-color than shades of pink and peach.

2. Complete any darts on the front and back stays, and press them toward the armscye or in the opposite direction of the darts on the blouse.

3. Finish the lower edge of the front and back stays by serging or pinking. You could also stitch a chiffon hem or hand overcast the edge.

Prepare the Blouse

1. Complete any darts and press them toward the garment center.

2. Baste any gathers, easing, pleats, or tucks in place.

Attach the Front and Back Stays

1. With wrong sides together, place each stay on top of each blouse section.

2. Match and pin the edges together at the neck, shoulders, and armscyes of the blouse front and the back, as shown in **Diagram 3.**

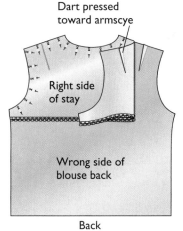

Diagram 3

3. Machine baste just inside the seamlines.

4. Finish the blouse.

■ SEWING SECRET: You can hand baste the front and back stays to the blouse if desired. Hand basting allows you to position the layers of fabric exactly, ensuring accurate machine stitching later.

The secret to taming a cowl neckline is an easy-to-sew stay.

The stay helps this cowl neckline drape attractively.

Cowl Stay

Cowl necklines with their soft folds of fabric have always been a favorite of mine, but no amount of weighting could coax them to stay attractively draped. Then I learned about cowl stays, and the battle was won.

This easy-to-sew cowl stay controls the drape of the front of the blouse. Similar to the blouse stay, the cowl stay fits the body while allowing the fullness of the blouse to drape attractively.

In these instructions, all measurements begin and end at the cutting, not the stitching, lines.

Tools & Supplies

♦ Pattern paper
♦ Lightweight fabric to match your flesh color or self-fabric

Plot the Cowl Stay

1. If the blouse has pleats at the shoulders, fold them in place on the pattern.

2. On a piece of pattern paper, trace the cutting lines of the blouse front pattern at the shoulder, the armscye, and the underarm. Remove the front pattern piece.

3. Aligning the shoulder seams, place the back pattern on top of the traced front pattern. Trace the cutting line of the back pattern at the shoulder, neckline, and garment center, as shown in **Diagram 1.** Then remove the back pattern.

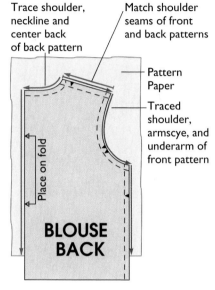

Trace shoulder, neckline and center back of back pattern

Match shoulder seams of front and back patterns

Pattern Paper

Traced shoulder, armscye, and underarm of front pattern

Place on fold

BLOUSE BACK

Diagram 1

4. On the traced pattern, measure and mark a point on the shoulder about 4 inches from the armscye, as shown in **Diagram 2,** so the stay won't extend into the neck area.

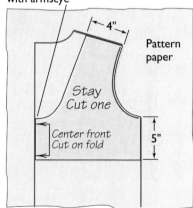

Mark deepest part of neckline even with armscye

4"

Pattern paper

Stay Cut one

Center front Cut on fold

5"

Diagram 2

5. At the center front, mark the deepest part of the neckline even

with the bottom of the armscye. Draw the neckline, as shown in **Diagram 2.**

6. Measure and mark a point on the underarm 5 inches below the armscye. Square a line from the center of the blouse to that marked point, as shown in **Diagram 2.** For instructions on how to square a line, see "Square a Line from a Line" on page 161.

7. Cut out the pattern, cutting along the neckline drawn in step 4.

8. Label the center of the pattern "Center front—Cut on fold," and mark the center of the pattern piece "Stay—Cut one," as shown in **Diagram 2.**

■ SEWING SECRET: To test the stay pattern, cut a full pattern for the stay. (For instructions, see "How to Make a Full Pattern" on page 10.) Place the stay pattern on top of the front pattern and pin the shoulder seams together. Examine the drape of the front pattern. If the stay is too tight, cut the pattern at the center front and add pattern paper as needed to get a perfect fit.

Make the Cowl Stay

1. Using the stay pattern, cut one stay from the fabric. For a tip on choosing fabric to match your skin color, see the Sewing Secret under step 1 of "Make the Stays" on page 133.

2. Hem the neckline and lower edge of the blouse stay with a chiffon hem. See "Chiffon Hem" on page 40 for instructions.

■ SEWING SECRET: Instead of stitching a chiffon hem, you can stitch a hand-rolled hem. For instructions, see "How to Hand Roll a Hem" on page 125.

Set the Cowl Stay

1. If the blouse has pleats at the shoulders, hand baste them in place.

■ SEWING SECRET: To mark pleats quickly and easily, use a clip and notch system. Mark the pleat foldline with a notch and the line it folds to meet with a clip.

2. With the blouse and the stay wrong sides together, place the stay on top of the blouse front.

3. Set the machine for 12 spi (2.0 mm) and stitch the two layers together just inside the seamline at the shoulders, the armscyes, and the underarms, as shown in **Diagram 3.**

Stitch blouse and stay together just inside the seamline at the shoulders, armscyes, and underarms

Right side of stay

Wrong side of blouse

Diagram 3

3. Finish the blouse.

Interfacings and Linings

Indispensable ingredients for beautifully tailored garments, interfacings and linings will improve the look of, preserve the shape of, and add comfort to most garments. To create high fashion with a professional look, use these essential how-tos.

Multiple layers of interfacing help this jacket retain its like-new shape.

Interfacing a Jacket

One of the features of designer jackets and suits is the ability to maintain a crisp silhouette for the life of the garment. To achieve this, the jackets, particularly the fronts, are interfaced with one or more layers of interfacing. The type of interfacing, the placement, and the number of layers will vary with the design and the designer.

These instructions focus on a pret-a-porter jacket from Yves Saint Laurent. Almost 15 years old, this jacket is definitely out of style, but it still retains its like-new shape.

The French term for ready-to-wear, *pret-a-porter* literally means ready to carry. The English term is "off the peg."

The front of this jacket has two layers of interfacing. One piece duplicates the shape of the front and the other, which is called the chest piece, fills the hollow area between the shoulder and bust so that the jacket will maintain a smooth line without collapsing to follow the contours of the body.

The front facing is completely interfaced. Many jackets do not have an interfacing on the facing except when the design has lapels.

The jacket back has a sew-in interfacing, but a second layer of fusible interfacing is often applied to it for additional body. Only the upper part of the jacket back is interfaced, so the jacket remains supple in the waist area and moves with the body.

The interfacing for the underarm panel follows the curve and reinforces the armscye. When the design has no underarm panel, the back interfacing extends 2 to 3 inches below the armscye.

The sleeve cap interfacing is generally called a sleeve backing. It is applied before the ease basting is stitched and eliminates the dimples that occur adjacent to the seamline by supporting the sleeve cap. This interfacing is used in addition to sleeve heads and shoulder pads.

Tools & Supplies

- Stiletto tracing wheel
- Pattern paper
- Fusible weft-insertion interfacing
- Lightweight fusible knit or weft-insertion interfacing
- Medium-weight fusible knit or weft-insertion interfacing
- Lightweight fusible interfacing
- Sew-in interfacing (such as hair canvas, muslin, wigan, or Armo Press Soft)

Plot the Interfacing Patterns

1. On the jacket front pattern, draw the chest piece, as shown in **Diagram 1.**

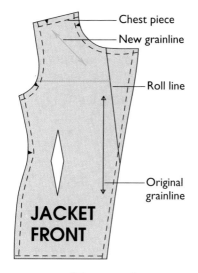

Diagram 1

■ SEWING SECRET: While you plot your patterns, preshrink your interfacing. Fold the interfacing and place it in a basin with hot water. Be sure all the layers are wet and leave it to cool. Then, let the water out of the basin and remove the excess water by pressing the interfacing against the drain. I usually hang it over the shower rod to dry.

2. On the jacket back pattern, draw the interfacing, as shown in **Diagram 2.** The large interfacing pattern ends 2½ inches from the bottom of the armscye. The small interfacing pattern ends 6 inches from the neckline.

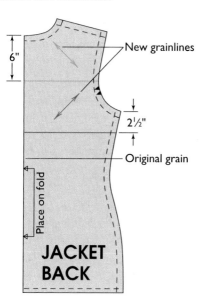

Diagram 2

3. On the sleeve pattern, draw the interfacing, as shown in **Diagram 3.**

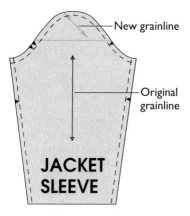

Diagram 3

4. Draw the new grainlines at a 45-degree angle to the original grainline so that the sections will be cut on the bias. Notice that the two back sections in **Diagram 2** on page 137 are cut on opposite grains.

■ SEWING SECRET: If the jacket pattern has an underarm panel, draw the interfacing so it is 2½ inches wide.

Trace the Patterns

1. Using a stiletto tracing wheel, trace the pattern for the chest piece onto a piece of pattern paper, as shown in **Diagram 4.** Trace the new grainline and label the pattern "Chest piece—Cut 2." (See "Resources" on page 243 for a source for the stiletto tracing wheel.)

2. Trace the patterns for the back interfacings. Trace the new grainlines. Label the larger pattern "Back interfacing 1—Cut 2," and label the smaller pattern "Back interfacing 2—Cut 2," as shown in **Diagram 4.**

3. Trace the pattern for the sleeve interfacing. Draw the new grainline and label the pattern "Sleeve interfacing—Cut 2."

4. Cut out all of the interfacing patterns.

■ SEWING SECRET: You can extend the life of your favorite patterns by fusing them to interfacing using a hot iron or cutting them from Swedish tracing paper. Then roll the patterns and store them in cardboard tubes.

Cut the Interfacings

1. Use the jacket front pattern to cut the full front interfacings from a fusible weft-insertion interfacing in a weight appropriate for the fabric. Mark the darts and cut them out of the interfacing, as shown in **Diagram 5.**

2. Use the upper collar pattern to cut the interfacing from a light- to medium-weight weft-insertion or knit interfacing. Use the under-collar pattern to cut the inter-

facing from a medium-weight weft-insertion or knit interfacing.

■ SEWING SECRET: Weft-insertion fusible interfacings are appropriate for wools, brocades, silk suitings, and heavy cottons and linens, but may be too heavy for many silks and summer fabrics. Experiment with crisp interfacings in lighter weights to find the perfect match for your fabric.

3. If the design has lapels, use the front facing pattern to cut the facing interfacings from a very lightweight fusible such as Whisper Weft, Touch 'o Gold, Stacy Easy-Knit, or SofKnit.

4. Cut the two Chest Piece interfacings from a lightweight-weft insertion or knit fusible interfacing.

5. Cut Back interfacing 1 from a sew-in interfacing such as hair canvas, muslin, wigan, or Armo Press Soft. Cut Back interfacing 2 from a fusible interfacing such as

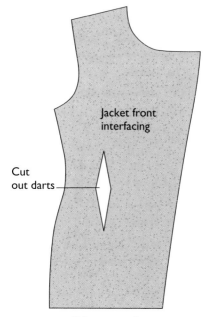

Diagram 5

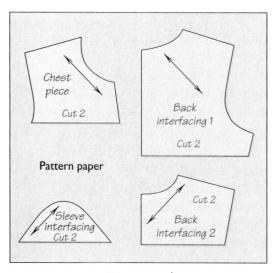

Diagram 4

Whisper Weft, Stacy Easy-Knit, or SofKnit.

■ SEWING SECRET: Used in tailoring, wigan is a cotton material similar to muslin, but it is more firmly woven.

6. Cut the two Sleeve interfacings from muslin, hair canvas, Armo Press Soft, or a lightweight fusible interfacing.

■ SEWING SECRET: When using a fusible interfacing, trim the lower edge with pinking shears. Before fusing it to the garment sections, make a test sample to check for a demarcation line and unwanted changes

in the character of the fabric. If you don't like what you see, experiment with another interfacing.

7. Cut any underarm interfacings from muslin, wigan, or a lightweight fusible interfacing.

8. From the sew-in interfacing, cut a bias strip 2¾ inches wide and long enough to interface the hems at the lower edge of the jacket and the sleeve hems.

■ SEWING SECRET: Better-quality tailored jackets and coats always have a bias-cut interfacing at the hemlines, even though they also may have underlinings. These interfacings can be applied before or after the vertical seams are stitched. On a two-piece sleeve, they are generally applied after the front seam is stitched.

Prepare the Interfacings

1. With one jacket front wrong side up, place one full front interfacing on top of the fashion fabric front, and fuse it in place following the manufacturer's directions.

2. Place one Chest Piece interfacing on top of the interfaced side of the jacket front, and fuse it in place following the manufacturer's directions.

3. Repeat steps 1 and 2 to fuse the interfacings to the remaining front section.

4. Place Back Interfacing 2 on top of Back Interfacing 1 and fuse the two back interfacings to-

gether following the manufacturer's directions.

5. With the jacket back wrong side up, place the back interfacing on top of it with the fusible section on top. Machine baste the layers together at the neckline, shoulders, and armscyes just inside the seamline.

6. With the upper sleeve wrong side up, place the interfacing on top and fuse the layers together following the manufacturer's directions, or machine baste the layers together just inside the seamline.

7. Repeat step 6 to apply the interfacing to the remaining sleeve, any underarm panels, the upper collar, undercollar, and lapels.

Apply the Hem Interfacings

1. With the garment sections wrong side up, place the bias strip of sew-in interfacing on the jacket and sleeve hems. Align and pin the raw edges together.

2. Set the machine for 12 spi (2.0 mm) and stitch ¼ inch from the raw edges.

■ SEWING SECRET: When you begin a new project, always put a new needle in your machine. Needles are inexpensive compared to the cost of a special fabric, which can be damaged by a worn needle. Some fabrics, such as synthetic suede, microfibers, and other synthetics dull the needle very quickly, and with these fabrics you may need more than one new needle.

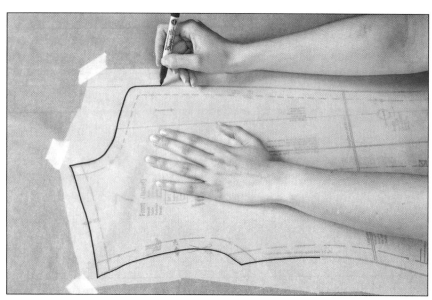

If your jacket pattern does not include a lining, you can draft your own.

Drafting a Jacket Lining Pattern

Lined jackets are more attractive, more comfortable to wear, and maintain their shape longer than unlined jackets.

Unfortunately, many sewing patterns do not include a pattern for the jacket lining. Those that do frequently need some minor adjustments so the lining will fit inside the jacket smoothly, and so that they can be sewn with the bagging technique.

These instructions will enable you to draft your own jacket lining pattern.

Tools & Supplies

♦ Pattern paper
♦ Curved ruler

Prepare the Pattern

1. Select the jacket pattern.

2. Press the pattern pieces for the jacket front, back, underarm panel (if any), front and back facings, and sleeves with a dry iron.

3. On a piece of pattern paper, trace the cutting lines of the jacket pattern pieces, all match points, hemlines, and grainlines.

4. Mark the front tracing "Lining Front" and the back tracing "Lining Back."

Plot the Lining Patterns

1. On the lining front and back patterns, trace the free or un-notched edge of the front and

back facing patterns, as shown in **Diagram 1.**

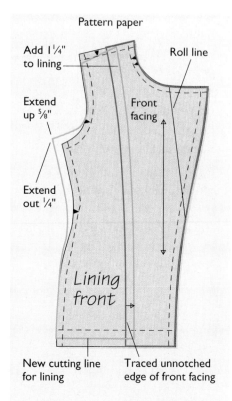

Pattern paper

Add 1¼" to lining

Extend up ⅝"

Extend out ¼"

Roll line

Front facing

Lining front

New cutting line for lining

Traced unnotched edge of front facing

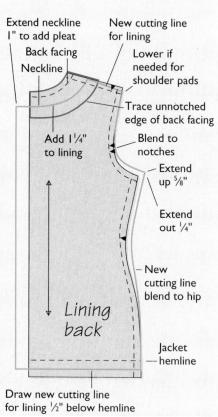

Extend neckline 1" to add pleat

Back facing

Neckline

Add 1¼" to lining

New cutting line for lining

Lower if needed for shoulder pads

Trace unnotched edge of back facing

Blend to notches

Extend up ⅝"

Extend out ¼"

New cutting line blend to hip

Lining back

Jacket hemline

Draw new cutting line for lining ½" below hemline

Diagram 1

2. To the lining patterns, add 1¼-inches—2 seam allowances—at the traced line of the facing on the front and back patterns. Indicate one or two match points

so the lining and facing will be easy to join together.

3. To adjust the front and back pattern shoulder seams for shoulder pads, see "How to

Prepare a Lining for Shoulder Pads," below, for instructions.

4. To adjust the front and back pattern seams at the underarm so the sleeves will hang attractively,

How to *Prepare a Lining* for *Shoulder Pads*

To make the lining fit inside the jacket smoothly, the armscye of the lining is cut and sewn smaller than the armscye of the jacket so the lining will fit smoothly without excess fullness to bunch up at the underarm. This is easy to visualize when you compare the arm and fabric layers to an onion. The shoulder is the center of the onion, and the lining is the first inner ring. The shoulder pad is a partial ring and covered by a larger full ring—the garment.

When the jacket has shoulder pads, the shoulder seams of the jacket are raised during the patternmaking process to accommodate the shoulder pads. The shoulder seams on the lining do not change because the lining fits the body and the shoulder pads are placed on top of the lining. The difference between the shoulder point of the garment shell and the lining equals the depth of the shoulder pad.

If no adjustment was made for the shoulder pads during the pattern development, you can do it before cutting the lining. But instead of adjusting the jacket pattern as you do in pattern development, you adjust the lining pattern to fit the body. The shoulder seams on the lining are redrawn to accommodate the thickness of the pad, so the slant of the shoulder seam increases as the depth of the pad increases.

Follow these instructions to adjust the lining at the shoulder.

1. Measure the depth of the shoulder pad at the armscye.
2. Place the lining pattern on top of the jacket front pattern, and examine the relationship of the cutting lines at the shoulder. At the armscye, the cutting line at the shoulder of the lining pattern should be lower than the cutting line on the jacket pattern—the amount is equal to the depth of the shoulder pad, as shown in **Lining Diagram 1**.
3. If the cutting lines at the shoulder are the same, measure and mark the new cutting line on the lining. For

example, if the shoulder pad is ½ inch thick, mark the shoulder point ½ inch below the original one, and connect it to the neck point.
4. Place the back lining pattern on top of the front lining pattern. Trace the new cutting line at the shoulder.
5. On the sleeve lining pattern, lower the cap at the shoulder point an equal amount, and blend to the notches, as shown in **Lining Diagram 2.**

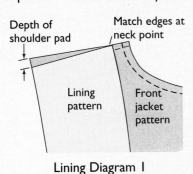

Depth of shoulder pad

Match edges at neck point

Lining pattern

Front jacket pattern

Lining Diagram 1

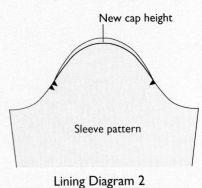

New cap height

Sleeve pattern

Lining Diagram 2

How to *Adjust a Lining* at the *Underarm*

To ensure that the sleeves will hang attractively and prevent stress and puckering at the underarm, the patterns for the front, back, side panel (if any), and sleeve lining are raised at the underarm so the lining will not flatten the armscye seam.

When checking the cut of the lining in a commercial pattern, compare each of the lining pattern pieces to the corresponding jacket pattern pieces. Many patterns have no adjustment, but some are adjusted on some sections but not on others.

Follow these steps when drafting a lining pattern or to improve the fit of a commercial pattern.

I. Tape the front lining pattern to a piece of pattern paper and raise the underarm seam into the armscye ⅝ inch by redrawing the armscye at the underarm, blending to the notch, as shown in **Adjust Diagram I.**

2. Repeat step 1 for the lining patterns for the back and the sleeve. If the design has a side panel or undersleeve, raise the armscye at the deepest point and blend to the notches, as shown in **Adjust Diagram 2.**

3. Cut out the patterns.

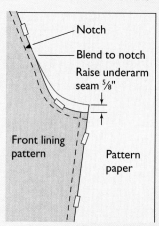

Adjust Diagram I

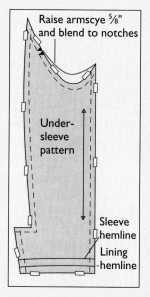

Adjust Diagram 2

see "How to Adjust a Lining at the Underarm," above, for instructions.

5. On the front and back patterns, extend the armscye seam ¼ inch, and redraw the side seam at the underarm, blending to nothing at the hips, as shown in **Diagram 1** on page 140.

6. Draw a new cutting line ½ inch below the jacket hemline on the front and back patterns, as shown in **Diagram 1** on page 140.

7. To add a pleat at the center back, extend the neckline 1 inch. Draw the pleat parallel to the center back, as shown in **Diagram 1** on page 140.

8. Trace the sleeve pattern, as shown in **Diagram 2.** Lower the shoulder as needed for shoulder pads. Extend the armscye seam ⅝ inch up and ¼ out at the underarm, blending to nothing at the notches and the hemline.

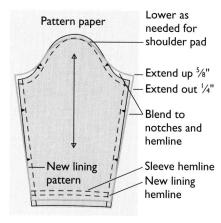

Diagram 2

Don't waste precious time hand stitching your next jacket lining when you can use the bagging method and sew it on the machine.

Bagging a Jacket

The bagging technique is used extensively in the fashion industry in all price ranges to stitch jacket linings completely by machine. By following these instructions, you'll find you can save time when lining your next jacket.

Tools & Supplies

♦ Paper-backed fusible web

Assemble the Jacket

1. Interface the jacket sections, following the instructions in "Interfacing a Jacket" on page 136.

2. Assemble and press the jacket. Press all hems in place.

3. Prepare the front facings and the jacket and sleeve hems for fuse hemming, following the instructions in "Prepare the Hem for Fusing" on page 146.

■ SEWING SECRET: If you want to finish the hems with traditional hemming instead of fuse hemming, hem the jacket and sleeves with a blindstitch or blind catchstitch now. Place the stitches at least ½ inch below the raw edge of the hem, as shown in **Diagram 1.**

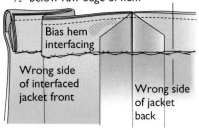

Place blind catchstitches at least ½" below raw edge of hem

Bias hem interfacing

Wrong side of interfaced jacket front

Wrong side of jacket back

Diagram 1

4. Pin the hems about ½ inch above the hemlines.

5. Set the sleeve heads and shoulder pads, following the instructions in "How to Stitch Sleeve Heads" on page 144.

6. Set the jacket aside and make the lining.

Prepare the Lining Pattern and Cut the Lining

1. Before cutting the lining, compare the lining patterns for the front, back, and sleeve to the corresponding patterns for the jacket sections to be sure the lining will fit smoothly and without bunching under the arm, but with enough length for the

How to *Stitch Sleeve Heads*

Sleeve heads are an essential feature of attractive sleeves. Used in addition to sleeve backings and shoulder pads, sleeve heads will improve the appearance of almost any set-in sleeve from traditional tailored wools to lightweight summer silks and washable sew-and-go designs. This technique from Christian Dior is the traditional method for making sleeve heads in tailored jackets.

TOOLS & SUPPLIES
♦ Cotton wadding or batting

PREPARE THE JACKET AND SLEEVE HEADS

1. For each sleeve head, cut a strip of cotton wadding 1½ inches wide and 8 inches long.

■ **SEWING SECRET:** *Similar to cotton batting, wadding has a glaze on one or both sides, and the cut edges can be torn and feathered to eliminate an unattractive ridge that might show on the right side of the sleeve. If wadding and cotton batting are not available, you can substitute a bias-cut strip of hair canvas, cotton flannel, or Armo Rite. See "Resources" on page 243 for sources of wadding.*

2. Set the sleeves in the jacket.

SET THE SLEEVE HEADS

1. With the jacket wrong side up and the sleeve head on top of the sleeve, align and pin one long edge of the sleeve head to the raw edges of the seam, as shown in **Stitch Diagram 1.**

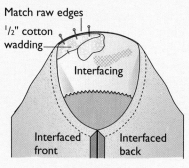

Match raw edges
½" cotton wadding
Interfacing
Interfaced front
Interfaced back

Stitch Diagram 1

2. Turn the seam over so you can see the seamline. Use a running stitch to sew through all layers on the seamline permanently.

3. Use your thumb and forefinger to tear-feather the edges of the wadding and round the ends so they will be inconspicuous when the garment is worn.

■ **SEWING SECRET:** *When making sleeve heads for lightweight silks, Dior uses bias-cut strips of silk organza. For added oomph, cut the strip 2¼ inches wide and fold it lengthwise. Lap and pin the folded edge ⅜ inch over the stitched line, as shown in **Stitch Diagram 2.** Secure the sleeve head with a running stitch on the seamline.*

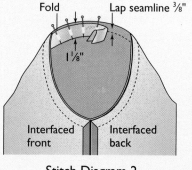

Fold   Lap seamline ⅜"
1⅛"
Interfaced front   Interfaced back

Stitch Diagram 2

jacket hem and sleeves to hang evenly. Make adjustments in the patterns as needed. (For directions, see "Drafting a Jacket Lining Pattern" on page 140.)

2. Cut out the lining.

3. With right sides together, stitch the vertical seams on the front and back and the shoulder seams.

4. Stitch the sleeve seams, leaving an 8- to 10-inch opening in the center of one seam on each sleeve, as shown in **Diagram 2.**

5. Set the machine for 10 spi (2.5 mm) and sew two rows of ease basting at the top of the sleeve cap.

6. With right sides together, sew the sleeves into the lining.

7. Press the lining.

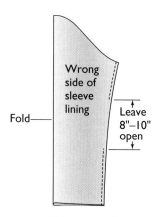

Wrong side of sleeve lining
Fold
Leave 8"–10" open

Diagram 2

Stitch the Lining

1. Place the jacket on the table with the right side up. Fold the jacket fronts back to expose the front facings.

2. With the lining wrong side up, place it on top of the jacket. As shown in **Diagram 3,** match the shoulder seams, notches, and raw edges on the front and back facings, pinning the edges of the lining to the facings.

3. Where the lining meets the front facings, fold the lining hem to the wrong side so the folded edge is ½ inch above the finished edge of the jacket, as shown in **Diagram 4.** Pin it in place.

4. To sew the lining, hold the jacket and lining out of the way. With the lining on top and the machine set at 12 spi (2.0 mm), stitch a ⅝-inch seam, removing the pins as you stitch. Press the seam toward the lining.

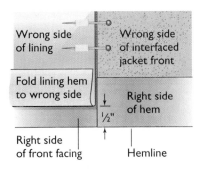

Diagram 4

5. Remove the paper from the fusible web on the front facings, jacket hem, and sleeve hems.

6. Turn the jacket right side out. Straighten the jacket and the lining.

Prepare and Finish the Hem

1. At the hemline, fold the raw edge of the lining under so the folded edge is ½ inch above the hemline. To establish the lining

length, pin the jacket and lining hems together at the center back and the seamlines.

■ **SEWING SECRET:** You can create a small tuck at the hemline for ease by setting the pin about ⅜ inch above the folded edge of the lining to mark the stitching line, as shown in **Diagram 5.**

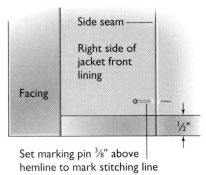

Set marking pin ⅜" above hemline to mark stitching line

Diagram 5

2. Reach into one of the open arm seams, and grasp the raw edges of the hem. Pull them out through the opening.

3. With the hems right sides together, reset the pins at the hem. Do not try to match the raw edges, but use the marking pins at the center back and side seams as guides for establishing the stitching line instead, as shown in **Diagram** 6 on page 146.

4. Hold the jacket and lining out of the way, and stitch the hems together, beginning and ending about 1 inch from the facings, as shown in **Diagram** 6 on page 146.

■ **SEWING SECRET:** This technique is called bagging because when you sew the hems together, the jacket forms a bag.

5. Turn the jacket right side out through one of the open arm seams and straighten the lining.

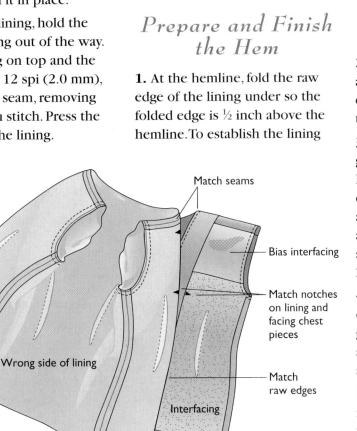

Diagram 3

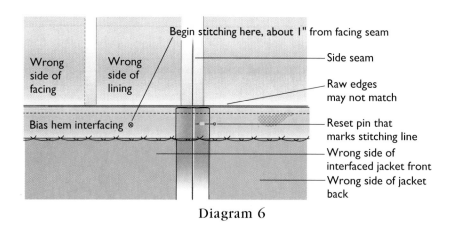

Begin stitching here, about 1" from facing seam

Wrong side of facing

Wrong side of lining

Side seam

Raw edges may not match

Bias hem interfacing ⊗

Reset pin that marks stitching line

Wrong side of interfaced jacket front

Wrong side of jacket back

Diagram 6

Anchor the Jacket Lining at the Underarms

1. With the lining side up, adjust and align the vertical seams on the lining with the seams on the jacket. At the underarm, the armscye seam on the jacket lining should be aligned with the raw edges of the armscye seam on the

How to *Fuse-Hem* a *Jacket*

Fuse-hemming is a very useful technique, especially for hemming jackets that will be bagged. Strips of paper-backed fusible web are applied to the wrong side of the facings and hems at the raw edges early in the construction process and sometimes immediately after the sections are interfaced, but the paper is not removed until just before fusing.

TOOLS & SUPPLIES
♦ Paper-backed fusible web

PREPARE THE HEM FOR FUSING

1. Cut the paper-backed fusible web into ½-inch-wide strips.

2. After the interfacings are applied to the facings and hems, place the strips fusible side down on the wrong sides of the garment sections about ¼ inch from the raw edges to be fused, as shown in **Fuse-Hem Diagram 1**.

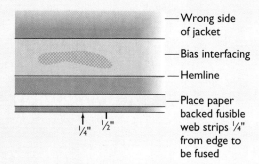

Wrong side of jacket

Bias interfacing

Hemline

Place paper backed fusible web strips ¼" from edge to be fused

¼" ½"

Fuse-Hem Diagram 1

■ SEWING SECRET: *If the hems have not been interfaced, interface them now or apply the fusible web only to the seam allowances to prevent it from showing on the finished jacket.*

3. Fuse the strips in place, following the instructions provided by the manufacturer. Do not remove the paper.

FUSE THE HEM

1. Assemble the jacket and lining. Stitch the lining into the jacket using your favorite method or the bagging method described on page 143.

2. Remove the paper backing from the fusible web at the hem and facings. When bagging a jacket, do this before closing the opening on the sleeve lining.

3. Smooth the lining in place so it is straight, as shown in **Fuse-Hem Diagram 2.**

4. With the lining side up, smooth one front facing.

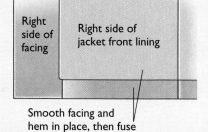

Right side of facing

Right side of jacket front lining

Smooth facing and hem in place, then fuse

Fuse-Hem Diagram 2

Cover it with a press cloth, and fuse it permanently. Repeat this step to fuse the remaining front facing, the jacket hem, and the sleeve hems.

jacket, or about ⅝ inch above the seamline.

2. Place a pin on the seamline approximately 1 inch below the armscye seam.

3. Reach into one of the open sleeve seams, and grasp the side seam allowances just below the pin. Pull them out.

4. With the side seam allowances right sides together, pin the raw edges together.

5. Then sew the seam allowances together by hand with a loose running stitch, beginning about 2 inches below the armscye seam and ending 3 to 4 inches above the hem.

6. Repeat steps 3 and 4 to anchor the jacket lining at the other underarm.

■ SEWING SECRET: To prevent pulling the knot through the fabric when hand sewing, always begin stitching with a backstitch.

7. Turn the jacket right side out, and straighten the lining.

Finish the Sleeve Linings

1. Straighten the lining inside one jacket sleeve.

2. Fold the raw edge of the lining under so the folded edge is ½ inch above the hemline. Pin the lining at the seamlines to establish the lining length, as shown in **Diagram 7.**

3. Reach into the open seam on the lining, and grasp the raw edges of the sleeve hems. Pull

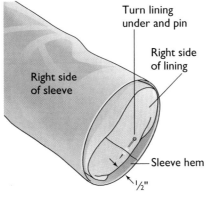

Diagram 7

them out through the opening in the sleeve lining.

4. With right sides together, reset the pin at the wrist. Pin the sleeve and lining hems together. Don't worry if the raw edges are not even. With the lining on top, stitch a ⅜-inch seam, as shown in **Diagram 8.**

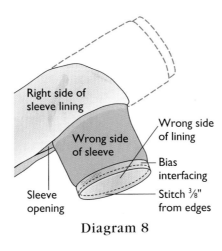

Diagram 8

5. Straighten the jacket sleeve. With the sleeve lining side out, close the opening on the seam by folding the lining seam allowances to the wrong side. Fold the lining on the seamline with the seam allowances together. Edgestitch along the folded edge to close the opening, as shown in **Diagram 9.** For

instructions, see "How to Edge-stitch," on page 6.

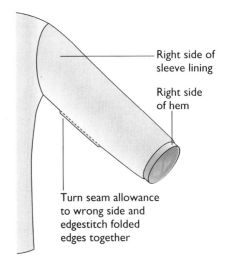

Diagram 9

6. Repeat steps 1 through 5 to finish the other sleeve.

Finish the Jacket

1. With the jacket lining side up, smooth the facings. If you choose to fuse-hem the jacket, steam-press the facings to fuse them in place.

2. Repeat step 1 to hem the jacket and sleeves. Press the lining lightly at the hems.

3. If you didn't anchor the underarm seams, ditch-stitch them together.

■ SEWING SECRET: To ditch-stitch at the underarm, straighten the lining in the jacket. Then align and pin the underarm seams together so the armscye seam on the jacket is about ⅝ inch below the corresponding seam on the jacket lining. Ditch-stitch in the wells of the underarm seams with a loose stab stitch, beginning about ½ inch below the armscye.

A lining adds body and helps maintain a skirt's shape by preventing the back from stretching out of shape.

Adding a Skirt Lining

Most expensive skirts have a separate lining, but sewing patterns rarely include a lining pattern for skirts. Even when they do, many of us eliminate the lining in our haste to finish and wear the garment.

Think twice next time. Most skirts will benefit from a lining. A lining adds body, reduces wrinkling, prevents seam slippage, and helps maintain the skirt's shape by reducing stress on seamlines and preventing the skirt back from "seating out" or stretching out of shape. The lining reduces the need to wear a slip, and it protects the seam allowances from abrasion and raveling.

Used on slim skirts, the lining duplicates the garment sections; on full skirts, it is often narrower.

Tools & Supplies

♦ Pattern paper
♦ Drafting or French curve

Prepare the Lining Pattern and Fabric

1. Select the skirt pattern and the fabric.

■ SEWING SECRET: If the skirt is straight, use the patterns for the skirt front and back patterns to make the lining. If it is full or flared, use a pattern for a straight skirt instead.

2. Press the pattern pieces for the body of the skirt with a dry iron. Generally this is a front and back section.

3. Mark the hemline for the lining on the skirt pattern pieces. For most skirts, the lining is finished ¾ to 1 inch shorter than the skirt.

4. Measure and mark the hem allowance for the lining.

■ SEWING SECRET: A double hem is used for linings on most

designer skirts. On straight skirts the hem is usually finished 2 inches wide, while on flared or tapered skirts it can be as narrow as ¾ inch.

5. Trace the skirt pattern pieces if needed to make separate lining patterns.

6. Select the lining.

■ SEWING SECRET: When selecting the lining, consider materials that are firmly woven, light-

weight, soft, and silky. Also, select a lining fabric that has care requirements similar to those of the fashion fabric.

7. Preshrink the lining fabric as needed.

8. Using the lining patterns, cut the lining.

■ SEWING SECRET: To keep the back of the skirt from stretching out of shape, cut the lining on the crossgrain of the fabric.

Assemble the Lining and the Skirt

1. With right sides together, assemble and fit the skirt. Press the seams open. Press any darts toward the garment centers, and set the zipper.

2. Repeat step 1 to assemble the lining. At the zipper opening, leave about 8½ inches unstitched. Press any darts away from the

How to *Dart* a *Skirt Lining*

By using darts in a skirt lining, you will reduce the amount of fabric in the tummy area—a place where few of us want any extra bulk. You can add darts to any skirt lining by following these steps.

1. Measure the entire lining at the waist edge. Subtract the finished length of the waistband plus 3¼ inches—2 inches ease plus two seam allowances—to determine the amount of fullness that must be darted out.

2. Divide the amount of fullness by the number of darts—usually four to eight. For example, if the fullness is 8 inches and there are 4 darts, each dart will be 2 inches. This is called a 1-inch dart—the width of the dart when it's folded for stitching.

3. At the waist edge, clip-mark the center of each dart about midway between the garment center and side seam.

4. With right sides together, fold the lining on the lengthwise grain at the clip-mark. Clip-mark the width of the dart at the waist edge, as shown in **Dart Diagram 1.**

5. Mark the end of the dart with a pin on the foldline about 3½ inches

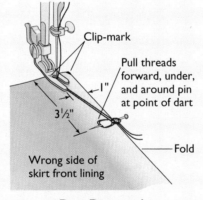

Clip-mark

Pull threads forward, under, and around pin at point of dart

1"

3½"

Fold

Wrong side of skirt front lining

Dart Diagram 1

from the waist edge on the skirt front, as shown in **Dart Diagram 1,** and about 4 inches from the waist edge on the skirt back.

6. Stitch the darts, beginning at the clip-marks and stitching to the pin at the dart point.

■ SEWING SECRET: *To mark the stitching line for the dart, pull the needle and bobbin threads forward 10 to 12 inches. Anchor the needle*

at the notches at the raw waist edge of the skirt. Lay the needle and bobbin threads on top of the fabric from the needle to the pin at the dart point. Wrap the threads under and around the pin, forming a figure eight, as shown in **Dart Diagram 1.** *Stitch the dart, using the needle and bobbin threads as a guide.*

7. Trim all of the darts so that they are ½ inch wide, as shown in **Dart Diagram 2,** and then press them toward the garment centers.

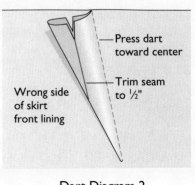

Press dart toward center

Trim seam to ½"

Wrong side of skirt front lining

Dart Diagram 2

garment centers. If the skirt has shirring instead of darts at the waist, use darts on the lining to reduce the bulk at the waist. See "How to Dart a Skirt Lining" on page 149 for directions.

Insert the Lining and Finish the Zipper

1. Arrange the skirt and lining wrong sides together with the lining side out.

2. Align the openings for the zipper placket and the raw edges at the waist edge.

3. At the zipper placket, fold the lining seam allowances to the wrong side. Pin-baste the folded edges to the back of the zipper tape, as shown in **Diagram 1**.

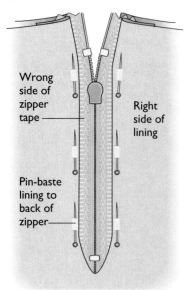

Wrong side of zipper tape

Right side of lining

Pin-baste lining to back of zipper

Diagram 1

4. Reach between the skirt and the lining, and grasp the seam allowances on one side of the

zipper. Pull the pins out and reset the pins on the wrong side of the lining, as shown in **Diagram 2**. Notice that the raw edges of the seam allowances do not match.

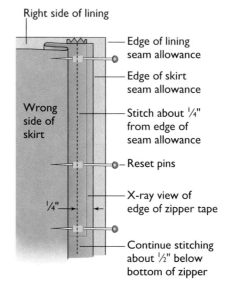

Right side of lining

Wrong side of skirt

Edge of lining seam allowance

Edge of skirt seam allowance

Stitch about 1/4" from edge of seam allowance

Reset pins

1/4"

X-ray view of edge of zipper tape

Continue stitching about 1/2" below bottom of zipper

Diagram 2

5. Hold the skirt and lining out of the way and stitch them together 1/4 inch from the raw edge of the seam allowance, as shown in **Diagram 2**. Continue stitching, stopping about 1/2 inch below the bottom of the zipper.

6. Repeat steps 4 and 5 to secure the lining on the other side of the zipper.

Finish the Waist Edge

1. Turn the skirt right side out with the lining inside so the wrong sides are together.

■ SEWING SECRET: If the skirt has darts, the waist edge should

be about 2 inches longer than the finished waistband so it can be eased to the band and will fit the body properly.

2. If the skirt is shirred at the waistline, adjust the rows of gathering stitches until the waist edge is the desired measurement.

3. Pin the skirt and lining together at the waist edge, matching the garment centers and side seams. If one edge is longer than the other, distribute the excess evenly.

4. With the skirt on top, stitch on the seamline to ease-baste the skirt and lining together at the waistline.

5. Position the hanger loops at the side seams on the lining side of the skirt. For directions, see "Hanger Loops" on page 130.

6. Stitch the waistband using your favorite method.

■ SEWING SECRET: When determining the length of the finished waistband, add 1 inch to your waist measurement. Your skirts will fit better and will be more comfortable to wear.

Hem the Skirt

1. Measure and mark the skirt hemline.

■ SEWING SECRET: To mark the hem on a long skirt easily, mark the hemline about 10 inches from the floor. Mark the finished length with a single pin at the center back.

How to *Tame* a *Free-Hanging Skirt Lining*

If your free-hanging skirt linings bunch up when you sit down, you can tame them by simply using a French tack to join the skirt and the lining at the hem. The following instructions tell you how.

1. With the lining wrong side up, begin the French tack about 1 inch above the hemline on the side seam.

2. Fasten a double strand of thread, and take a small backstitch. Pull the thread through, leaving a 3- to 4-inch loop.

3. Hold the loop open with your left thumb and forefinger while you hold the supply thread taut between your right thumb and forefinger, as shown in **Lining Diagram 1A.**

4. Use the left middle finger as a crochet hook, and reach through the loop and pull the supply thread through to make a new loop, as shown in **Lining Diagram 1A.** Let the first

loop fall off the fingers as you pull on the new loop, as shown in **1B.**

5. Pull on the new loop until the previous loop is taut on the chain. Continue making loops until the chain is the desired length.

6. To fasten the chain, take a small stitch on the garment hem. Then slip the needle through the last loop, as shown in **Lining Diagram 2.** Pull the loop taut and fasten the thread.

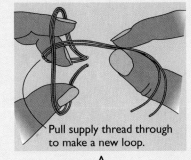

Pull supply thread through to make a new loop.

A

Let first loop fall off fingers as you pull on new loop.

B

Lining Diagram 1

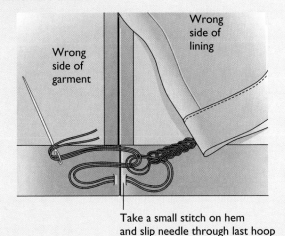

Wrong side of garment

Wrong side of lining

Take a small stitch on hem and slip needle through last hoop

Lining Diagram 2

2. Hem and press the skirt.

3. Mark the hemline on the lining ¾ to 1 inch shorter than the skirt.

■ SEWING SECRET: To mark the lining hem easily, put the skirt on a hanger. Pin the skirt and

lining together about 6 inches above the hem, and then mark the hem.

4. Measure and mark the hem allowance twice the finished width of the hem. Press a double-fold lining on the hem.

■ SEWING SECRET: To press the double-fold hem easily, press first on the finished hemline, then fold the raw edge in to meet the pressed hemline and press again.

5. Machine stitch the hem permanently.

A fashion model waits patiently as a designer puts his finishing touch on the uppermost tier of an exquisite ruffled organdy gown created during the 1950s.

PART II

Design Basics

"If there is no copying, how are you going to have fashion?"
—Coco Chanel

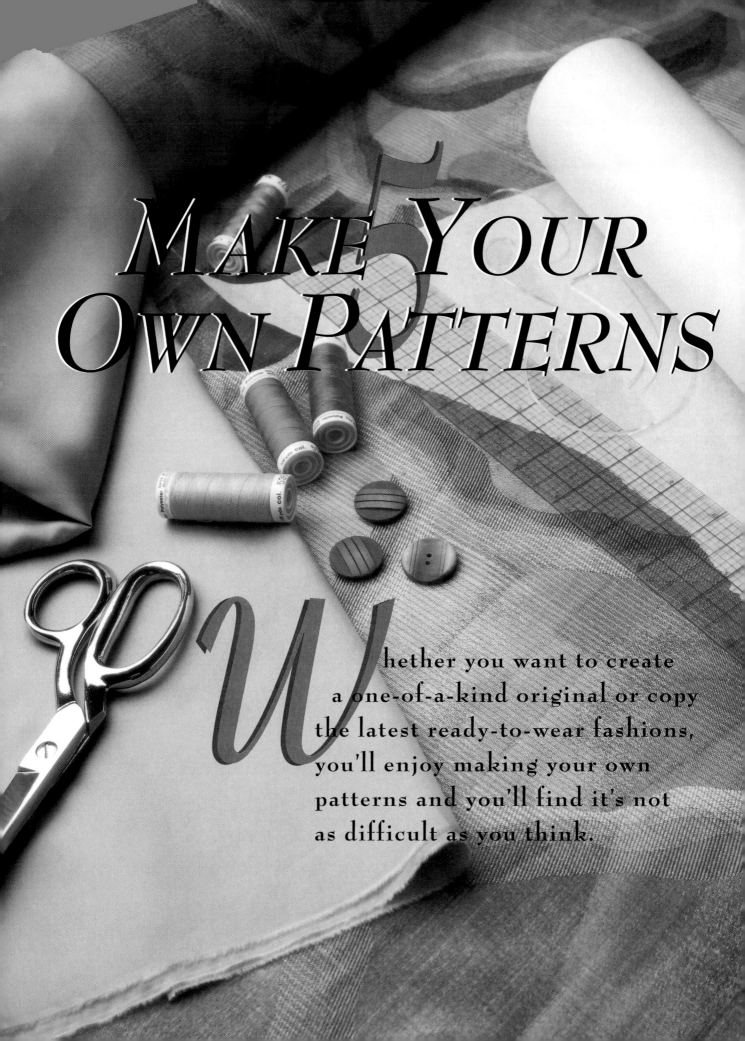

MAKE YOUR OWN PATTERNS

5

Whether you want to create a one-of-a-kind original or copy the latest ready-to-wear fashions, you'll enjoy making your own patterns and you'll find it's not as difficult as you think.

Preparing to Make a Pattern

Patternmaking is a very precise and exact science. It is based on drafting and patternmaking principles and skills that, once mastered, are applied every time a pattern is made.

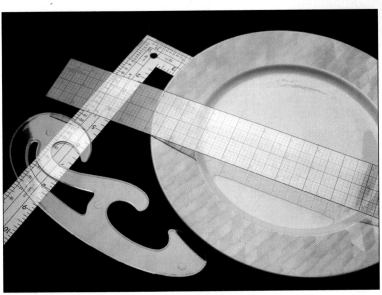

You may already own many of the tools used in patternmaking. If you don't have a French curve, substitute an ordinary dinner plate.

Tools and Supplies

To draft or alter patterns with precision, you must have the proper tools and supplies in your sewing room.

Precision is critical in patternmaking, so if you don't own a see-through ruler with a grid, you will want to invest in one now.

However, many of the tools listed here you may already own, or you may want to substitute one tool for another.

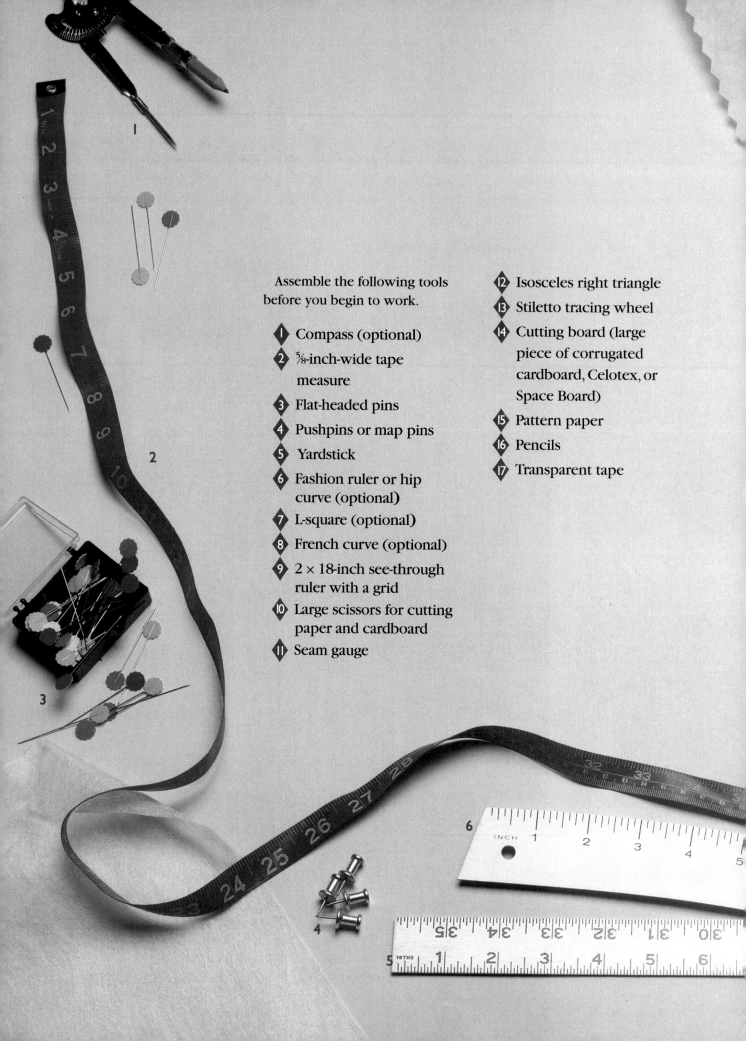

Assemble the following tools
before you begin to work.

1 Compass (optional)
2 ⅝-inch-wide tape
  measure
3 Flat-headed pins
4 Pushpins or map pins
5 Yardstick
6 Fashion ruler or hip
  curve (optional)
7 L-square (optional)
8 French curve (optional)
9 2 × 18-inch see-through
  ruler with a grid
10 Large scissors for cutting
  paper and cardboard
11 Seam gauge
12 Isosceles right triangle
13 Stiletto tracing wheel
14 Cutting board (large
  piece of corrugated
  cardboard, Celotex, or
  Space Board)
15 Pattern paper
16 Pencils
17 Transparent tape

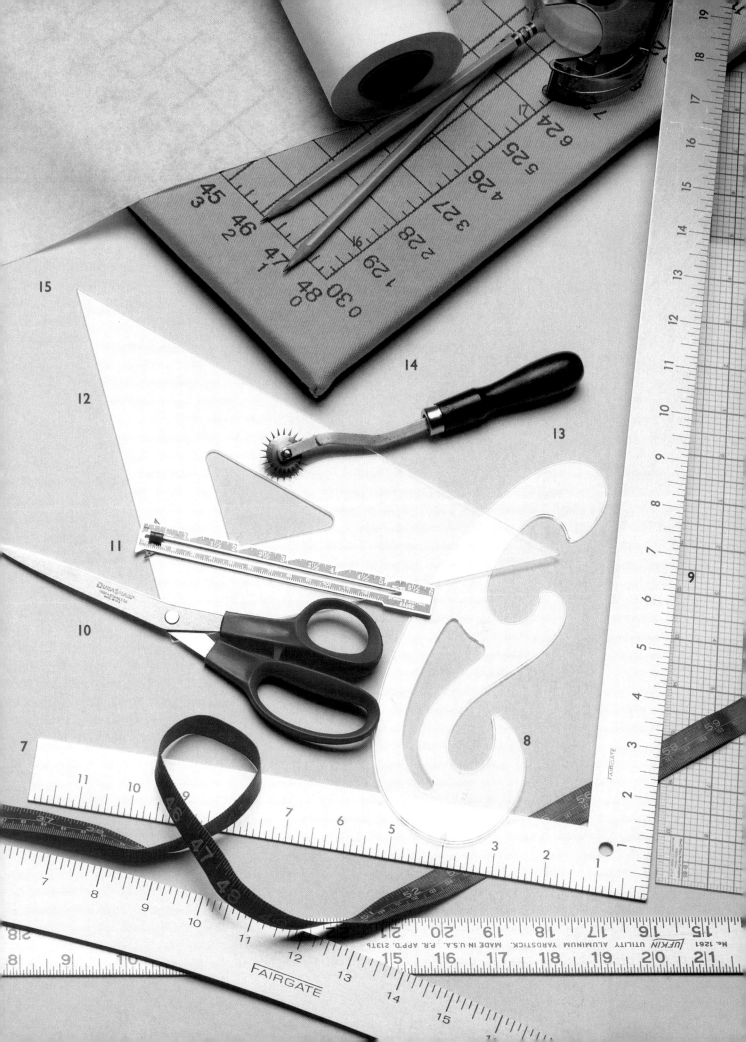

This basic pattern set features a fitted bodice with a jewel neckline, a center front opening, a straight skirt, and long sleeves.

Essential Patterns

To begin patternmaking, you need a simple pattern set or block. You will use that set of patterns to develop a master pattern or fashion silhouette.

While the basic pattern set will help you to understand your figure and its particular fitting problems, a master pattern allows you to create a fashionable design. Plus, once you learn how to modify a master pattern, you will be able to create an infinite number of stylish creations.

Patternmaking begins with a simple pattern set or block. This set of patterns is used to develop a master pattern or fashion silhouette.

The Basic Pattern Set

The basic pattern set is a simple, close-fitting design that has no design interest. It fits the natural outline of the figure and has a jewel neckline, natural shoulders and armscyes, long and fitted sleeves, and a straight skirt.

Sometimes called a block or foundation pattern, the basic pattern set has only five pieces—the bodice front and back, the skirt front and back, and a long, fitted sleeve, as shown in **Diagram 1** on the opposite page.

The basic pattern can be drafted from individual measurements or a standard set of measurements, or it can be a purchased pattern.

The basic pattern has only the minimum ease required to

cover the body, compared to the design ease included in commercial fashion patterns. It is used to develop master patterns with attractive fashion silhouettes as well as master patterns for pants, jackets, and coats. It also provides a clear base for illustrating patternmaking techniques. The basic pattern is rarely used for creating fashion garments.

Master Patterns

Known by a variety of names such as slopers, fashion slopers, basic bodies, and body styles, master patterns are developed from the basic pattern set.

Master patterns are simple but fashionable silhouettes that can be modified by changing or adding features within the silhouette to create an infinite variety of new styles, such as by adding buttons and buttonholes down the center front of a simple dirndl skirt. For instructions, see "Adding Buttons and Buttonholes" on page 235.

Master patterns can also be changed to create new silhouettes, such as by adding a flare to a straight skirt.

Master pattern styles can be simple variations created with trims, pockets, and interesting construction techniques, or they can be more complex designs created by adding or changing features such as seams, tucks, pleats, necklines, collars, closures, sleeves, and darts.

There are many sources for master patterns. The most frequently used are fashion patterns produced by commercial pattern companies, patterns taken from ready-made garments, and patterns generated by computer programs.

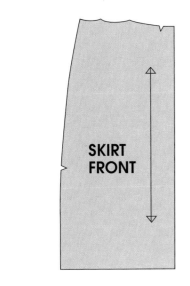
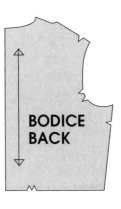

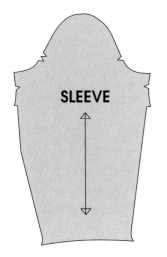
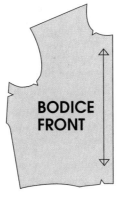

Diagram 1

*d*esign studio
secret

ACCURACY COUNTS

Unfortunately, many home sewing tools are not printed accurately. Check the accuracy of your measuring equipment by comparing it to a metal drafting ruler. Most art and hobby shops should have one in stock.

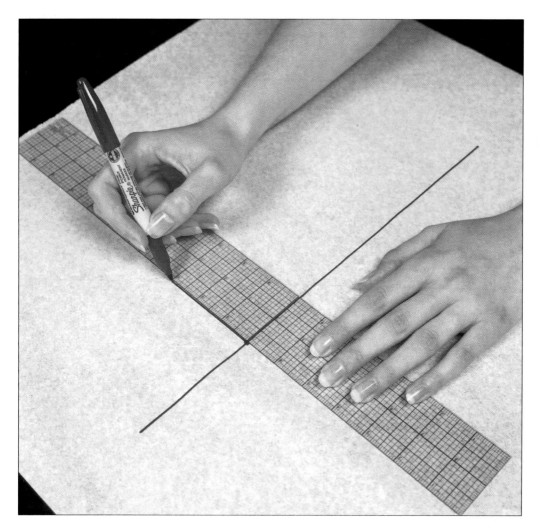

Squaring a line is one of the simplest drafting techniques, and it is used in all aspects of patternmaking.

Basic Drafting Techniques

Before you can devote your attention to the more creative aspects of patternmaking, you must master a few drafting techniques.

Used in all aspects of patternmaking, squaring a line is one of the easiest techniques. It is the process of drawing one line perpendicular to another line with a 90-degree or right angle at the intersection. This drafting technique is used for transferring matchpoints from the seamline to the cutting line, for establishing cutting lines and other parallel lines, for truing pattern edges, for adding fullness, and for squaring a line from a point on another line or from a point to a line.

Parallel lines, which run side by side with equidistant spacing at all points, are used extensively in patternmaking for adding seam allowances, hems, facings, tucks, pleats, fullness, and button and buttonhole extensions.

If you have some patternmaking experience or remember the skills you learned in geometry, these techniques will appear elementary. However, they are essential for making accurate patterns.

Square a Line from a Line

1. Draw a straight vertical line on a piece of pattern paper.

2. Mark a point anywhere on the line. Label it A.

3. To square a line using a see-through ruler, place the ruler on top of the line so one long edge of the ruler is at the marked point and one of the grid lines on the ruler is aligned with the original line.

4. Draw the squared line along the long edge of the ruler and to Point A, as shown in **Diagram 1.**

Most patternmakers prefer to use an isosceles right triangle or an L-square. To square a line using one of these tools, align one short edge of the triangle or square with the line and the right-angle corner with Point A, and draw the squared line, as shown in **Diagram 1.** Many patternmaking directions show a small triangle or right angle at the corner to indicate a squared corner, as shown at the bottom of **Diagram 1.**

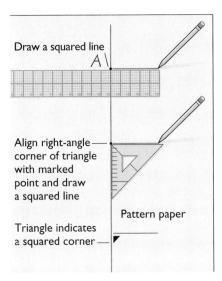

Diagram 1

5. Draw a curved line on the paper and mark Point A on it.

6. Place the see-through ruler on top of the line so one long edge of the ruler is at Point A and a short grid line on the ruler is aligned with the curved line.

■ **SEWING SECRET:** Since the first line is curved, you cannot align the grid on the ruler with the entire line. Align only 1/16 or 1/8 inch of the line with the ruler, as shown in **Diagram 2.**

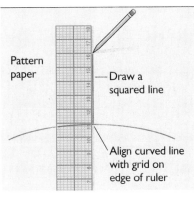

Diagram 2

7. Draw the squared line along the long edge of the ruler and through Point A, as shown in **Diagram 2.**

Square a Line to a Point

1. Draw another straight vertical line on the pattern paper.

2. Mark Point A about 6 inches to the right of the line.

3. Place the see-through ruler on top of the line so one of the grid lines on the long edge of the ruler is aligned with the vertical line. Slide the ruler along the vertical line until the long edge touches Point A.

4. Draw the squared line along the long edge of the ruler from Point A to the vertical line, as shown in **Diagram 3.**

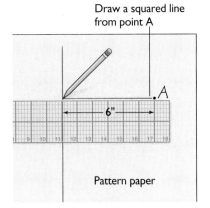

Diagram 3

5. Draw a curved line on the piece of pattern paper, as shown in **Diagram 4.**

6. Mark Point A about 6 inches above the curved line.

7. Place the see-through ruler on top of the curved line so between 1/16 and 1/8 inch of one of the short grid lines on the ruler is aligned with the curved line. Slide the ruler along the line until the long edge touches Point A, as shown in **Diagram 4.**

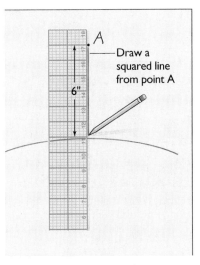

Diagram 4

8. Draw the squared line along the long edge of the ruler from Point A to the curved line.

Draw a Parallel Line

1. Draw a vertical straight line (Line A) on the pattern paper.

2. Square a 4-inch line (Line B) from Line A. At the end of Line B, mark Point C, as shown in **Diagram 5.**

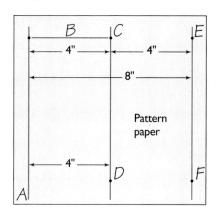

Diagram 5

3. As shown in **Diagram 5**, mark Point D 4 inches to the right of Line A, and several inches below Point C.

4. Draw a line through Points C and D to draw a line parallel to line A. As shown in **Diagram 5**, the distance between the lines will be 4 inches.

5. Repeat steps 2 through 4 to mark Points E and F.

6. Check the widths between the lines to be sure the lines are accurate by measuring the distance between the two outside lines. That distance should equal the sum of the parallel widths (4 inches plus 4 inches), which

is 8 inches, as shown in **Diagram 5.**

■ SEWING SECRET: When the distance between the parallel lines is less than the width of the ruler, use this shortcut. Locate the line marking the ⅝-inch width on the see-through ruler and align it with Line A. Draw the new Line B and then measure the distance between Lines A and B to be sure they are spaced accurately, as shown in **Diagram 6.**

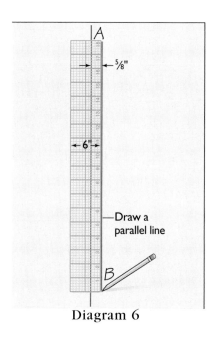

Diagram 6

7. Draw a curved line on the pattern paper.

8. Mark several points ⅝ inch away from the curved line, as shown in **Diagram 7.** Where the line is sharply curved, mark the points closer together. Connect the marked points, as shown in **Diagram 7.**

■ SEWING SECRET: You will get a cleaner line if you use a fashion ruler or French curve to connect the points.

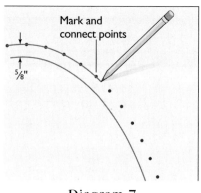

Diagram 7

Draw a Circle

1. Fold a piece of pattern paper into quarters.

2. Mark the radius of the circle—the distance from the center to the edge—on the tape measure.

3. Pin the marked point to the circle center—the folded corner of the paper—with a pushpin, as shown in **Diagram 8.**

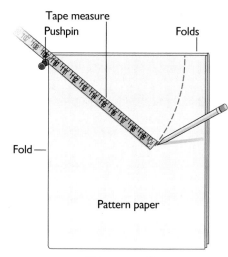

Diagram 8

4. Use a pencil to mark the edge of the circle at the end of the tape measure. Move the tape and mark the edge of the circle until the entire quarter is marked.

5. Connect the marked points.

Plotting a Pattern

The procedure for making all patterns—no matter how intricate the design—is the same: Define what you want, select a pattern similar in silhouette, and then apply patternmaking techniques to alter it.

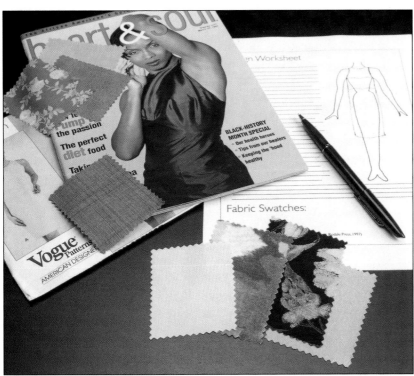

Combine inspiration, imagination, a master pattern, and patternmaking skills to create a one-of-a-kind design.

Basic Patternmaking

Basic patternmaking starts with a design that can be simple or complex. The design can come from your own imagination, a photograph, a magazine, or even a garment in a department store.

Once you have a design in mind, select a pattern that is similar, adjust it to fit your figure, and apply patternmaking techniques to create the specific details you have included in your design.

Tips for Successful Patternmaking

To ensure accurate patternmaking, take your measurements carefully and record them accurately—and doublecheck your work.

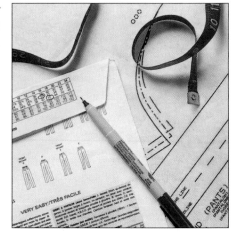

A fashion design does not have to be complicated or intricate to be attractive, but patternmaking requires accuracy at every step to ensure a perfect pattern. If the finished pattern isn't perfect, the garment will be difficult, perhaps impossible, to assemble. Check and recheck your work before making the final pattern.

These simple tips for patternmaking will help you save time and avoid disappointment.

♦ All design details are introduced within the seamlines. When working with patterns that have seam allowances added, mark the stitching lines or trim away the seam allowances to avoid confusing the cutting and stitching lines.
♦ When adding or changing design details, adjust the corresponding pattern sections as needed.

♦ Label the pattern accurately.
♦ When creating an asymmetrical design, mark the right and left sides distinctly to avoid cutting errors.
♦ Mark the pattern clearly to indicate seam and hem widths.
♦ Check to be sure seam and hem allowances have been added before laying out the pattern.

The following step-by-step instructions will help you to make your own pattern for your next creation.

Create the Design

1. Analyze the design you have chosen and describe the design verbally. Initially this may appear to be a waste of time, but it will help you become more observant and to identify the details that initially attracted you to the design.

2. Draw a sketch of the design. If you can't sketch well, photo-copy the fashion figure on page 238, which is used by designer Victor Costa, and add your design to it.

Select and Alter the Master Pattern

1. Select a sloper from your library of master patterns.

2. Alter and correct the sloper as needed so it fits your figure.

3. Trace the sloper to make a working pattern. Trace only the elements you need: the cutting and/or stitching lines, the match-points and notches, garment centers, and grainlines.

■ SEWING SECRET: You can trace the sloper with a pencil or pattern tracer. When using a pencil, cover the original pattern with pattern paper and then trace. When using the pattern tracer, place the pattern on top of the pattern paper and wheel over the lines to transfer them to the paper.

4. Create the new design using the patternmaking techniques found in Chapter 7 on page 202.

5. Indicate new matchpoints and grainlines.

How to *Draw Matchpoints* and *Notches*

Matchpoints and notches are guides that indicate how the sections are to be matched so the garment can be assembled accurately and easily. When matchpoints are omitted or misplaced, the comfort and the appearance of the finished design can be affected, and the garment may not fit or drape correctly.

Matchpoints are located on corresponding seamlines of patterns and garment sections. They are used in patternmaking to establish the notch locations. On commercial patterns, they are shown as circles, squares, and triangles.

Notches are located on the raw edges of garment sections. On commercial patterns, notches are shown as diamond shapes on the cutting lines and are frequently numbered in the order in which they are sewn. Notches are used in pairs—one on each garment section—of single, double, and triple notches.

Notches are usually located on every seamline so garments can be assembled easily and accurately. They are used to mark the starting and ending of ease, gathers, and shirring, and the positioning of pleats and tucks.

In garment construction, they are also used to mark the garment centers, the beginnings of darts, unusual seam widths, and foldlines of hems, edges, tucks, and pleats.

You can indicate as many or as few matchpoints and notches as you want. However, if you add too many, you will find them confusing when you assemble the garment. If you have too few, matching the garment sections may be difficult and the result may not be what you originally had intended.

If several sections of the garment look alike, notches can be used to tell them apart. Use single notches on the first seam to be stitched, double notches on the second, and triple notches on the third. On armscye seams, use a single notch on the front and a double notch on the back.

To avoid confusion, do not place notches in the center of a seamline. On long seams, space the notches about 15 inches apart.

Follow these simple steps to indicate notches:

1. To transfer a match point to the cutting edge, square a line from the seamline to the cutting line, as shown. For instructions, see "Square a Line from a Line" on page 161.

2. To make a double notch, mark a second match point ½ inch away from the first. Then square a line from each matchpoint to the cutting line, as shown.

3. Mark the ends of the notches with a bar, as shown.

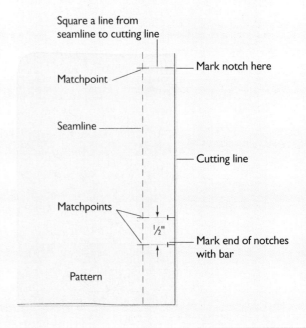

Square a line from seamline to cutting line

Matchpoint

Mark notch here

Seamline

Cutting line

Matchpoints

½"

Mark end of notches with bar

Pattern

■ SEWING SECRET: When creating your own design, always remember the lengthwise grain has less give than the cross-grain.

6. Add seam and hem allowances, true the patterns following the instructions that start on page 168, and transfer the matchpoints to the cutting lines.

■ SEWING SECRET: To add seam allowances and narrow hems easily, use a double tracing wheel. This sewing tool features two tracing wheels that, on some models, can be adjusted to the desired width of the seam allowance. (See "Resources" on page 243.)

7. Plot the facings. Trace the facing patterns, and reverse the facing patterns so they are for the right side of the garment. For instructions, see "Making a Neckline Facing" on page 210.

Make the Final Pattern

1. Trace the working pattern onto a fresh piece of pattern paper to make a clean copy. Most often the pattern will be for the right side of the figure, like most commercial patterns, but it can be a complete-figure pattern, like industry production patterns.

■ SEWING SECRET: Use non-woven interfacing or Swedish tracing paper (see "Resources" on page 243) when making a pattern that requires fitting. Either can be stitched together, fitted, and used for the layout and cutting.

2. Label the pattern pieces and include any notes that will be useful when you assemble the garment.

■ SEWING SECRET: Do not be afraid to make notes on the pattern pieces. This is your pattern, and jotting down a quick note when you create the

pattern may save you a lot of time later.

Make a Test Garment

1. Cut the entire garment out of paper and try it on, or make a test garment if needed. If you are using a master pattern, you may only need to make a test or muslin garment when you have a complicated design, a very expensive fabric, or an unusual style for your figure type. A paper pin-up or a muslin test garment allows you to check the design before cutting the fabric and help you perfect your sewing skills before you begin.

2. Correct and revise the pattern as needed.

3. Store the pattern. Place the pattern, design sketch, and a fabric swatch in a large envelope or plastic bag along with the date the design was made and the amount and width of the fabric used.

■ SEWING SECRET: In the French couture houses, the original muslin patterns are stored in large manila envelopes with all the pertinent information written on the outside so it is easy to see. If you prefer a plastic bag, write on the pattern and position it so you can read it without opening the bag.

design studio secret

FULL PATTERNS

Sometimes called full patterns, complete-figure patterns include a piece for each garment section. They are laid on a single layer of fabric, which is called an open lay. With these patterns, you can match printed and plaid fabrics faster and with greater accuracy, plus you can create a tighter layout on expensive fabrics.

How to *Label* a *Pattern*

The primary reason for labeling a pattern is so that the garment can be cut out and assembled accurately and easily. Labeling also allows you to resume work immediately if you're interrupted, and it allows you to reuse a pattern if you want to make another design at a later date.

The most common pattern labels and markings are listed below.

- Cutting lines
- Pattern piece name
- Number of pieces to cut
- Size
- Place on fold
- Bust point
- Dart end
- Dart lines
- Center front (CF) or center back (CB)
- Waistline
- Notches
- Matchpoints
- Stitching lines
- Button/buttonhole placement
- Foldline
- Lengthwise grain (grainline)
- Pleats
- Right side (RS), left side (LS) on asymmetrical designs
- Cut with right side up (RSU)
- Cut with nap
- Pocket placement
- Hemline
- Gathers

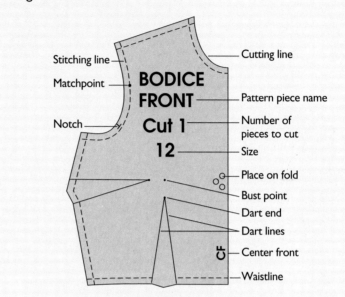

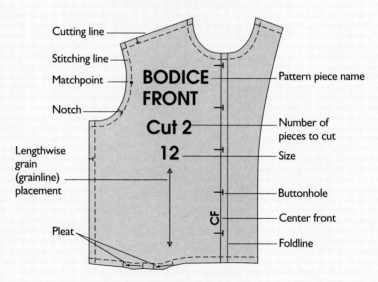

SEWING SECRET: *Store the patterns for your original designs in a clear plastic bag. Include a photograph of the completed garment for easy reference.*

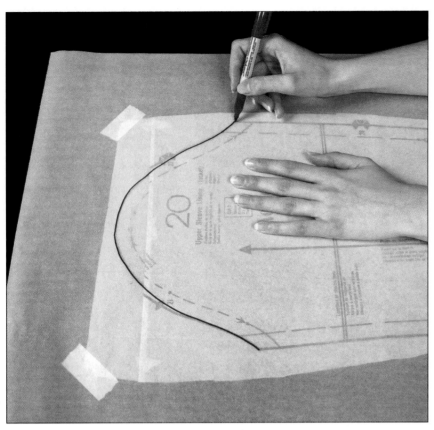

Blending is frequently used to remove ease from the cap of a sleeve pattern.

Precision Patternmaking

Every pattern must be measured and checked to be sure that the garment can be assembled accurately. This process is called truing. It includes blending and equalizing stitching and cutting lines as well as establishing jog-lines at the edges of the pattern for seams, darts, pleats, tucks, and other folded edges.

Blending

Blending is used to establish seamlines, hemlines, and cutting lines; to connect broken lines smoothly; and to eliminate sharp angles. Blending is frequently used in home sewing to remove excess ease from the cap of a sleeve pattern.

1. Fold a small horizontal pleat in the sleeve cap. To reduce the length of the sleeve cap ½ inch, make a ⅛-inch pleat, as shown in **Diagram 1.**

2. Blend a new line from the folded pleat to the top of the sleeve cap, as shown in **Diagram 1.**

■ SEWING SECRET: When reducing the ease on the sleeve cap, do not reduce the width of the sleeve.

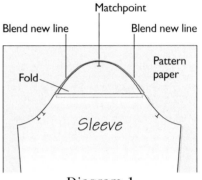

Diagram 1

Equalizing Seamlines

Generally seams that will be joined together are the same length except when one is eased, gathered, or pleated.

1. To check seamlines that have the same shape, place one pattern section on top of the other. Verify the seamline lengths and the locations of matchpoints.

2. If they are not equal, correct them as needed, as shown in **Diagram 2.**

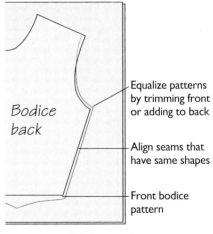

Diagram 2

■ SEWING SECRET: To equalize the seamlines, use your own judgment in making additions and subtractions. You can add a small amount to one or both ends of the shorter seamline, you can reduce the corresponding seamline by a small amount, or you can do both.

3. Use the stiletto tracing wheel to add matchpoints as needed.

4. Add seam allowances when needed.

5. To check seamlines such as reverse curves and corners that do not have the same shape, measure the stitching lines carefully.

■ SEWING SECRET: To measure curved lines accurately, use a flexible metal ruler or tape measure. Stand the ruler or tape measure on its edge, and fit it to the curve, as shown in **Diagram 3.**

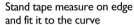

Stand tape measure on edge and fit it to the curve

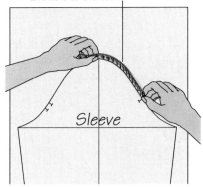

Sleeve

Diagram 3

6. Repeat steps 2 through 4 as needed until all of the seams are checked.

■ SEWING SECRET: Generally, the seamline on the sleeve cap is 1 to 2 inches larger than the bodice so it can be eased to the armscye.

Truing Horizontal Seams

When horizontal seamlines intersect the garment centers, they must form a right angle for ¹⁄₁₆ to ⅛ inch to keep a small V from forming when stitched.

1. To check horizontal seamlines, align the right-angle corner of the isosceles triangle with the garment center.

2. Examine the horizontal seamline to be sure it is squared for at least ¹⁄₁₆ inch at the garment center.

Truing Intersecting Seamlines

When two seamlines intersect, the seams are trued to establish the jogline—the edge that must change direction when there is a fold in the fabric—so the garment will be easier to assemble and the fabric will drape correctly on the body.

When they are not trued, the seam allowances can be too long or too short and sometimes affect the drape of the fabric.

Both of these can occur on seams that intersect with the armscye. For example, seam allowances on a princess seam can extend to ridiculous lengths, as shown in **Diagram 4,** while those on the shoulder seam allowances are generally too short at both the neckline and armscye.

Most commercial patterns are trued for the princess seam, but many are not trued at the shoulder. If you do not trim the ends of the seam so they won't

*d*esign studio secret

TRUING SEAMS
Truing seams is an important pattern-making concept in the fashion industry, but it is not always necessary in home sewing if you trim away the triangles at the seam ends before crossing the seam with another row of stitching.

be caught in the seamline, the seam will be too short when the raw edges are matched at the armscye, creating an unattractive pull at the shoulder point.

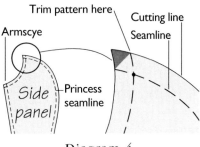

Trim pattern here
Cutting line
Seamline
Armscye
Side panel
Princess seamline

Diagram 4

1. Begin truing with the basic bodice front.

2. Determine which seam will be stitched first. Usually the shoulder seam is stitched before the armscye seam.

3. If the shoulder seam will be pressed open, fold the bodice front on the seamline and trace the cutting line of the seam allowance to match the cutting line of the bodice front, as shown in **Diagram 5**.

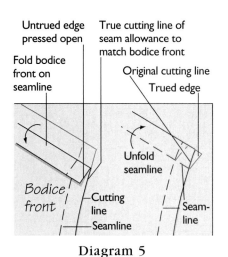

Diagram 5

4. Trim away any excess paper at the neck and armscye.

5. Repeat steps 3 and 4 to true the seam on the bodice back pattern.

6. If the shoulder seam will be pressed toward the front, fold the seam allowance at the front bodice shoulder toward the front.

7. Align and pin the folded edge with the seamline on the bodice back pattern.

8. Trim the excess paper on the cutting lines at the neckline and armscye.

Truing Darts

Truing darts determines the jogline at the end of the dart so all the raw edges are aligned on the finished garment.

These directions are applied to the basic bodice front pattern that has a horizontal bust dart and a vertical waist dart (see the diagrams on page 167), but they can be applied to any pattern with darts.

1. On a piece of pattern paper, trace the stitching and cutting lines of the basic bodice front pattern. Do not trace any joglines at the bottom of the dart.

2. Fold the waist dart into the position it will have on the finished garment by creasing one dart line near the center and aligning it with the remaining dart line.

■ SEWING SECRET: Vertical darts that originate at horizontal seamlines are generally folded toward the garment center, while horizontal darts that originate at vertical seamlines are folded down. The darts can be folded in the reverse direction to eliminate bulk. For example, darts placed on the shoulder seams near the neckline are generally folded away from the center so they won't be stitched into the neckline seam. Darts placed near a center fold should be folded away from the center to prevent them from overlapping.

3. Pin the dart closed.

■ SEWING SECRET: If there is an awkward angle at the bottom of the dart, redraw and blend the seamline.

4. Cup the dart by folding the pattern at the end of dart, as shown in **Diagram 6**.

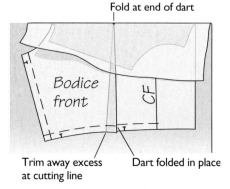

Diagram 6

5. Trim the excess paper at the pattern cutting line to establish the dart jogline, as shown in **Diagram 6**.

6. Wheel over the seamline with the stiletto tracing wheel to mark the stitching line.

7. Repeat steps 2 through 4 to establish the jogline on the bust dart.

8. Open the pattern and examine the joglines, as shown in **Diagram 7**.

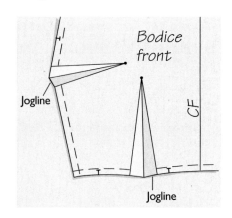

Diagram 7

9. Examine the difference in the joglines for a bust dart that is set on a diagonal, as shown in **Diagram 8.**

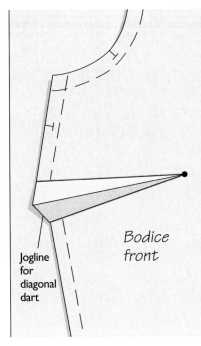

Diagram 8

Truing Hems

Hems on sleeves, pants, and pegged skirts are often trued, while hems on flared skirts are not, because it would make it difficult to lengthen the garment.

These directions are for truing a plain hem and a cuffed hem on pants. They can also be applied to sleeves and pegged skirts.

1. On a piece of pattern paper, trace the stitching, cutting, and hem lines of the pants' leg.

2. For a plain hem, add a 1¼-inch hem allowance.

3. Fold the pattern at the hemline.

4. With the hem folded, trace the seamlines with a stiletto tracing wheel, add seam

allowances as needed, and trim the excess paper at the cutting line, as shown in **Diagram 9.**

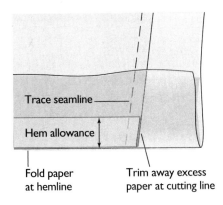

Diagram 9

5. Open the pattern and examine the trued edge, as shown in **Diagram 10.**

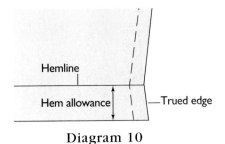

Diagram 10

6. For a cuffed hem, add twice the width of the cuff (for example, for a 2 inch cuff, add 4 inches). Then add a 1¼-inch hem allowance, as shown in **Diagram 11.**

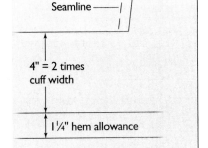

Diagram 11

7. Fold the pant cuff into the position it will have on the finished garment.

8. Repeat step 4 to true the pattern, as shown in **Diagram 12.**

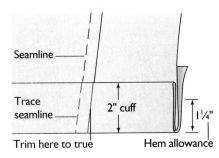

Diagram 12

9. Open the pattern out and examine the trued edge, as shown in **Diagram 13.**

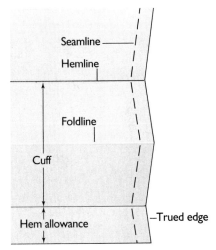

Diagram 13

■ SEWING SECRET: If your pants design features cuffs, use lightweight fabrics so the pants will drape more attractively. You can choose from lightweight polyesters, silks, synthetic suedes, and wool.

6
COPY
A GARMENT

One of the best sources for master patterns is a pattern taken from a ready-made garment because you can easily see how the design fits and looks. Use one of the three methods for taking patterns from ready-to-wear—measurements, tracings, and rub-offs—individually or together.

Prepare to Copy a Garment

Before you actually begin copying a garment, there are several important steps you must take. If you take the time now, the copying process will be easier and you will save time later.

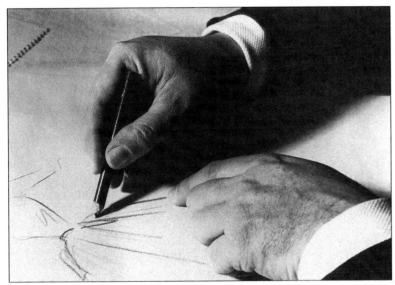

Christian Dior makes a fashion sketch shortly before his death in 1957.

Tools for Copying

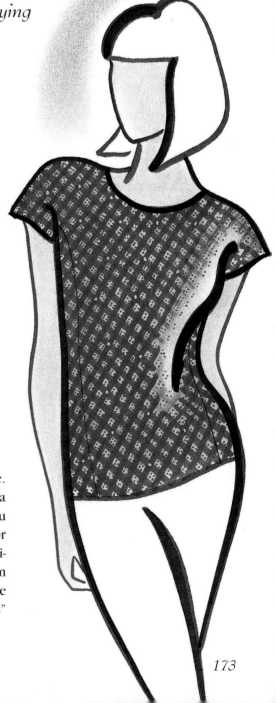

You must have a number of tools on hand to be able to properly copy a garment. Not all of these tools are essential, but they will make the task easier.

You may already have many of these tools in your sewing room, and you can substitute items you have around the house for the tools that you don't have. For instance, if you don't have a French curve or curved ruler you can substitute plates or bowls for those tools. If you don't own a triangle, you can make one from cardboard or an envelope. (See "How to Cut and Join Bias Strips" on page 5.)

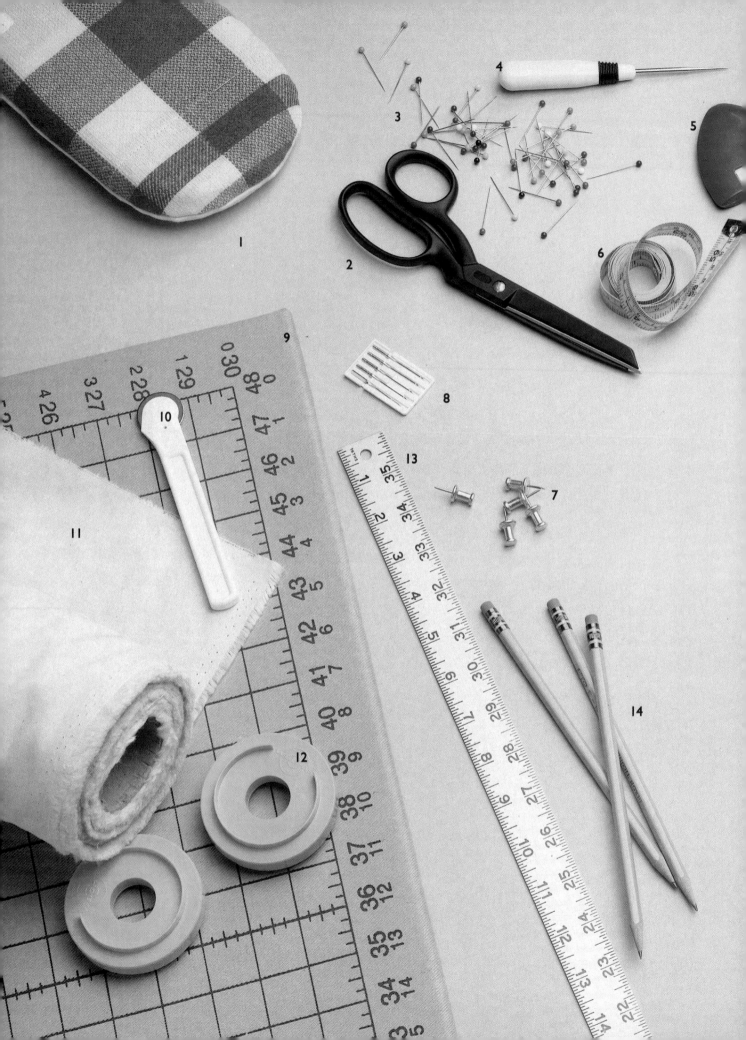

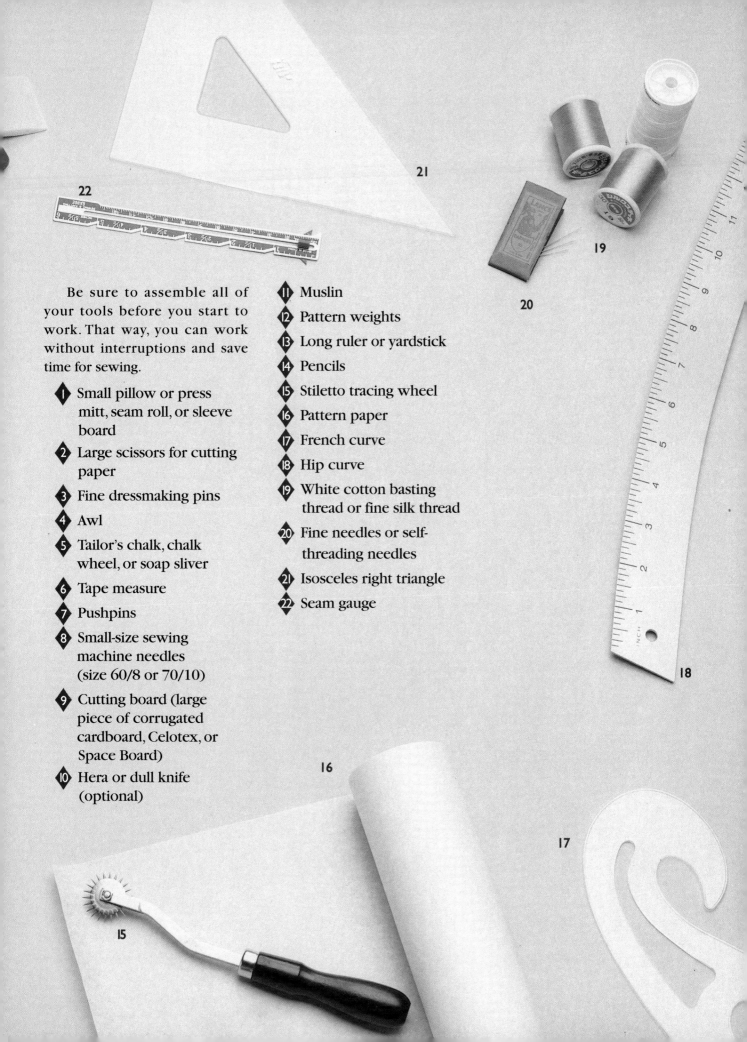

Be sure to assemble all of your tools before you start to work. That way, you can work without interruptions and save time for sewing.

1 Small pillow or press mitt, seam roll, or sleeve board

2 Large scissors for cutting paper

3 Fine dressmaking pins

4 Awl

5 Tailor's chalk, chalk wheel, or soap sliver

6 Tape measure

7 Pushpins

8 Small-size sewing machine needles (size 60/8 or 70/10)

9 Cutting board (large piece of corrugated cardboard, Celotex, or Space Board)

10 Hera or dull knife (optional)

11 Muslin

12 Pattern weights

13 Long ruler or yardstick

14 Pencils

15 Stiletto tracing wheel

16 Pattern paper

17 French curve

18 Hip curve

19 White cotton basting thread or fine silk thread

20 Fine needles or self-threading needles

21 Isosceles right triangle

22 Seam gauge

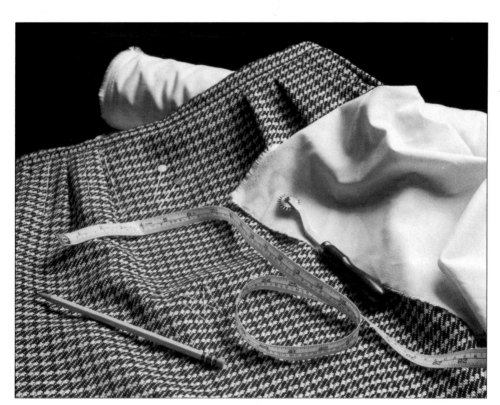

You will find it surprisingly easy to copy that favorite straight wool skirt.

Copying Basics

These basic instructions for copying can be applied to all of your garments.

It doesn't matter if the garment is faded, an unattractive color, or made from cheap fabric, because you can use this technique to create a new design in the fabric and color of your choice. You can even use a garment that requires minor alterations to adjust the fit.

Before you start to copy a garment, read all of these instructions carefully and keep this information in the back of your mind as you work. By following these basic steps, you will find that you can copy garments easily and accurately.

1. Assemble the tools and supplies, as described on page 175.

2. Select the garment. Garments with many small sections are surprisingly easy to copy. Flat garments without pleats, gathers, tucks, darts, or easing are easier to copy than designs with gathers and draping. Garments with prominent grainlines, plaids, or stripes are easy to copy, while twill weaves and knits are generally more difficult. If the garment is not cut on-grain, it will be difficult and perhaps impossible to copy.

3. If the garment is not new, have it dry cleaned or laundered before copying, or you can press it as needed to remove any wrinkles or creases that might affect the accuracy of the pattern.

4. Analyze the design carefully. Keep your sewing ability and past experiences in mind, because you will have no guide sheet. If you need additional sewing directions, refer to the sewing books listed in the Bibliography on page 242.

5. Examine the design to determine which copying techniques will be easiest to use on which sections. There is no reason not to use several different techniques on one garment. For instructions see "Measuring" on page 180, "Tracing" on page 186, or "Rub-Off" on page 192.

6. Carefully examine the garment. Analyze and describe the design. Identify areas of fullness such as darts, gathers, tucks, pleats, and ease.

7. Identify the lengthwise grain and landmarks on each garment section.

■ SEWING SECRET: Landmarks are frequently used in pattern-making and in copying to identify key points on the body or garment sections. Some frequently used landmarks along with their abbreviations are the center front (CF), center back (CB), bust point (BP), neck point (NP), shoulder point (SP), mid-arm front, and mid-arm back.

8. Use your knowledge of garment construction and pattern-making as guides. And while you are copying, observe how the garment was put together.

■ SEWING SECRET: Listen to the garment as you work; it can teach you new techniques. Through careful observation and after working with many different garments, you will find you will be able to recognize quality construction methods.

9. Mark the garment carefully and accurately, following the instructions in "How to Mark a Garment," below.

10. Copy each garment section separately.

■ SEWING SECRET: When copying a section, it is easier to begin with a flat area (frequently the hem) and work toward the shaped areas.

How to *Mark* a *Garment*

Examine the garment carefully before you start to mark it. If it is cut off-grain, select another garment or ignore the grains.

Use fine pins or needles, soap, temporary marking pens, and hand basting to mark the garment. When marking delicate fabrics, mark with fine needles instead of pins or mark with a needle and white thread. When marking wools, loosely woven fabrics, or coarse fabrics with thread, use self-threading needles.

Before marking the garment, check to be sure the marking tools will not mar the fabric permanently. After you've examined the garment and gathered the necessary tools, follow these instructions to mark each section.

1. Mark each garment section separately. Do not extend marking lines across seamlines, darts, or other stitching lines.

■ SEWING SECRET: *When pin marking, I prefer to use pins with flower heads because the heads lie flat.*

2. When marking garment centers, do not assume the center is on grain; instead, fold the section in half, and mark the foldline as described in steps 1 and 2 of "Mark the Blouse Front" on page 187.

3. Mark each garment section with at least two lines—one on the lengthwise grain and one on the crossgrain.
4. Locate and mark landmarks such as neck and shoulder points and other key points such as the beginning of gathers or ease.
5. Identify and mark at least one matchpoint on each seamline. Mark one matchpoint on the front armscye and two on the back.
6. Use a magnifying lamp as an aid when marking grainlines that are difficult to see.
7. If you can't identify the grains on

the face of fabrics such as twill, flannel, satin, and pile materials, turn the garment wrong side up and mark the wrong side.
8. When marking large sections, use pins or thread tracing to divide them into several small sections so you can mark each section independently.
9. When marking darts, isolate the dart in a thread-traced box.
10. When marking sleeves, work with the garment on a dress form or on a clothes hanger so that you are working with the sleeve in the position it will be in when it is worn.

design studio secret

ADJUSTING FOR FIT

When restyling the design or copying a garment that needs to be adjusted for your figure, copy the original design first. Then try on and mark the pattern as needed to fit your body shape. Make any adjustments to personalize the fit. Then restyle the individual pattern pieces before adding seam and hem allowances. Remember, a garment's fit may change if you construct it from a different fabric.

11. Copy major garment sections with the garment right side out, referring to the wrong side only when needed.

■ SEWING SECRET: If the garment is symmetrical, mark and copy only the right-hand side. On asymmetrical garments, mark and copy both sides.

12. Copy set-in and inseam pockets and facings with the garment wrong side out.

13. When copying jeans or trousers with a fly placket, mark the front with the overlap.

14. Once the design is copied, complete the pattern, following the directions in "How to Complete the Pattern," below.

15. Estimate the required yardage following the instructions in "How to Estimate the Fabric Yardage," on the opposite page.

16. Purchase the fabric.

■ SEWING SECRET: Although many designs can be made up in a variety of fabrics, your success will be greater if you use a fabric that is similar to the original garment. If you make up a garment in a fabric that has different drape and flexibility, it won't fit the same as the original garment did.

17. Cut out the garment using the pattern pieces.

How to *Complete* the *Pattern*

After you have copied the garment design, complete the patternmaking process by following these simple steps.

1. Use the ruler and French curve to true seams and darts. For directions, see "Precision Patternmaking" on page 168.
2. To be sure the pattern sections are accurate, baste or pin the sections together, aligning any matchpoints.
3. Correct the pattern sections as needed.
4. Remove the pins and press the patterns as needed.
5. Add hem and seam allowances. For guidelines on hem allowances, see "How to Add Hems" on page 208. For information on seam allowances, see "Adding a Seam" on page 201.
6. Make the lining, facing, and interfacing patterns.
7. Check to be sure you have labeled all of the patterns. (See "How to Label a Pattern" on page 167.)
8. Cut out the patterns.

How to *Estimate* the *Fabric Yardage*

When estimating the amount of fabric required, the most important factors to consider are: the fabric width; whether the fabric has a pattern, plaid, or nap that will require matching or one-way layouts; the type of layout (single or double layer of fabric); and the number and size of the pattern pieces.

The most precise method for estimating the yardage is to plan the layout before purchasing the fabric. However, you can also use the requirements for a similar commercial pattern as a guide.

Follow these steps to plan the pattern layout.

1. Press all of the pattern pieces with a warm, dry iron.

2. Plan the layout on a similar piece of fabric or on an old sheet or tablecloth.

■ **SEWING SECRET:** *You can use an old double bedsheet to make a reusable layout planner. Simply draw vertical lines on the sheet to indicate the layout widths you use for most fabrics. The measurements I use are 22 and 27 inches for cutting a double layer, and 36, 42, and 54 inches for cutting a single layer. Use a different color permanent marker to mark and label each width.*

3. When possible, position the pattern sections for a "with nap" layout so the tops of the pattern pieces are all facing in the same direction.

■ **SEWING SECRET:** *Many fabrics have a one-way design, or nap, that may not be apparent until the garment is made up. Fabrics with nap also include pile fabrics and knit fabrics. When using a napped fabric, remember that your design will require additional fabric. Also, most napped fabrics are cut with the nap running downward.*

4. Lay out all the large pieces first.

5. Lay out the remaining small pieces, dovetailing sections wherever possible.

6. When planning an open lay, make a complete pattern by cutting a pattern piece for each garment section. This way you will avoid cutting two left sleeves or forgetting to lay out a section.

■ **SEWING SECRET:** *An open lay is the fashion industry term for cutting on a single layer of fabric.*

7. Check to be sure all the pattern sections for the garment are on the layout.

8. Measure the number of yards of fabric covered by the pattern.

Foolproof Copying

Garments can be copied by one of three methods—measuring, tracing, or rub-off. Measuring and tracing are the easiest. The rub-off method is the most time consuming, but it is also the most versatile, since it can be used for almost any garment or garment section no matter how complex.

Add depth to your hemline by stitching contrasting fabric to the straight sides of the godets before you set them into the skirt.

Measuring

You can easily copy many ready-made garments and garment sections simply by measuring them. This method is even easier when the individual sections are rectangular, but that is not a prerequisite. Used most often for copying designer details such as waistbands, cuffs, pockets, collars, and plackets, the measuring method can also be used for copying entire garments.

This technique works well on simple, flat garments or garment sections such as collars, cuffs, and pockets that have no shaping devices. Although it is easier to measure garment sections that are rectangular, sections with other shapes can be measured as well.

This knock-off of a Diane Fries skirt is a little more complex than many of the designs you will measure, but it is still easy to copy. I particularly like the design because it flatters many figure types and because the godets provide an opportunity to perfect two different sewing techniques—joining reverse corners and joining three seams at a point. Since the godets are near the hem and not at eye level, small imperfections on your first attempts are less likely to be noticed.

Analyze and Measure the Design

1. Examine and describe the design. The rectangular skirt is divided into eight equal sections. There are eight pie-shaped godets located at the side seams, garment centers, and midway between the side seam and center. The top of the skirt is finished with a straight elasticized band, and the skirt is gathered to the band. The front and back sections are identical. All of the seams are ¼ inch wide.

2. Draw a sketch of the skirt, as shown in **Diagram 1**. Don't be concerned if you can't draw well. The sketch is just for your information, and you will find it helpful during the copying process.

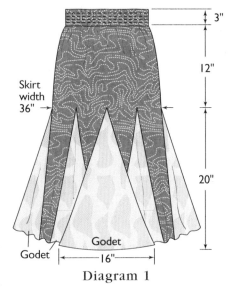

Skirt width 36"

Godet

Godet

3"

12"

20"

16"

Diagram 1

3. Pin-mark the grainlines.

4. Measure the godet: the length of the godet seamlines, the length of the godet at the center, and the width at the hem.

5. Measure the skirt: the width of the skirt at the waist with the elastic fully stretched, the width of the skirt at the top of the godets, and the length of the skirt at the side seams. To measure the skirt width, pull the skirt taut and measure it from the top of the godet on the right side to the top of the godet on the left side, as shown in **Diagram 1**.

6. Measure the waistband: the width of the band and the waistband length. To measure the length, hold the band taut and measure from one side to the other to determine half the

length. Multiply by two to determine the finished band length.

■ SEWING SECRET: To avoid errors when multiplying or adding fractions, let your tape measure do the work for you. Instead of multiplying the initial waistband measurement by two, fold the tape at that measurement, and read the measurement where the end of the tape meets the tape itself.

7. Measure the distance between the top of the godets and the waistband, as shown in **Diagram 1**.

design studio secret

MEASURING A DESIGN

When measuring a design in a store, I use my hand to estimate the measurements. My extended hand measures 8 inches from the tip of my thumb to the tip of my little finger. Find out what yours measures, and use it as a gauge.

Make the Waistband Pattern

1. Since the waistband pattern for this skirt is a simple rectangle, seam allowances can be added to the finished measurements before the pattern is plotted. That way you won't have to draw them onto the pattern. On a piece of pattern paper, draw a rectangle using the waistband measurements taken in step 6 of "Analyze and Measure the Design" on page 181. Add two seam allowances—two times ⅝ inch, or 1¼ inches—to the full length, as shown in **Diagram 2**. For the width, double the finished width of the waistband and add two seam allowances—1¼ inches.

Divide that number in two to define the foldline. Indicate the foldline, and mark the pattern "Waistband—Cut 1."

■ SEWING SECRET: When making a paper pattern, do not draw the pattern on the edge of the paper, because the edge is frequently damaged and no longer straight. Instead, draw one edge of the pattern parallel to and about 1 inch away from the edge of the paper.

2. Draw the grainline parallel, as shown in **Diagram 2**, or perpendicular to the waist edge.

■ SEWING SECRET: Before proceeding, be sure the length of the waistband is sufficient to slide over your hips easily. Measure your hips at the widest point and compare the measurement to the total waistband length.

3. Cut out the pattern.

Make the Skirt Pattern

1. A variation of a dirndl skirt, this skirt is rectangular. It requires only one pattern piece because the front and back are identical. On a piece of pattern paper, as shown in **Diagram 3**, draw a rectangle using the measurements taken in step 5 of "Analyze and Measure the Design" on page 181.

2. Indicate the grainline. Do not add seam or hem allowances now. This pattern is slightly more complex than the waistband pattern, so it is easier to add the seam and hem allowances after marking the godet positions.

■ SEWING SECRET: Although this skirt fits bodies of many different sizes, you can make it larger by adding to the width of the skirt.

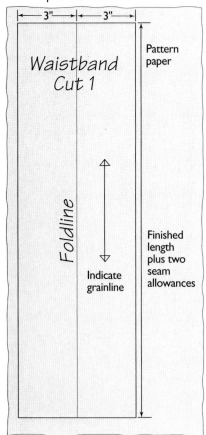

Double finished width
plus two seam allowances

Waistband Cut 1

Pattern paper

Foldline

Indicate grainline

Finished length plus two seam allowances

3"   3"

Diagram 2

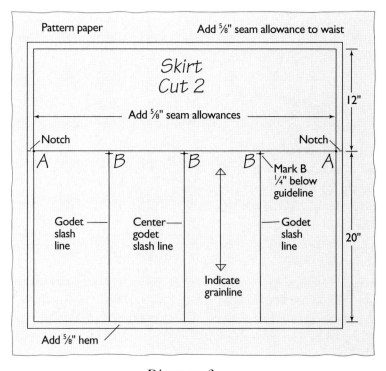

Pattern paper   Add ⅝" seam allowance to waist

Skirt Cut 2

Add ⅝" seam allowances

Notch   Notch

A   B   B   B   A

Mark B ¼" below guideline

Godet slash line   Center godet slash line   Godet slash line

Indicate grainline

12"

20"

Add ⅝" hem

Diagram 3

3. Use the measurement from step 7 in "Analyze and Measure the Design" on page 181—the distance between the waistband and godets—to measure and mark Point A (the top of the godets) on each side seam, as shown in **Diagram 3.**

4. Draw a line from Point A on the left to Point A on the right to establish a guideline for marking the godet positions, as shown in **Diagram 3.**

5. Draw a slash line for the center godet parallel to the side seams and midway between them, as shown in **Diagram 3.** Mark Point B—the end of the slash line—¼ inch below the guideline.

6. Repeat step 4 to draw the slash lines for the godets midway between the center front and the side seam and to mark Point B, as shown in **Diagram 3.**

7. Add ⅝-inch seam allowances to the waist and to the side seams, as shown in **Diagram 3.** No seam allowances are added to the skirt pattern along the slash lines.

■ SEWING SECRET: Although the width of seam allowances on American-made patterns is ⅝ inch, you can use a narrower seam allowance if desired.

8. Add a ⅝-inch hem allowance to the bottom of the skirt pattern.

■ SEWING SECRET: To add a cutting line parallel to a stitching line, use a tape measure or ruler to measure the desired seam or hem allowance from several points along the stitching line. Then connect the points to draw the cutting line.

9. Mark the grainline parallel to the center front. Then mark the notches on the side seams at each Point A, as shown in **Diagram 3.**

10. Label the pattern "Skirt—Cut 2," as shown in **Diagram 3.**

11. Cut out the pattern.

Make the Godet Patterns

1. On a piece of pattern paper, draw the godet without seam allowances using the measurements that were taken in step 4 in "Analyze and Measure the Design" on page 181 as a guide.

2. Draw the hemline for the godet so all points are an even distance from the top of the godet. For directions, see "Draw a Circle" on page 162.

3. Indicate the grainline at the center of the godet, as shown in **Diagram 4.**

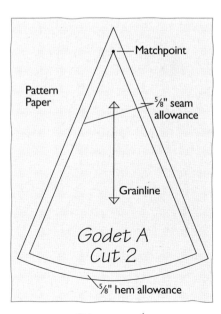

Diagram 4

■ SEWING SECRET: When the grainline is placed at the center of the godet, the godet will flare evenly at the seamlines. If you would like the godet to flare only at one seamline, draw the grainline on the opposite seamline.

4. Mark a matchpoint at the end of the godet.

5. Trace the godet pattern onto a piece of pattern paper.

6. To make the pattern for the godet that will be stitched into the side seams of the skirt, add seam allowances to the sides and a ⅝-inch hem allowance at the hemline of the traced godet pattern. Label the pattern "Godet A—Cut 2," as shown in **Diagram 4.**

7. To make the remaining godet pattern, add ¼-inch seam allowances to the sides and a ⅝-inch hem allowance to the bottom of the original godet pattern. Label the pattern "Godet B—Cut 6," as shown in **Diagram 5.**

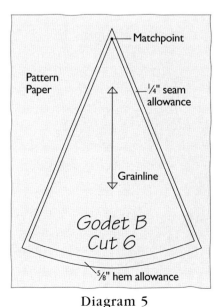

Diagram 5

8. Cut out the godet patterns.

How to *Sew* a *Godet*

Godets can have many shapes, but most godets are wedge shaped and are sewn into a slash.

PREPARE THE SKIRT SECTIONS

1. Cut out the skirt and godet sections.

2. Using the pattern as a guide, mark the godet slash lines on the skirt sections. Mark the ends of the godets ¼ inch above the slashes. Mark the notches at Point A on the skirt side seams.

REINFORCE THE SLASH ENDS

1. Cut six 1-inch-square pieces of self-fabric or silk organza. These will be used as facings at the ends of the godets.

2. With the skirt right side up, center and pin the facing wrong side up over the mark at the top of one godet slash, as shown in **Godet Diagram 1**.

High-fashion designers have used godets since the nineteenth century to add fullness to the hemline of a dress or a skirt.

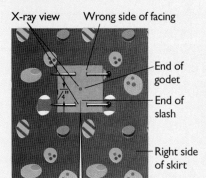

X-ray view · Wrong side of facing · End of godet · End of slash · Right side of skirt

Godet Diagram 1

3. Turn the skirt wrong side up. Be sure the facing is not rumpled. Set the stitch length on the machine to about 20 spi (1.0 mm). Begin stitching a small V-shape about

½ inch from the marked point. Taper the stitching to almost 0 at the end of the slash. Take two stitches across the end of the slash, and then stitch away from the point about ½ inch toward the hemline, gradually increasing the seam width from almost 0 to ½ inch, as shown in **Godet Diagram 2**.

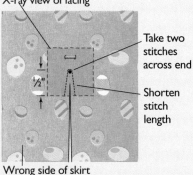

X-ray view of facing · Take two stitches across end · Shorten stitch length · Wrong side of skirt

Godet Diagram 2

4. Extend the slash of the godet to the stitched line, and turn the facing to the wrong side. Press the end of the slash with the wrong side up, as shown in **Godet Diagram 3**.

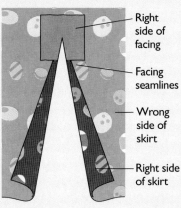

Right side of facing · Facing seamlines · Wrong side of skirt · Right side of skirt

Godet Diagram 3

5. Repeat steps 2 through 5 for each slash.

STITCH THE GODETS IN A SLASH

1. With right sides up, place the skirt on top of the godet. Align the end of the slash with the marked point on the godet, as shown in **Godet Diagram 4.** Pin and then slipstitch them together for about 1 inch on each side of the point.

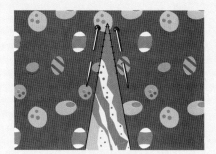

Godet Diagram 4

2. Reposition and pin the fabric layers with the right sides together.
3. Stitch a ¼-inch seam at 15 spi (1.5 mm) from the hem to the facing. At the facing, set the machine for 20 spi (1.0 mm) and stitch just alongside the little facing seam so it won't show on the garment, as shown in **Godet Diagram 5.** Pivot at the

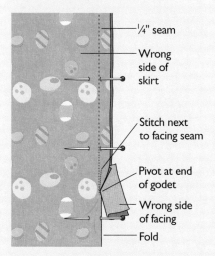

- ¼" seam
- Wrong side of skirt
- Stitch next to facing seam
- Pivot at end of godet
- Wrong side of facing
- Fold

Godet Diagram 5

point, and in the same manner stitch the other side of the godet to the hem.
4. Repeat steps 1 through 3 to stitch the remaining godets in the slashes.

STITCH THE GODETS IN A SEAM

1. With right sides together, stitch the side seams from the waist to Point A. Backtack and press the seam open.
2. With right sides up, place the skirt on top of the godet. Align the end of the seam with the marked point on the godet. Pin and then slipstitch them together for about 1 inch on each side of the point.
3. Reposition and pin the fabric layers with the right sides together.
4. Spot-tack at the point and then stitch toward the hem at 15 spi (1.5 mm) with a ⅝-inch seam, as shown in **Godet Diagram 6.** Repeat to stitch the other side of the godet.

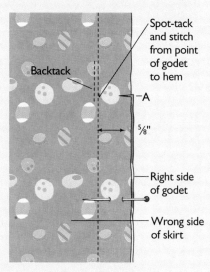

- Spot-tack and stitch from point of godet to hem
- Backtack
- A
- ⅝"
- Right side of godet
- Wrong side of skirt

Godet Diagram 6

To get a sharp corner at the point of the godet, as shown in **Godet Diagram 7,** be sure the adja-

cent seam allowances are held out of the way as you stitch.

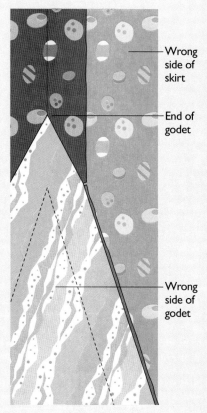

- Wrong side of skirt
- End of godet
- Wrong side of godet

Godet Diagram 7

SEWING SECRET: *Always begin stitching at the point of difficulty to ensure a perfect corner.*

5. Tie the thread ends at the point and trim.
6. Repeat steps 2 and 3 to stitch the remaining godet in the other side seam.

FINISH THE GODETS

1. Overlock or serge the edges of the seam allowances and godets. When overlocking, work carefully so you don't cut into the skirt at the top of the godets.
2. Press all the godets and seams.

Create your own version of this chic designer blouse by using the tracing method.

*T*racing

Sometimes called spiking, fold and spike, or pricking, tracing is another easy method of copying ready-made garments.

You can use the tracing method, like measuring, to copy entire garments, garment sections, or details. It is a good technique for simple, flat garments such as blouses and shirts that are shaped with seams instead of garments with fullness in the form of darts, pleats, tucks, or gathers.

Select and Analyze the Garment

1. Choose a simple garment like a blouse or shirt, and press it to remove any creases that might affect the accuracy of the pattern.

2. Examine the garment and make a sketch.

The Christian Dior blouse in the photo above has three main sections—a front, a back, and a side

panel—with no side seams. The center front is on the lengthwise grain. The side panel joins the front and back and is cut with the lengthwise grain at the center. The back has a button/buttonhole closure that laps right over left.

The back opening is finished with an extended facing, while the neck and armscyes are finished with a separate all-in-one facing. The all-in-one facing duplicates the shape of the blouse, but it is cut in two pieces, instead of three like the garment, to reduce bulk at the seamlines.

The blouse fabric is a small print with vertical and horizontal lines on the grains, making it very easy to identify the grains.

■ SEWING SECRET: American-made garments generally lap left over right on the back, while European-made designs lap right over left.

3. Locate landmarks such as shoulder and neck points and garment centers.

Mark the Blouse Front

1. Fold the front in half lengthwise.

2. Match and pin the shoulder seams together at the neck and shoulder points. Match and pin the tops and bottoms of the side/front seams, and mark the lengthwise grain at the center front with pins, as shown in **Diagram 1**.

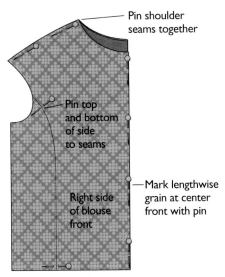

Pin shoulder seams together

Pin top and bottom of side to seams

Right side of blouse front

Mark lengthwise grain at center front with pin

Diagram 1

■ SEWING SECRET: If the garment center is off-grain, ignore the grain and use the foldline as the lengthwise grain.

3. Remove all pins except those marking the center front, and open the blouse flat.

4. Pin-mark the crossgrain either at the bustline or about 2 inches below the armscye.

5. Mark a matchpoint on the shoulder seam about 2 inches from the neckline and on the side front seam about 4 inches from the armscye, using tailor's chalk or basting stitches. For in-structions, see "How to Mark a Garment" on page 177.

■ SEWING SECRET: To avoid confusion when sewing, never position a matchpoint or notch at the middle of the seam during the patternmaking process. That way you don't have to worry about identifying the top or bottom of the garment sections.

Prepare the Pattern Paper

1. Measure the length and width of the garment section. Add several inches to each measurement, and cut a piece of pattern paper that size. If you are working with narrow pattern paper, cut two lengths and join them together with transparent tape.

2. Cover a cutting board, large piece of corrugated cardboard, Celotex, Space Board, or other pliable surface with pattern paper.

3. As shown in **Diagram 2**, on the paper, draw a vertical line parallel to the right edge of the

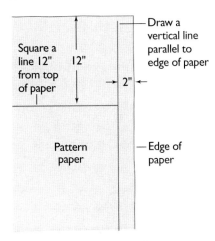

Square a line 12" from top of paper

12"

2"

Draw a vertical line parallel to edge of paper

Pattern paper

Edge of paper

Diagram 2

paper and about 2 inches away. Then square a second line about 12 inches from the top of the paper.

Trace the Blouse Front

1. With the blouse flat and right side up, place the garment on the pattern paper. Align the intersections of the pin-marked lengthwise and crosswise grains on the garment with those drawn on the pattern paper.

2. Beginning at the intersection of the grainlines, anchor the lines at the center front of the blouse using fine dressmaking pins. Smooth the blouse toward the front/side seam, and anchor the crossgrain. Then, beginning with the lower half of the blouse, smooth the blouse away from the center and crossgrain, and anchor the side/front seam at the top and bottom using fine dressmaking pins, as shown in **Diagram 3**.

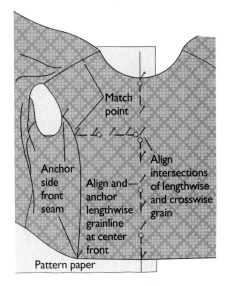

Match point

Anchor side front seam

Align and anchor lengthwise grainline at center front

Align intersections of lengthwise and crosswise grain

Pattern paper

Diagram 3

design studio secret

Tracing Garments

When tracing garment edges, avoid tracing them with pencil, which may rub off and leave a smudge on the garment that may be difficult or impossible to remove. To prevent the garment from slipping when marking with a pattern tracer or hera, place the fingertips of one hand close to the seamline, and move the wheel about 6 inches, then move your fingers and repeat until the entire seam is marked. When marking delicate fabrics, use a fine needle to prick the seamline.

■ SEWING SECRET: When anchoring a garment at a seam, set the pins between the stitches.

3. Check to be sure the front/side section of the blouse is flat, and then trace the hemline using a stiletto tracing wheel.

4. Trace the seamline with the stiletto tracing wheel, beginning at the underarm.

5. Mark the matchpoint on the side/front seam, and remove all the pins below the marked crossgrain.

6. Smooth the upper part of the blouse away from the marked lines, and anchor the shoulder seam.

7. Check to be sure the section is flat, and then trace the edges and mark the seamlines and matchpoints using the stiletto tracing wheel.

Prepare and Trace the Blouse Back

1. Measure the width of the button extension—the distance between the center back and garment edge.

2. Identify and pin-mark the center back on the right-hand side.

■ SEWING SECRET: On a garment with a button/buttonhole closure, the buttonholes begin ⅛ inch toward the edge so the centers match when the garment is buttoned. On the Dior blouse, the center back is ¾ inch from the edge.

3. Pin-mark the crossgrain just below the armscye.

4. Using basting stitches or chalk, mark two matchpoints—½ inch apart—on the side/back seam about 5 inches below the armscye.

5. Measure the blouse back, and cut a piece of pattern paper.

6. On the paper, draw the center back parallel to the left edge of the paper and about 6 inches away, as shown in **Diagram 4**.

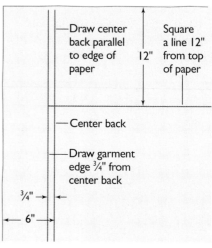

Diagram 4

7. Draw the garment edge—for the extension to the left of the center back—as shown in **Diagram 4**.

8. Square a line through the two parallel lines about 12 inches from the top of the paper, as shown in **Diagram 4**.

9. To trace the blouse back, repeat steps 1 through 7 of "Trace the Blouse Front" on page 187.

10. Mark the buttonhole locations using the stiletto tracing wheel.

11. Remove the blouse from the paper. Turn the blouse wrong side up, and measure the width of the facing at the back opening.

12. From the line marking the garment edge, measure the

width of the facing (in this case, 2 inches). Draw a parallel line to mark the facing edge and indicate the grainline on the back pattern parallel to the center back, as shown in **Diagram 5.**

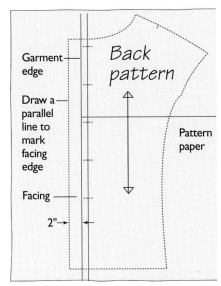

Diagram 5

Trace the Side Panel

1. Open the side panel flat, and mark and trace it in the same manner as the blouse front and back. (See **Diagram 6** for the shape of the side panel.)

2. Indicate the grainline at the center.

Proof the Patterns

1. Pin the pattern sections together on the seamlines.

2. Check to be sure that the pattern is accurate, matchpoints match, and the seams are equal in length unless otherwise designed. Re-mark or retrace as needed until the seams and markings are correct.

Finish the Pattern

1. With a pencil and French curve or ruler, trace over the pricked lines on the patterns so the outlines are crisp and clean.

2. Label the patterns "Back—Cut 2," "Side—Cut 2," and "Front—Cut 1." For instructions see "How to Label a Pattern" on page 167.

3. Add seam allowances to each pattern piece, as shown in **Diagram 6.**

home sewing. An added advantage is that the narrower seam allowances do not require trimming after stitching.

4. Add a hem allowance to each pattern using the hem on the garment as a guide, as shown in **Diagram 6.**

5. On the front pattern, indicate a fold at the center front, as shown in **Diagram 6.**

6. Transfer the matchpoints to the cutting lines.

7. Fold the back pattern at the edge of the button extension, then trim the hem and neck edge to true the pattern.

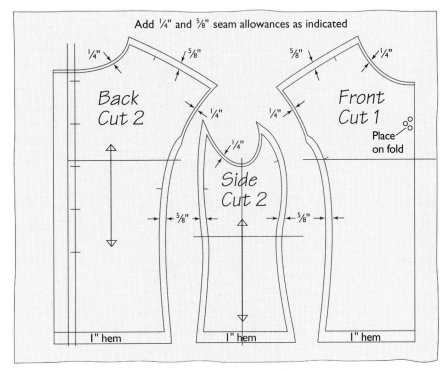

Diagram 6

■ SEWING SECRET: In the fashion industry, seam allowances at the neckline and armscye are only ¼ inch because they are easier to match accurately than the ⅝ inch used in

8. True the back facing at the neck and hem, following the instructions in "Precision Patternmaking" on page 168.

9. Cut out the back, front, and side panel patterns.

Make the Facing Patterns

The Christian Dior blouse has three facings: a front facing, a back facing, and a facing at the back opening. The front and back facings are cut separately, and they finish the neckline and armscye all in one piece. The facing at the back opening is an extended facing, which was added to the pattern when the back was traced.

1. Starting at the armscye, pin the front, back, and side panel together for about 4 inches.

2. Fold the extended facing at the back opening to the right side of the pattern.

3. Draw the facings on the patterns, as shown in **Diagram 7**, and indicate the seamlines and the foldline at the center front. For directions, see "All-in-One Facing" on page 213.

4. On the patterns, mark the grainlines on each of the three facings parallel to the garment centers.

How to *Trace* a *Shirt Sleeve*

Even though sleeves can be very difficult to copy, many shirt and blouse sleeves can be copied by tracing because the sleeve cap has little ease.

SELECT AND PREPARE THE SLEEVE

1. Select the shirt that you would like to trace.

■ **SEWING SECRET:** *A man's plaid shirt is the easiest to copy. Men's shirts have less fullness at the armscye, and the pleated fullness at the wrist is easier to copy than gathers. Since the plaid pattern is easy to follow, it makes copying even the most difficult section—the section just above the cuff—easier.*

2. Examine and describe the skirt sleeve. This sleeve has a cuff with a bound underlap. At the wrist, the fullness is held in with two ½-inch pleats. The first pleat is at the center of the sleeve and the second pleat is ¼ inch away.

3. Using fine dressmaking pins, pin-mark the matchpoints on the armscye seam on the front and the back of the shirt.

■ **SEWING SECRET:** *Mark the matchpoints with a temporary marking pen instead of using pins.*

4. Fold the sleeve in half. One wrist pleat is at the fold and the other is on the front of the sleeve.

5. Mark the crossgrains with hand basting or pins about 3 inches above the cuff and at the cap line.

TRACE THE SLEEVE

1. Place a piece of pattern paper on a pliable surface.

2. Draw a vertical line down the center of the pattern paper. Mark a point on the vertical line about 5 inches from the bottom of the paper and square a line through it.

3. Place the right sleeve on the pattern paper with the front of the sleeve on top. Align the folded edge of the sleeve with the vertical line and the marked crossgrain near the cuff with the horizontal line. Anchor the sleeve in place with dressmaking pins at the intersection of the two lines.

4. Smooth the fabric toward the underarm seam so the sleeve lies flat. Beginning at the cuff, anchor the seam with dressmaking pins or pushpins. Don't be concerned if the foldline on the lower part of the sleeve doesn't touch the armscye.

5. Trace the underarm seam and then trace the cuff seam using the stiletto tracing wheel, as shown in **Sleeve Diagram 1**.

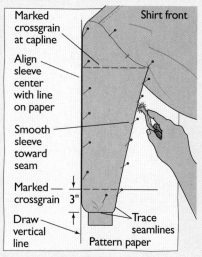

Sleeve Diagram 1

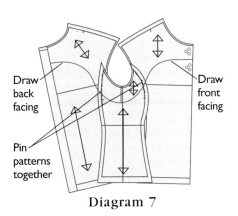

Draw back facing

Draw front facing

Pin patterns together

Diagram 7

5. Place a piece of pattern paper on top of the blouse patterns. Use the stiletto tracing wheel to trace the front and back neckline facings and the facing at the back opening.

6. Add seam allowances to the shoulder, underarm, armscye, neckline, and at the end of the back facing. For information on adding seam allowances, see "Adding a Seam" on page 201.

7. Turn the facing patterns over and label the facing patterns appropriately.

■ SEWING SECRET: Mark the matchpoints and notches carefully. These are the guides that will help you to assemble the garment accurately and easily.

6. If the sleeve cap doesn't lie smoothly, remove the pins from the foldline at the top of the cap until it does.

7. Smooth the sleeve cap toward the armscye and anchor it at the matchpoint with pins.

8. Trace the armscye seam to the matchpoint and mark the matchpoint, as shown in **Sleeve Diagram 2.**

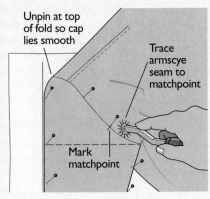

Unpin at top of fold so cap lies smooth

Trace armscye seam to matchpoint

Mark matchpoint

Sleeve Diagram 2

9. Remove the pins below the cap.

10. Continue smoothing the cap and anchoring the armscye seamline. If the sleeve has any fullness or ease, there will be a small gap between the sleeve fabric and the line drawn on the paper at the shoulder point.

11. Remove the pins on the armscye seam and repin the sleeve cap so that the folded edge at the shoulder point is aligned with the marked line on the paper.

12. Use a stiletto tracing wheel to trace the seamline at the sleeve cap, as shown in **Sleeve Diagram 3.**

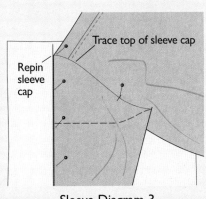

Repin sleeve cap

Trace top of sleeve cap

Sleeve Diagram 3

13. Remove the pins and turn the sleeve over.

14. Repeat steps 1 through 7 to trace the back armscye.

FINISH THE PATTERN

1. If there are pleats at the cuff edge of the sleeve, measure the pleats on the pattern. Compare them to the pleats on the shirt, and make any corrections.

■ SEWING SECRET: *If you are tracing a plaid shirt, use the plaid pattern as a guide to correct and draw the cuff seamline.*

2. Fold the pleats in place and true them, following the directions in "Precision Patternmaking" on page 168.

3. True and proof the seams. To proof the armscye, pin the seams joining the front and backs to the yoke; then measure the seamline at the armscye from the front notch to the shoulder point to the back notches. Repeat to measure the seamline on the sleeve. For additional instructions on truing, see "Precision Patternmaking" on page 168.

4. Add seam and hem allowances. For directions see "Adding a Seam" on page 201 and "How to Add Hems" on page 208.

5. Indicate the grainline on the pattern pieces.

6. Label the pattern pieces. For directions, see "How to Label a Pattern" on page 167.

7. Copy the remaining sections of the shirt following the instructions in "Measuring" on page 180 or "Tracing" on page 186.

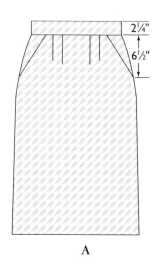

Even a skirt with pleats and tucks can be copied in just a few hours when you use the rub-off technique.

Rub-Off

The rub-off technique is the most versatile method of copying a ready-made garment. Although the process of rubbing-off is very time-consuming, it can be used to copy almost any type of garment.

The rub-off method is well suited for designs that feature traditional set-in sleeves, ease, gathers, darts, pleats, and tucks, as well as tailored and draped garments.

You can use this technique to copy an entire garment, or you can rub-off only one or two sections of a garment and use the measuring or tracing techniques to copy the other sections of the garment.

Analyze the Garment

1. Begin with a simple garment like a skirt. Press the garment to remove any creases that might affect the accuracy of the pattern.

2. Examine the garment and make a sketch, as shown in **Diagram 1A.** This Yves Saint Laurent skirt has a straight line with slash pockets at the waist. As shown in **Diagram 1B,** it is shaped with two dart-tucks on the front and two darts on the back. The front is cut without a seam. The back has a seam on the lengthwise grain at the center back. There are four visible

Diagram 1

pieces: the front, back, waistband, and pocket underlay—the visible part of the slash pocket. It also has an underpocket that faces the pocket opening and front and back linings.

Mark the Skirt Front

1. On the skirt front, mark the lengthwise grain at the center front and midway between the two dart-tucks. Mark the crossgrain

How to *Copy* a *Dart*

The easiest way to copy a dart is to isolate it in a box by marking the grainlines on each side of the dart stitching lines and at the dart ends.

These directions focus only on the process of copying darts and dart tucks.

BOX THE DARTS

1. Analyze the darts. On the skirt back, there are two vertical darts on each side, and they begin at the waist seam.

2. Using hand basting stitches or pins, mark the lengthwise grain on each side of the darts. Mark the crosswise grain ½ to 1 inch from the end of the longest dart. Then mark the lengthwise grain between the darts so each dart is isolated in a box, as shown in **Dart Diagram 1**.

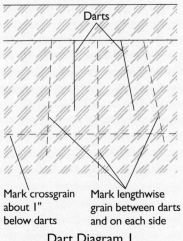

Mark crossgrain about 1" below darts

Mark lengthwise grain between darts and on each side

Dart Diagram 1

When marking a horizontal dart, mark the crossgrain on each side of the dart. Then mark the lengthwise grain at the end.

When marking a double-pointed dart that you might have on a jacket or sheath dress, mark the crossgrain at both ends.

PREPARE THE MUSLIN

1. Cut a 12-inch square of muslin.

2. Using a pencil, mark the lengthwise grain at the center of the muslin, and then mark the crossgrain about 8 inches from the top.

COPY THE DARTS

1. Place the muslin on top of the darts.

2. Align the intersection of the lengthwise and crosswise grainlines on the muslin with the intersection of the grainlines on the skirt. Pin them together.

3. Smooth the muslin away from the intersection and pin the lengthwise grains together. Then pin the crossgrains together to the right of the intersection.

4. When you reach next marked lengthwise grainline on the skirt, pull a thread on the muslin and pin the grainlines together. The excess muslin will bubble between the pins.

5. Smooth the muslin and pin the layers together at the dart point, as shown in **Dart Diagram 2**.

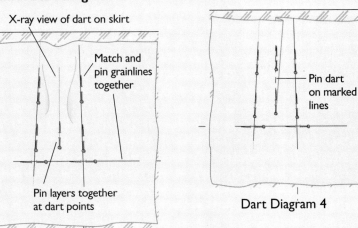

X-ray view of dart on skirt

Match and pin grainlines together

Pin layers together at dart points

Dart Diagram 2

6. Smooth the muslin on one side of the dart, and mark the dart seamline from the point to the waist seam. Then smooth the muslin to the other side of the dart to mark that side of the dart, as shown in **Dart Diagram 3**. Mark the end of the dart with a crossmark.

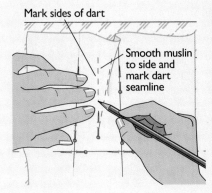

Mark sides of dart

Smooth muslin to side and mark dart seamline

Dart Diagram 3

7. To check the dart, fold and pin it in place, as shown in **Dart Diagram 4**. If it has been marked correctly, it will fit smoothly over the skirt.

Pin dart on marked lines

Dart Diagram 4

8. Repeat steps 4 through 7 to mark the remaining dart.

just below the darts and at the hipline, as shown in **Diagram 2**.

◼ SEWING SECRET: It is usually better to mark the grains using thread, but on fabrics such as wool, you can mark with pins or small-size sewing-machine needles because they will not mar the fabric. When marking plaids and stripes, it's tempting to simply use the color bars instead of marking, but you may become confused and end up wasting time or fabric.

2. As shown in **Diagram 2**, mark a matchpoint on the side seam about 9 inches below the waist. Mark a matchpoint at the waist about 1 inch from the top of the pocket opening.

3. Mark the lengthwise grain on each side of the dart tucks to isolate each tuck in a box, as shown in **Diagram 2**. For instructions, see "How to Copy a Dart" on page 193.

4. Use your fingers to feel the edges of the pocket bag. Mark the edges with basting stitches or pins, as shown in **Diagram 2**.

5. Mark the lengthwise grain and crossgrain on the pocket underlay, as shown in **Diagram 2**. Mark a matchpoint on the side seam.

Prepare the Muslin

1. Steam-press the muslin.

◼ SEWING SECRET: Pattern cloth that is printed with a grid works well when copying simple garment sections. However, it is

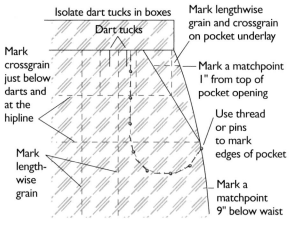

Diagram 2

more difficult to use when the section has several grainlines marked.

2. Measure the length and width of the skirt front, and add several inches to each measurement. Use these dimensions to cut the muslin.

◼ SEWING SECRET: If you misjudge and cut the muslin too short or too narrow, you can piece it as needed by hand or machine—just match and join the sections on the grainlines.

3. Mark the lengthwise grain at the center of the muslin.

◼ SEWING SECRET: To mark the grains, pull a thread using a tapestry needle. Or, if the muslin is on-grain, mark the grain using a well-sharpened pencil (with 2B lead) and a ruler.

4. Mark the crossgrain about 9 inches from the top of the muslin.

Copy the Skirt Front

1. With the skirt front right side up, place the muslin on top.

◼ SEWING SECRET: Most garments are easier to copy if they

are placed on a shaped form such as a pillow, ham, seam roll, or sleeve board.

2. Align and pin the intersection of the lengthwise grain and the crossgrain at the hipline to the corresponding intersection on the skirt.

3. Pin the grainlines together so the skirt is divided into quarters.

4. Smooth the muslin away from the pinned grainlines over the lower part of the skirt toward the side seam and hem. Pin the muslin to the skirt and pencil-mark the seams on the muslin.

5. Smooth the muslin from the pinned grainlines toward the center front. Pin it in place.

6. To check the center front grainline, fold the muslin so the folded edge is aligned with the thread tracing at the center front of the garment. Be sure the fold is on the grainline. If it isn't, examine the pinned muslin and repin the muslin until it is correct. Pin the folded edge to the center front, as shown in **Diagram 3**.

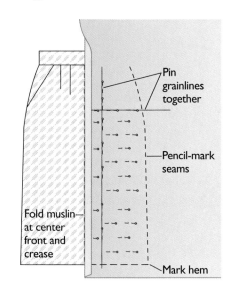

Diagram 3

How to *Mark Seams* and *Edges*

There are several techniques for identifying darts and seamlines and for pencil-marking the seams and edges. Here are two methods that can be adapted for most designs.

DITCH MARKING

The "Ditch Marking" technique is well-suited for fabrics that have a definite well or ditch at seams and darts. These are usually bulky, textured, or medium- to heavyweight fabrics.

1. Use your fingers to feel the seamline. Then, with a very sharp pencil, mark the seamline indentation or ditch with short dashes, as shown in **Seams Diagram 1.** On long, straight seams, you can space the dashes several inches apart. On curved seams, space them close together.

2. When marking the edges of hems, facings, pockets, collars, and flaps, mark outside the edge instead of on top of it so the new garment will be the same size as the original. As shown in **Seams Diagram 2,**

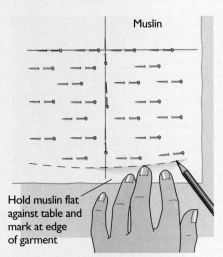

Hold muslin flat against table and mark at edge of garment

Seams Diagram 1

Crosswise grainline — Lengthwise grainline

Mark in ditch of seam

Muslin

Muslin

Seams Diagram 2

position the fingertips of your left hand so they hold the muslin taut against the table or garment section.
3. Use a pencil to mark close to the edge.

CREASE MARKING

This technique can be used on all types of fabrics, but it is particularly useful when there is no definite well at the seamline. These fabrics are generally lightweight, smooth, and silky.

1. Smooth the muslin to the seamline then fold it back so the folded edge is aligned with the seam, as shown in **Seams Diagram 3.**

2. Crease the folded edge of the muslin where it is aligned with the seamline, as shown in **Seams Diagram 3.**

3. Open the creased muslin and, with a very sharp pencil, mark along the crease with short dashes.

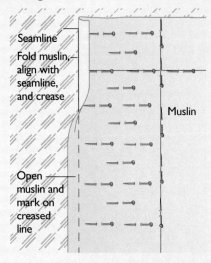

Seamline

Fold muslin, align with seamline, and crease

Muslin

Open muslin and mark on creased line

Seams Diagram 3

■ **SEWING SECRET:** *You can use your thumbnail, a wooden or plastic hera, or a dull knife to make a crease along the seamline of a garment. Then mark the crease with a sharp pencil. Wooden or plastic heras are available at your favorite fabric and notions shop, or you can purchase one by mail order. See "Resources" on page 243.*

■ SEWING SECRET: When preparing the muslin, you may be tempted to mark the grain at the outset, but if your measurements are not accurate, the marked line on the muslin won't match the marked line on the garment.

7. Open the crease at the center front and pencil-mark it following the instructions in "How to Mark Seams and Edges" on the opposite page.

8. Smooth and pin the muslin above the crossgrain. When you reach the marked grain at the dart tuck, pull a thread on the muslin to correspond, but before pulling the thread, examine the muslin to be sure it is pinned correctly at the top of the skirt. Pin the muslin to the marked grain.

9. Mark and pin the dart-tucks in place, as shown in **Diagram 4.** (For directions, see "How to Copy a Dart" on page 193.)

10. Continue pinning the muslin to the top of the skirt.

11. Mark the pocket opening and the waist and side seams, as shown in **Diagram 4.** Pencil-mark the opening, seamlines, matchpoints, and pocket sack following the instructions in "How to Mark Seams and Edges" on page 195.

■ SEWING SECRET: Since the skirt is eased to the waistband, the muslin may not be smooth at the top of the skirt.

12. Mark all the matchpoints following the instructions in "How to Draw Matchpoints and Notches" on page 165.

13. Check the muslin and remove it from the skirt.

Copy the Pocket Underlay

1. Cut a piece of muslin for the pocket underlay—the exposed section of the pocket. Mark it on the lengthwise grain at the center and on the crossgrain about 5 inches from the top.

2. With the skirt right side up, place the muslin on the underlay.

3. Align and pin the intersection of the crossgrain and lengthwise grain to the corresponding intersection on the pocket underlay.

4. Pin the grainlines together and mark the waist and side seams. Mark the pocket opening and the edges of the pocket sack. Then mark all the pocket matchpoints, as shown in **Diagram 5.**

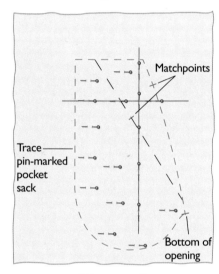

Diagram 5

5. Check the muslin, and remove it from the skirt.

Copy the Skirt Back and Waistband

1. Mark the skirt back and prepare the muslin, then copy the back as described in "Copy the Skirt Front" on page 194.

2. Copy the waistband following the instructions in step 6 of "Analyze and Measure the Design" on page 181.

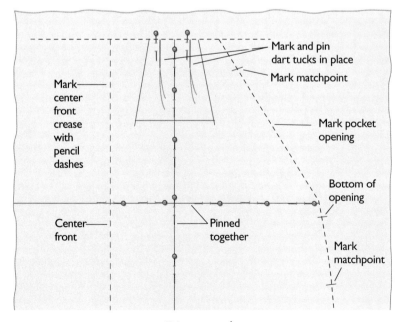

Diagram 4

Proof the Muslin

1. Pin the skirt front to the pocket underlay at the pocket opening.

2. Pin the front and back of the muslin together on the seamlines.

3. Check to be sure the pattern is accurate, the matchpoints match, and the seams are equal in length. Re-mark or retrace the seamlines as needed until they are correct.

■ SEWING SECRET: If the fit of the garment requires fine tuning, cut out the muslin sections, baste them together, and try the muslin on. Check the silhouette and design lines. Check the ease, the darts, and the length of the garment. Mark the muslin as needed so that you will be able to make adjustments to it.

Finish the Pattern

1. Once the fit is finalized, use a straight edge or curve and a sharp pencil to redraw the traced lines on the muslin. Correct and blend any irregularities and mark the matchpoints.

2. Add seam and hem allowances. (For instructions, see "Adding a

Seam" on page 201 and "How to Add Hems" on page 208.)

3. True the pattern sections. (For directions, see "Precision Patternmaking" on page 168.)

4. Place the skirt front pattern on a piece of pattern paper and then trace the outline of the upper pocket with a stiletto tracing wheel, as shown in **Diagram 6.**

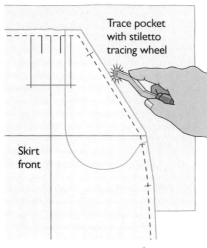

Trace pocket with stiletto tracing wheel

Skirt front

Diagram 6

5. Indicate the grainline and a matchpoint at the opening of the pocket. (For directions, see "Tracing" on page 186.)

6. Label all of the pattern pieces. (For directions, see "How to Label a Pattern" on page 167.)

*d*esign studio secret

SHARPEN YOUR PENCIL

It's important for you to keep your pencil very sharp when patternmaking so that your lines are precise. When I learned patternmaking, I was instructed to use sandpaper to sharpen my pencil. You can also use an emery board.

How to *Copy* a *Sleeve*

You can copy a basic one-piece sleeve by following these instructions, or you can adapt the instructions to copy a two-piece sleeve.

MARK THE SLEEVE

1. Using basting stitches or pins, mark the lengthwise grain at the center of the sleeve. On the sleeve cap, mark the lengthwise grains an additional two times, about 3 inches from each side of the center. Then mark the crossgrain at the cap line, biceps, and elbow, as shown in **Sleeve Diagram 1.**

2. Mark as needed for an elbow dart, following the directions in "How to Copy a Dart" on page 193. If there is no dart, indicate matchpoints about 1½ inches above and below the elbow line to mark the location of the ease.

3. Mark as needed for darts or pleats on the sleeve cap.

4. Mark the matchpoints on the armscye.

■ SEWING SECRET: *I mark about five matchpoints at the armscye: one at the shoulder point with two on each side of the sleeve, as shown in* **Sleeve Diagram 1,** *spaced 2 to 2½ inches apart.*

COPY THE SLEEVE

1. Cut and prepare the muslin so you can begin pinning it to the garment at the capline.

2. Insert a sleeve roll or board into the sleeve, and begin pinning with the sleeve center facing up.

3. Place the muslin on the sleeve, and align and pin the lengthwise grains together, beginning at the capline intersection. Pin the marked caplines.

4. Pin and mark the lower part of the sleeve.

5. To copy the cap, smooth the muslin over the cap, matching the grainlines as you work. Pin and mark the front of the cap, as shown in **Sleeve Diagram 2.** Pin and mark the back of the cap.

■ SEWING SECRET: *When copying the fullness at the top, work with the sleeve in the position it is in when worn so the cap on the pattern won't be too short. If you have a dress form, place the garment on the form, then smooth the muslin over the cap.*

FINISH THE PATTERN

1. Remove the muslin from the sleeve.

2. Following the instructions in "Precision Patternmaking" on page 168, true and blend the seamlines and mark the matchpoints, as shown in **Sleeve Diagram 3.**

3. Finish the pattern, following the directions in "How to Complete a Pattern" on page 178.

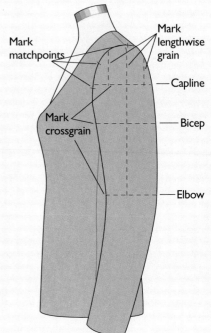

Mark matchpoints

Mark lengthwise grain

Mark crossgrain

— Capline

— Bicep

— Elbow

Sleeve Diagram 1

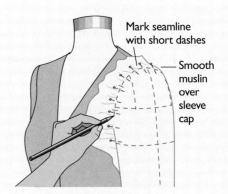

Mark seamline with short dashes

Smooth muslin over sleeve cap

Sleeve Diagram 2

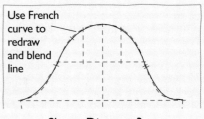

Use French curve to redraw and blend line

Sleeve Diagram 3

How to *Copy Pants*

Pants are among the most frequently copied garments, and if the grainlines are easy to see, they are no more difficult to copy than a skirt.

Always examine the pants carefully before beginning. Like skirts, pants generally have about 2 inches of ease at the waist that is eased to the waistband. The front crease is frequently, but not always, on the lengthwise grain.

PREPARE THE GARMENT AND MUSLIN

1. Sketch, examine, and describe the pants.

2. Using hand basting stitches or pins, mark the lengthwise grain at the center of the leg, as shown in **Pants Diagram 1.**

■ **SEWING SECRET:** *If you can't see the grain, begin at the center of the hem and mark to the center of the knee. Align a long ruler with the marked line to identify the lengthwise center above the knee.*

3. Mark the crossgrain at the knee, crotch, and about 7 inches below the waist, as shown in **Pants Diagram 1.**

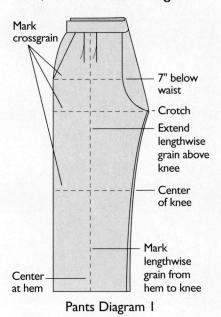

Mark crossgrain

7" below waist

Crotch

Extend lengthwise grain above knee

Center of knee

Mark lengthwise grain from hem to knee

Center at hem

Pants Diagram 1

4. Mark as needed for darts, pleats, and tucks.

COPY THE PANTS

1. Cut and prepare the muslin pieces so you can begin pinning at the crotch line.

2. Align and pin the lengthwise grains of the muslin and the pant leg together.

3. Pin and mark the back pant leg between the crotch and knee, then pin and mark from the knee to the hem.

■ **SEWING SECRET:** *Clip-mark the inseams on the back of the pant legs midway between the knee and crotch lines. Then, before joining the pant legs, stretch and press the curved section of the crotch and the inseam beginning at the clip-mark for a better fitting crotch and back leg.*

4. Copy the back above the crotch line. If the muslin doesn't lie flat, unpin the areas that have already been copied or clip and trim the muslin as needed.

5. Repeat steps 1 through 4 to copy the front pant leg.

■ **SEWING SECRET:** *When copying fullness at the top, examine the wrong side of the pants to determine the widths of the tucks and pleats.*

6. Pin the fullness at the top of the pants into place to check your work, as shown in **Pants Diagram 2.**

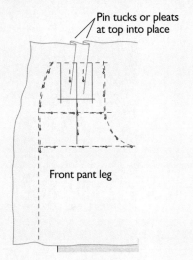

Pin tucks or pleats at top into place

Front pant leg

Pants Diagram 2

■ **SEWING SECRET:** *To prevent baggy knees from forming when you wear pants, stretch the front pant leg from the knee to the hem during stitching or scoop the inseam and outer seam slightly at the knee line. To do this, draw the knee line on the pant leg patterns. On both the cutting lines of the inseam and outseam, mark a point 2 inches above and 2 inches below the kneeline. Then mark a point on the kneeline $1/4$ inch from the raw edge and toward the center of the pant leg. Connect the points with a gentle curve.*

PATTERNMAKING BASICS

Every sewer wants to create a captivating, one-of-a-kind garment. Use one of these techniques to transform your master patterns.

Elements of Design

Seams, hems, and facings are basic elements of a garment's design and are essential to its structure. Although they perform their functions more or less inconspicuously, you can use them imaginatively to create stunning designs.

The contrasting fabric on the hemline of this casual split skirt adds design interest to the garment.

Adding a Seam

Seams are the basic structural element of a garment and one of the simplest design elements. Literally the threads that hold the garment together, seams range from simple, utilitarian, inconspicuous components to eye-catching, decorative details that transform plain garments into extraordinary creations.

Seams can be used to add design interest, to improve fit, and

design studio secret

AVOID PATTERNMAKING ERRORS

The two most common mistakes made in patternmaking are (1) forgetting to add seam allowances and (2) confusing the stitching and cutting lines. To avoid confusion when I make my own patterns, I use a red pen or marker to draw the seamline. Then, when I'm ready to cut the fabric, the red line immediately tells me that I have not added seam allowances.

to add shape, and they can be added to create a design accent.

During the patternmaking stage, nonfitting seamlines can be introduced or eliminated anywhere within the silhouette of the garment without changing the shape or fit of the design. However, they can make a remarkable difference in the appearance of the finished design.

In home sewing, seam allowances are generally ⅝ inch wide. In the fashion industry, seam widths vary, depending on the location and type of seam, the fabric, and the garment quality.

Most seams in ready-to-wear garments are ⅜ to ½ inch wide, but there are two common exceptions. The first is enclosed seams, which are rarely more than ¼ inch wide; these are the seams at garment edges that, in home sewing, are trimmed after stitching. The second exception applies to vertical seams located at the center back and the underarms of better garments. These seam allowances are cut wider to allow for alterations.

When making your own patterns or altering commercial patterns, choose the seam allowance that best suits the stitching operation.

Analyze the Design

1. Sketch the garment and examine the design. The basic split skirt in the photo on page 201 has a horizontal seamline on the front and back 5 inches above the hemline.

2. Select a split skirt pattern with the desired silhouette.

Prepare the Working Pattern

1. On a piece of pattern paper, trace the front and back split skirt patterns.

2. On the traced front pattern, use a red pen or marker to draw the new seam parallel to the hemline and 5 inches away, as shown in **Diagram 1**. Repeat to draw the new seamline on the traced back pattern.

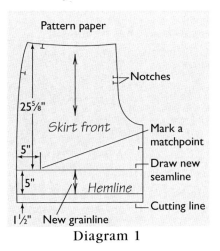

Diagram 1

3. As shown in **Diagram 1**, mark a matchpoint at one end of the seamline on the traced front pattern about 5 inches from the side seam. Do the same on the traced back pattern. For instructions, see "How to Draw Matchpoints and Notches" on page 165.

4. Mark the grainline on the new pattern sections, as shown in **Diagram 1**.

◼ SEWING SECRET: The grainline is usually parallel to the garment center, perpendicular to it, or at

How to *Replace* a *Fold* with a *Seam*

You may want to replace a foldline with a seam to create a tighter layout on the fabric, to add a fastener, to change the fabric grain, or to use a contrasting fabric.

To change a fold to a seam, follow these simple steps:

1. Tape the pattern section to a piece of pattern paper.

2. Add a seam allowance and notches or matchpoints at the foldline, as shown. Cross out the "Place on Fold of Fabric" label. If desired, change the grainline, as shown.

3. Label the pattern "Cut 2."

4. Cut out the new pattern.

■ **SEWING SECRET:** *I frequently like to add a seam at the center back on jackets. That way I can fit the jacket at the waistline and at the shoulders, avoiding a boxy look at the upper back.*

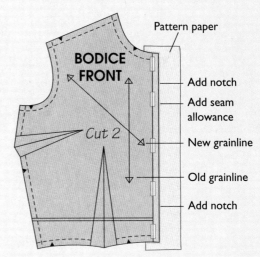

a 45-degree angle (true bias) to it, depending on the garment design.

5. Cut the working patterns apart on the new seamline.

6. Tape each front pattern section to another piece of pattern paper and add a ⅝-inch seam allowance to each section, as shown in **Diagram 2.**

■ SEWING SECRET: When taping pattern sections to paper, use removable transparent tape so you can easily reposition the patterns as needed.

7. Repeat step 6 for the back pattern.

8. On each pattern section, mark notches on the cutting

lines of the new seam allowances, using the matchpoints as guides, as shown in **Diagram 2.**

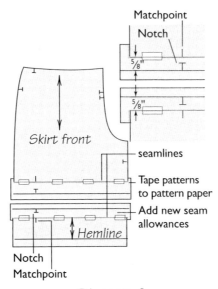

Diagram 2

Finish the Split Skirt Pattern

1. True the seams on all of the pattern pieces for the split skirt. For directions on truing seams, see "Precision Patternmaking" on page 168.

2. Trace the new pattern pieces on pattern paper.

3. Label the new pattern pieces, following the instructions in "How to Label a Pattern" on page 167.

4. Cut out each of the pattern pieces.

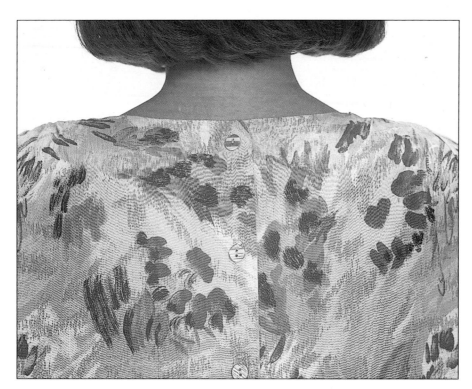

You can also save fabric by eliminating the seam that joins the back facing and the bodice back.

Eliminating a Seam

Seams can be eliminated to reduce bulk or to save fabric or time. Seams also can be eliminated to change the design, and in this way garments can be transformed from plain to fancy with very little effort.

Some seams that are frequently eliminated include non-fitting seams such as seams at garment centers, shoulder seams, decorative seams, and the front/front facing seam. You can also convert fitting seams such as side seams and raglan shoulder seams to darts. (See "How to Change a Seam to a Dart" on the opposite page.)

Follow the instructions here to eliminate the seam that joins a blouse front and the front facing.

Analyze the Design

1. Analyze the pattern and sketch the design. The blouse pattern in **Diagram 1** has a separate facing that is stitched to the bodice front. Since the separate facing is easier to place on many fabric widths, it is frequently used to create a tighter layout.

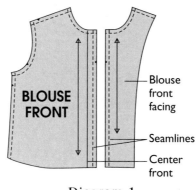

Diagram 1

2. If the stitching lines on the blouse front and front facing patterns are not marked, draw them at the front edge so you can match the two garment sections accurately.

Prepare and Finish the Pattern

1. Fold under the seam allowance on the front edge of the blouse front pattern.

2. Align the folded edge of the blouse pattern front with the stitching line on the blouse front facing pattern.

3. Pin the blouse front pattern and the blouse front facing

How to *Change a Seam* to a *Dart*

Frequently used on Chanel skirts, this design has no side seam; instead the side seam is eliminated and replaced with a dart. It can be used as a wrap design or with a flattering front panel.

ANALYZE THE DESIGN

1. Analyze and sketch the design. This simple lined lapped skirt is composed of only two sections—the right front/back and the left front/back; the side seams have been converted to darts. The right front laps the center front by 4 inches, and although the skirt appears to be a wrap-around lapped design, it actually zips in the back.

2. Select a straight skirt pattern.

■ **SEWING SECRET:** *To be sure the design is a straight skirt, compare the measurements at the hem and hip. If it is wider at the hemline, draw a new seamline from the hip to the hem that is parallel to the center front.*

MAKE THE WORKING PATTERN

1. If the pattern does not have stitching lines, draw them at the side seams on the front and back patterns. Then trim the seam allowances on each section.

2. Beginning at the hem, match and tape the front and back pattern sections together at the side seam, as shown in **Dart Diagram 1.** Continue taping as long as the pattern sections remain flat. The untaped section

will be stitched as a dart to shape the sides of the skirt.

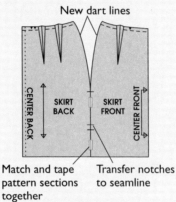

Dart Diagram 1

3. Indicate matchpoints at the beginning of the hip curve, as shown in **Dart Diagram 1.** For instructions, see "How to Draw Matchpoints and Notches" on page 165.

4. Trace the pattern on a piece of pattern paper. To mark the dart at the top of the side seam, trace the stitching lines and mark the end of the dart at the matchpoints.

5. To add a lap, draw the edge parallel to the center front and 4 inches away. Then add a seam allowance at the edge of the lap extension. See "Adding a Seam" on page 201 for instructions.

FINISH THE PATTERN

1. True the top of the new dart following the instructions in "Truing

What looks like a side seam on this skirt is actually a dart.

Darts" on page 170. To true the top of the lap extension, pin the front dart closed and fold the skirt pattern at the center front. Trim the pattern edges at the waist and the hem, cut out the rest of the pattern, and unfold, as shown in **Dart Diagram 2.**

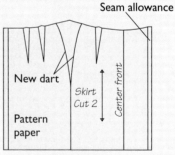

Dart Diagram 2

2. Label the pattern "Cut 2," as shown above.

■ **SEWING SECRET:** *Use the skirt pattern to cut the lining as well as the skirt.*

*d*esign studio secret

FIGURE-FLATTERING SEAMS

Think twice before eliminating a seam at the center back of a skirt or jacket. Eliminating that seam will make a figure look wider. On a shirt the seam is especially flattering on larger figures, and on a skirt the seam allows you to fine-tune the fit.

How to *Replace* a *Seam* with a *Fold*

You may want to replace a straight seam with a fold to avoid interrupting the fabric pattern, to create a tighter layout on the fabric, to reduce bulk, to flatter the figure, or to add a bound zipper placket. (See "How to Sew a Bound Placket with a Zipper" on page 94 for instructions.)

To replace a seam with a fold, just follow these directions.

1. Check the seamline to be sure it is straight.

2. Cross off the original seam allowance, mark the pattern section for cutting on a fold, and label the pattern "Cut 1," as shown.

3. Trim away the original seam allowance.

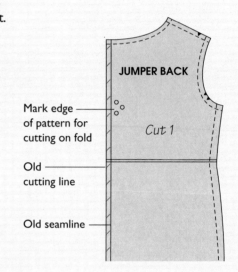

■ **SEWING SECRET:** *Examine the pattern carefully. Many center back seams are shaped, and if they are eliminated, the garment will not fit as attractively.*

---

pattern together, as shown in **Diagram 2**.

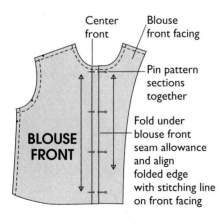

Diagram 2

4. Trace the new blouse front pattern onto pattern paper, as shown in **Diagram 3**.

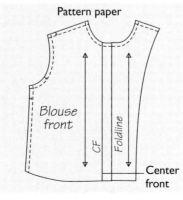

Diagram 3

■ SEWING SECRET: Place a piece of pattern paper on top of the commercial patterns, and trace them with a stiletto tracing wheel. If you do not have a stiletto tracing wheel, trace the pattern with a fine-point permanent marker.

5. Label the traced pattern, following the instructions in "How to Label a Pattern" on page 167.

Transferring a Seam

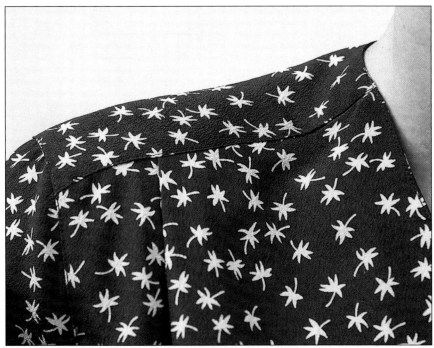

To camouflage a large bustline, shift the shoulder seams forward and add tucks to your favorite blouse pattern.

*d*esign studio
secret

DESIGNING
SHOULDER SEAMS
*The forward shoulder
seam is generally used
with a back yoke. When
it is not, the seam is
rarely more than 1¹/₂
inches below the original
shoulder seam.*

Transferring a seam combines the procedures of eliminating and adding seams. You can use this technique to move decorative seams or to create forward shoulder seams, as described here.

This design is particularly attractive for figures with a large bust and narrow shoulders when combined with pleats, released tucks, or gathers.

Analyze the Design

1. Sketch and describe the design. The shoulder seam is repositioned on the blouse front 1⅜ inches below the original seam, which is eliminated. The back wraps over the shoulder, as shown in the photo above.

2. Select a blouse pattern.

Add the New Seam

1. Trace the blouse front pattern onto a piece of pattern paper.

2. Using a red pen or marker, draw the new seamline 1⅜ inches away from the old seamline, as shown in **Diagram 1.** Mark one or two matchpoints on the new seamline.

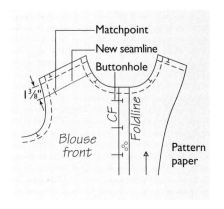

Diagram 1

■ SEWING SECRET: One match-point is enough, except when there is shirring. Then you will need a matchpoint to identify the beginning and end of the shirring.

3. Cut the pattern apart on the new seamline, tape each pattern section to another piece of pattern paper, and draw a ⁵⁄₈-inch seam allowance on each section, as shown in **Diagram 2.**

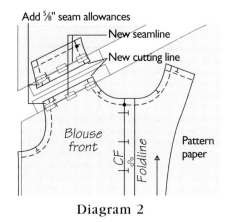

Diagram 2

Eliminate the Original Seam

1. Trace the blouse back pattern on a piece of pattern paper.

2. If there is a dart at the shoulder on the blouse back pattern, transfer that dart to the neckline or to a yoke seamline following the instructions in "How to Move a Back Shoulder Dart" on page 220.

3. At the back pattern shoulder seam, fold under the seam allowance.

4. Align the seamline on the traced blouse back pattern with the old seamline from the section cut from the traced blouse front pattern. Use transparent tape to tape the two pattern sections together, as shown in **Diagram 3.**

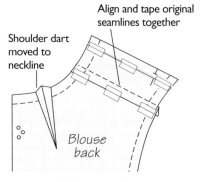

Diagram 3

Finish the Pattern

1. To true the seams, see "Equalizing Seamlines" on page 168. Mark the notches on the shoulder seam cutting lines following the instructions in "How to Draw Matchpoints and Notches" on page 165.

2. Trace and label the new pattern sections. See "How to Label a Pattern" on page 167.

How to *Add Hems*

Hems are used at the lower edges of garments or garment sections to finish a straight or slightly curved edge. Generally, hems are cut as an extension of the garment section and folded back against the garment.

The hem or hem allowance is the area between the hemline—the garment edge—and the cutting line. The width of the hem varies with the garment type, the design, and the quality of the fabric used. In most cases, the directions for adding seams can be adapted for hems.

Use these hem allowances as a guide when patternmaking.

Type of Garment	Hem Allowance
BLOUSES (tuck-in)	⁵⁄₈ inch
COATS	2 to 2½ inches
JACKETS	1¼ to 1½ inches
OVERBLOUSES AND TUNICS	⁵⁄₈ to 2 inches
PANTS	1¼ to 1½ inches
SKIRTS	
Circular	⁵⁄₈ to 1 inch
Flared	1 to 1½ inches
Sheer	½ to ⁵⁄₈ inch
SLEEVES	⁵⁄₈ to 1¼ inches

How to *Subtract* from and *Add* to *Garment Sections*

When you subtract an equal amount from one edge of a garment and add it to the corresponding edge, the fit of the garment is not affected, but the appearance may be dramatically improved.

The following instructions focus on reshaping the edges of a bodice back pattern for a yoke, but they can be adapted for any seam.

TRACE THE PATTERNS

1. On a piece of pattern paper, trace the back and yoke patterns that are created in "Converting Darts to Seams" on page 221.
2. Trim away the seam allowances on the yoke/back seam on both pattern pieces.
3. Cut out the yoke pattern.
4. Tape the yoke pattern to a piece of pattern paper, as shown in **Edges Diagram 1**.

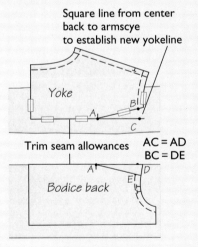

Square line from center back to armscye to establish new yokeline

Yoke

Trim seam allowances   AC = AD
BC = DE

Bodice back

Edges Diagram 1

ALTER THE YOKE PATTERN

1. On the yoke pattern, extend the squared yoke line to the armscye to establish the new seamline, as shown in **Edges Diagram 1**.
2. Mark point A on the yoke line and point B on the armscye, as shown above, and measure the distance between them. Mark point C on the yoke line so AC equals AB, as shown in **Edges Diagram 1**. At the armscye, measure BC—the distance from the squared yoke line to the original seamline.

ALTER THE BACK PATTERN

1. On the back pattern, mark point D at the armscye on the original seamline, as shown in **Edges Diagram 1**.
2. Mark point E on the armscye seamline so DE on the back pattern equals BC on the yoke pattern.
3. Mark point A on the back pattern yoke line so AD on the back pattern equals AC on the yoke pattern.
4. Trim off the triangle ADE from the back pattern, turn it over so that the wrong side is up, and tape it to the yoke pattern to establish the armscye, as shown in **Edges**

Diagram 2.

5. Indicate the grainlines, as shown in **Edges Diagram 2**.

Cut off triangle ADE, turn it wrong side is up, and tape it to yoke pattern

Yoke

Pattern paper

Bodice back

Edges Diagram 2

6. Mark the matchpoints following the instructions in "How to Draw Matchpoints and Notches" on page 165.
7. Add seam allowances following the instructions in "Adding a Seam" on page 201.
8. Finish the pattern and label the pieces following the directions in "How to Label a Pattern" on page 167.
9. Cut out the pattern pieces.

■ **SEWING SECRET:** *To add ⅝-inch seam allowances to your patterns, use the width of the tape measure. Always use a tape measure that is made from a material that will not stretch.*

If you've been inspired to copy a ready-made garment, you can easily draft your own neckline facings.

Making a Neckline Facing

Facings, like hems, are used to finish the raw edges of garments to prevent raveling at the neckline, armholes, and front and back openings. Essential to the garment's structure, facings perform their functions more or less inconspicuously. However, like the world's best fashion designers, you can use facings imaginatively with little effort to create an infinite variety of new designs.

More versatile than hems, facings can finish curved as well as straight edges, duplicating the shape and grain of the garment sections that they face.

At curved edges such as necklines, armholes, closures, and shaped hemlines, facings are cut as separate sections and seamed to the garment. On straight edges, facings can be cut separately or as extensions, like hems.

Separate facings are used on curved edges such as necklines, armholes, and waistlines, and they can replace hems on skirts, sleeves, and slacks. Most often they are applied so they are on the inside of the finished garment, but they can also be applied as a trim on the outside. (See "Facing as a Trim" on page 27.)

Most facings are cut from the same fabric as the garment, but they can be cut from other materials to reduce bulk or cost, add stability, improve comfort, or add design interest.

When you create a new design, you must create new facing patterns. Different sections of the garment and different designs require different kinds of facings.

Facing patterns are usually plotted on the main pattern sections after seam and hem allowances are added, but they can be plotted before those elements are added. Separate facings are outlined on the working pattern.

Facings turned to the wrong side of the garment are cut slightly smaller than the sections they face. Facings used as trims are cut slightly larger. Facings usually do not have darts and should not extend into the bust or shoulder blade area.

The neckline facing is one of the most common separate facings. Used to finish the neck edge of a garment, the neckline facing is usually a separate facing because it must fit the neckline curve.

These directions for a simple neckline facing are applied to the basic bodice pattern, but they can be applied to almost any neckline. The facing is deeper at the garment centers than facings provided with commercial patterns so the facing will protect the garment from skin oils and will stay inside the garment when worn.

Plot the Facing Patterns

1. Trace the front and back bodice patterns, adding seam allowances as needed.

2. On the bodice front pattern, measure and mark the facing 2⅝ inches wide at the shoulder seam and 3 to 5 inches deep at the center front, as shown in **Diagram 1A.**

■ SEWING SECRET: When the neckline is scooped or deep, mark the facing an even width around the entire neckline.

3. On the bodice back pattern, measure and mark the facing 2⅝ inches wide at the shoulder seam and 5 to 7 inches deep at the center back, as shown in **Diagram 1B.**

4. Shorten the ends of the facings, as shown in **Diagrams 1A** and **1B**, so they will fit smoothly inside the garment. Then indicate the grainlines on the facings.

■ SEWING SECRET: The grainline on a facing can be parallel to the grainline on the garment or it can be placed on the bias for a more flexible facing.

5. Draw matchpoints or notches at the neck edge, following the instructions in "How to Draw Matchpoints and Notches" on page 165.

Make the Facing Patterns

1. Place a piece of pattern paper under the front and back patterns.

2. Use a stiletto tracing wheel to trace the facings.

3. Turn the patterns over to make the facing patterns for the right side of the garment, as shown in **Diagram 2.**

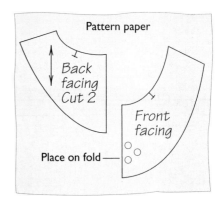

Diagram 2

4. On the front pattern, label the foldline at the center front. On the back pattern, indicate the grainline parallel to the center back and label the pattern "Cut 2" as shown in **Diagram 2.**

5. Cut out the facing patterns.

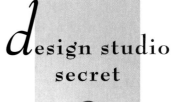

design studio secret

FITTING A FACING

When a facing fits inside a garment, the facing is slightly smaller than the garment. But if you want to use a facing as trim, be sure the facing is slightly larger than the garment.

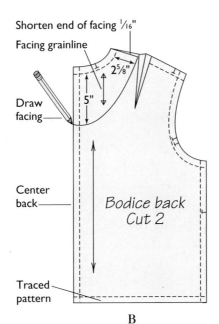

Diagram 1

211

How to *Add* an *Extended, Interfaced Facing*

The extended, interfaced facing is a narrow, straight facing cut in one piece with the garment, and in these directions it is self-interfaced. This facing is suitable for lightweight, transparent fabrics. Generally it is less conspicuous than the traditional shaped facing.

PREPARE THE PATTERN

1. Examine the commercial front pattern or the pattern you have traced or created. Locate the fold or seamline at the front edge and trim the pattern along that line.

2. Tape the pattern to a piece of pattern paper.

3. Measure the width of the button stand—the distance between the center front of the garment and the edge of the pattern.

4. Multiply the width of the button stand by two to determine the minimum finished width of the front facing. For example, if the button stand is ¾ inch wide, the finished front facing will be 1½ inches wide.

DRAW THE FRONT FACING PATTERN

1. To draw the facing, draw a line parallel to and 1½ inches—the facing width—from the front edge, as shown in

Facing Diagram 1.

2. To draw a second line for the self-fabric interfacing, subtract ⅛ inch from the facing width, and draw a line 1⅜ inches from and parallel to the first

line, as shown in **Facing Diagram 1.**
This is the new cutting line of the pattern.

3. Label the extended facing and self-fabric interfacing on the pattern.

SHAPE THE NECKLINE

1. Cut the pattern along the new front edge.

2. To shape the neckline, fold the pattern paper on the two vertical lines so the facing and interfacing are in the position they will have on the finished garment.

3. Trim the excess paper at the neckline and the hem, using the cutting line on the pattern as a guide, as shown in **Facing Diagram 2A.**

4. Open the pattern flat and mark notches at the fold-lines, as shown in **Facing Diagram 2B.**

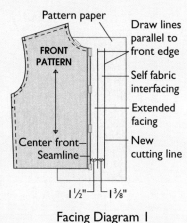

Facing Diagram 1

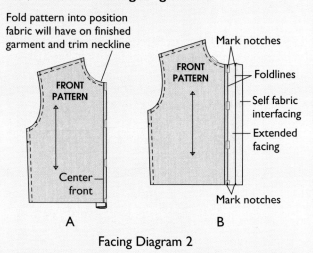

Fold pattern into position fabric will have on finished garment and trim neckline

Facing Diagram 2

■ **SEWING SECRET:** *To secure facings so they won't pop out when the garment is worn, ditch stitch on the seamline through all the layers from the right side of the garment.*

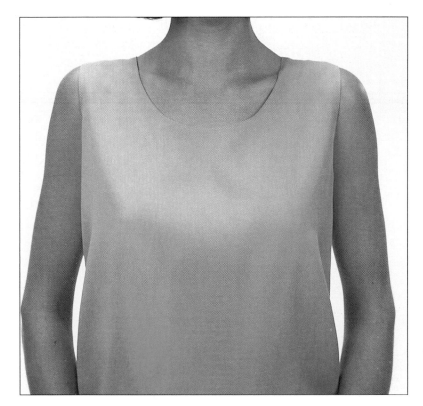

An all-in-one facing gives this lightweight silk shell more body so it holds its shape better in the area above the bust.

All-in-One Facing

Sometimes called combination or neckline-armhole facings, all-in-one facings are frequently used in place of separate facings to finish the neckline and armscyes on sleeveless designs. The all-in-one facing reduces the bulk in the facing, which gives the garment a neater appearance.

These instructions are for the basic bodice pattern but can be adapted for a variety of sleeveless designs, including cut-away armholes, halters, and one-shoulder designs.

Plot the Facings

1. On the commercial pattern or the one you have traced or created, trim the seam allowances to ¼ inch at the neck and armscyes.

2. Measure and mark the facing at least 2⅝ inches wide at the side

seams and up to 4 inches wide at the center front and center back, as shown in **Diagram 1**. Draw the facing cutting lines with a smooth curve.

■ SEWING SECRET: When the design has a high neckline, the facing can be 3 to 4 inches deep

at the center front and the center back, but the facing should not extend into the bust or the shoulder blade area.

3. Mark matchpoints or notches at the neck and armscye.

4. Fold out and pin any darts on the back pattern.

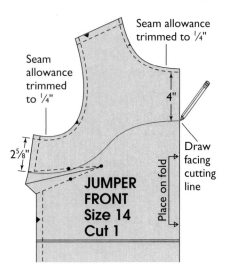

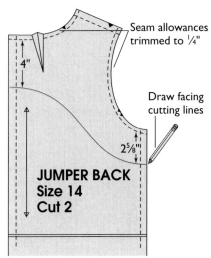

Diagram 1

Make the Facing Patterns

1. Place the front and back patterns under a piece of pattern paper. Trace the facings using the stiletto tracing wheel.

2. Turn the pattern paper over for the right side and redraw the neckline and armscye, trimming ⅛ inch, as shown in **Diagram 2**, so the seams will roll to the inside of the garment.

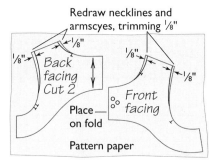

Diagram 2

3. On the front facing, label the fold at the center front, as shown in **Diagram 2**.

4. Mark the matchpoints and notches following the instructions in "How to Draw Matchpoints and Notches" on page 165.

5. On the back facing pattern, indicate the grainline parallel to the center back and label the pattern "Cut 2," as shown in **Diagram 2**.

6. Cut out the facing patterns.

7. Stitch the facings following the directions in "How to Sew All-in-One Facings," below, and complete the garment.

How to *Sew All-in-One Facings*

If you avoid all-in-one facings because they are difficult to sew, here is an easy method that you will enjoy stitching. This flip facing method, the most popular and easiest all-in-one facing, requires a center front or back opening and shoulder seams that are at least 4 inches wide.

PREPARE THE GARMENT AND THE FACING

1. If the garment has ⅝-inch seam allowances at the neckline and armscyes, trim them to ¼ inch.

2. Stitch, press open, and trim the ends of the shoulder seams on the garment and the facing, leaving the underarm seams open.

3. Serge or pink the unnotched edges of the facing sections.

JOIN THE GARMENT AND THE FACING

1. With right sides together, place the facing on top of the garment, matching the notches. Stitch ¼-inch seams at the neckline and armscyes, as shown in **Facing Diagram 1**.

2. Clip the curves to, but not through, the seamline.

3. Gently pull the garment through the shoulders to turn it right side out.

4. With the facing side up, under-press the edges.

5. Understitch the neckline and the armscyes, as shown in **Facing Diagram 2**.

6. With right sides together and starting at the facing edge, stitch and press the vertical seams at the underarm and the garment center, as shown in **Facing Diagram 3**.

7. Complete the garment.

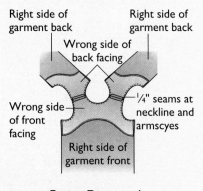

Facing Diagram 1

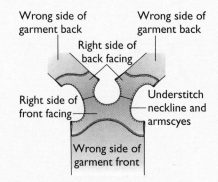

Facing Diagram 2

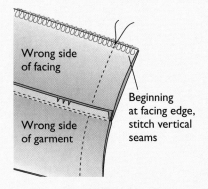

Facing Diagram 3

How to *Sew* a *Narrow* *All-in-One Shoulder Facing*

This method for stitching all-in-one facings can be used for shoulders as narrow as 1 inch wide.

PREPARE THE GARMENT AND THE FACING

1. If the garment has ⅝-inch seam allowances at the neckline and armscyes, trim them to ¼ inch.
2. Stitch and press the seams at the underarms and the garment center on the garment, leaving the shoulder seams open.
3. Repeat step 2 to assemble the garment facings.
4. Serge or pink the unnotched edges of the facing sections.

JOIN THE GARMENT AND THE FACING

1. With right sides together, place the facing on top of the garment.
2. Stitch ¼-inch seams at the garment neckline and the armscyes, stopping 2 inches from the shoulders, as shown in **Narrow Diagram 1.**

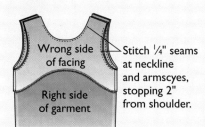

Stitch ¼" seams at neckline and armscyes, stopping 2" from shoulder.

Wrong side of facing

Right side of garment

Narrow Diagram 1

3. Clip the neckline and armscye curves to, but not through, the seamlines.
4. Turn the all-in-one facing right side out, as shown in **Narrow Diagram 2.**

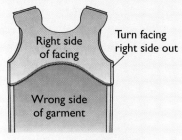

Right side of facing

Turn facing right side out

Wrong side of garment

Narrow Diagram 2

SEW THE SHOULDER

1. With right sides together, stitch the shoulder seams of the garment with a ⅝-inch seam, as shown in **Narrow Diagram 3.** Press the seam allowances open.

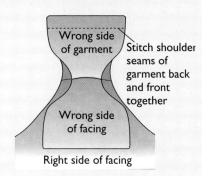

Wrong side of garment

Stitch shoulder seams of garment back and front together

Wrong side of facing

Right side of facing

Narrow Diagram 3

2. Reach between the back and back facing. Grasp the stitched shoulder seam, and pull it out between the layers.
3. With right sides together, stitch the shoulder seam on the facing, as shown in **Narrow Diagram 4.** Press the seam allowance open, trim it to ¼ inch, and clip the ends on an angle.

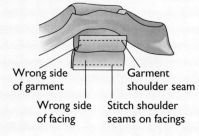

Wrong side of garment

Garment shoulder seam

Wrong side of facing

Stitch shoulder seams on facings

Narrow Diagram 4

4. Adjust the shoulder of the garment so you can complete the unstitched sections at the neckline and armscye. When stitching the shoulder, overlap the previous stitching at the beginning and the end by about ¼ inch, as shown in **Narrow Diagram 5.**

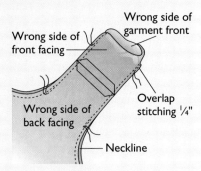

Wrong side of front facing

Wrong side of garment front

Wrong side of back facing

Overlap stitching ¼"

Neckline

Narrow Diagram 5

5. Repeat Steps 2 through 4 to complete the remaining shoulder.

FINISH THE GARMENT

1. Straighten the shoulders and understitch or edgestitch the edges.
2. With the facing side up, press the neckline and armscyes.
3. Complete the garment.

Darts

Darts are one of the most versatile fashion design elements. They are also used to improve the design's fit.

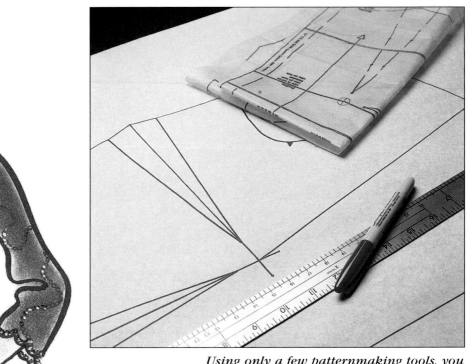

Using only a few patternmaking tools, you can transfer darts on your own designs.

Transferring Darts

A dart is simply a stitched triangular fold that is used to shape a flat, two-dimensional piece of fabric to fit a three-dimensional figure.

Darts can be transferred from one seamline to another, combined, divided, released, or left unstitched. They can be converted to seamlines, dart-tucks, gathers, flares, or pleats; but on fitted designs made from woven fabrics, darts usually cannot be eliminated.

In the fashion industry, the process of transferring darts is called dart manipulation. By following these step-by-step instructions, you'll find it easy to transfer darts on your own designs.

Prepare the Working Pattern

1. Analyze and sketch the design. Then select a sloper.

2. Trace the original bodice front pattern onto a piece of pattern paper.

3. Locate the bust point on the pattern. If the bust point is not marked on the pattern, extend the center lines of the underarm and waist darts until they intersect, as shown in **Diagram 1**. Then draw the new dart line at the shoulder seam. Cut out the pattern.

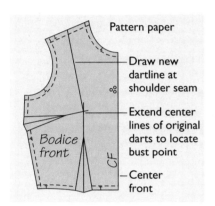

Diagram 1

Slash and Spread

1. Slash one leg of the underarm dart to the bust point.

2. Slash the new dart line to, but not through, the bust point.

3. To close the underarm dart, match the dart lines at the side seam and tape the edges together.

■ SEWING SECRET: When the original dart is closed, the new dart opens.

4. Tape a piece of pattern paper under the new dart to create the dart take-up.

■ SEWING SECRET: Sometimes called the dart underlay, the dart take-up is the excess fabric on the wrong side of the finished garment.

5. On the pattern paper, mark the center of the dart at the shoulder seamline and connect it to the bust point to establish the center line of the dart, as shown in **Diagram 2**.

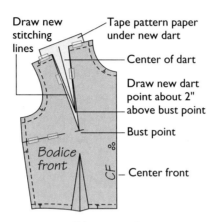

Diagram 2

6. Mark the dart end on the fold-line about 2 inches above the bust point, as shown in **Diagram 2**.

■ SEWING SECRET: The distance between the bust point and the end of the dart depends on the number, size, and location of the darts, the garment design and fit, the bust size, and personal preference.

7. Draw the new stitching or dart lines for the shoulder dart, as shown in **Diagram 2**.

Finish the Pattern

1. True the dart and establish the jog line at the edge of the pattern. (For directions, see "Truing Darts" on page 170.) Trim away the pattern paper at the shoulder seam, as shown in **Diagram 3**.

2. Add seam allowances if needed. (For instructions, see "Adding a Seam" on page 201.)

design studio secret

WORKING WITH SEAM ALLOWANCES

When working with a commercial pattern that has seam allowances, you may initially find the seam allowances confusing. If so, mark the seamlines with a red pen or marker and cut off the seam allowances before tracing the original pattern.

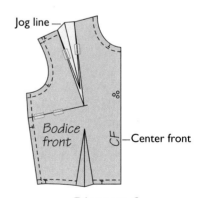

Diagram 3

3. Trace the pattern, including the dart lines and dart point, onto a piece of pattern paper.

4. Indicate the grainline, and cut out and label the pattern.

Tips for Sewing Darts

Darts are used to shape flat pieces of fabric to fit a three-dimensional figure. Darts are not only functional; they also can be used to create design interest. Follow these tips to sew perfect darts every time.

READY

♦ Darts can be transferred easily from one seamline to another, combined, divided, released, or left un-stitched.

♦ Darts can be converted to equivalent shaping devices such as seamlines, dart-tucks, gathers, flares, or pleats; but on fitted designs made from woven fabrics, darts generally cannot be eliminated.

♦ Darts can be transferred by two methods of pattern alteration: slash and spread (see "Transferring Darts" on page 216) and pivoting (see "How to Move a Back Shoulder Dart" on page 220).

♦ Darts that control fit point toward the bust point on the bodice front and the shoulder blades on the back.

♦ The bust and pivot point on the back bodice is located at the intersection of the center foldlines of the dart.

♦ Dart lines are equal in length except when designed otherwise.

♦ Many darts, such as shoulder, underarm, neck, and waist darts, are named for the seams where they originate.

♦ Vertical darts originate on horizontal seamlines and horizontal darts originate on vertical seamlines.

SET

♦ The distance between the bust point and end of the dart depends on the number of darts, the size and location of the dart, the garment design and fit, the bust size, and personal preference.

♦ In most cases, darts above the bust end farther from the bust point than those below or at the side seam.

♦ When fitting a large bust, the dart will appear crooked if the dart end is too close to the bust point.

♦ If the garment requires fitting, first baste the dart together by hand or machine and then try on the garment and make adjustments as needed.

♦ Underarm darts are more flattering when they point upward toward the bust. On small-busted figures they can be horizontal.

♦ Darts set at an angle frequently will have unusual jog lines. (See **Diagram 8** under "Truing Darts" on page 170.)

SEW

♦ Always stitch darts from the raw edge of the fabric to the points.

♦ When sewing darts, the ends are tapered smoothly to avoid a pucker at the end.

♦ Darts are rarely stitched to the bust point and never extend beyond it.

♦ On large darts, the dart take-up—the excess fabric on the wrong side of the garment—should be trimmed to 5/8 inch to reduce bulk.

♦ When sewing darts, always stitch a thread chain at the point of the dart for several inches. Then tie the thread chain into a tailor's knot following the instructions in "How to Fasten Threads" on page 35.

♦ To stitch a perfectly straight dart, fold the dart into position and place a piece of removable tape next to the stitching line. Then stitch next to, not on, the tape.

♦ Insert pins into the dart so that you can stitch them without stopping the machine.

♦ In general, vertical darts are pressed toward the center and horizontal darts are pressed downward.

♦ Always check the fit of a garment before pressing the darts, and always press the darts flat before you press them to one side.

♦ For a high-fashion finish, slash the darts in bulky fabrics and press them open so they will lie flat, preventing a ridge from forming at the dartline.

Converting Darts to Dart Tucks

The dart tuck is used to replace the stitched dart while retaining the fit of the design. Dart tucks and other dart equivalents such as gathers, pleats, and flares are attractive for large- or small-busted figures, particularly when used with yokes or forward shoulder seams.

Replace a dart but retain fit by using a dart tuck.

Prepare the Pattern

1. Sketch and describe the design. This V-neck design has a forward shoulder with a back yoke. On the front, the seamline is 1½ inches below the natural shoulder; on the back it is 4 inches below the center back at the neckline. The dart tuck is placed 2 inches from the armscye.

2. Trace the original bodice front pattern onto a piece of pattern paper, as shown in **Diagram 1.** Then transfer the shoulder seam to a yoke seam on the front pattern. (For instructions, see "Transferring a Seam" on page 207.)

3. Locate the bust point and draw the new dart line, beginning at the yoke seamline, as shown in **Diagram 1.** (For instructions, see step 3 of "Prepare the Working Pattern" on page 217.)

4. Transfer the side dart to the new dart line using either the slash-and-spread method described on page 217 or the pivot method described on page 220 in "Trace and Pivot."

5. Cut out the pattern.

True the Pattern

1. To true the pattern, fold the tuck at the new dart line. Pin the tuck in place and trim the paper at the cutting line. (See "Precision Patternmaking" on page 168.)

2. As shown in **Diagram 2,** open the pattern and examine the jog line. Mark the beginning and end of the tuck.

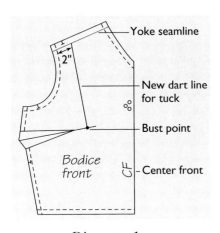

Diagram 1

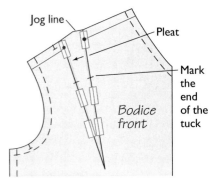

Diagram 2

3. Complete the pattern.

How to *Move a Back Shoulder Dart*

The shoulder dart can be moved from the top of the shoulder to the back neckline, as shown in **Dart Diagram 1,** or into a yoke seam. When the shoulder dart is moved to the back neckline, the dart can be parallel to the center back or can slant toward the shoulder blade, as shown.

The shoulder dart can be moved using the slash-and-spread method as described in "Transferring Darts" on page 216, but it is usually easier to move it using the trace and pivot method that is described here.

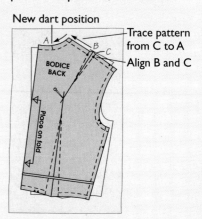

Shoulder darts moved to back neckline

Dart Diagram 1

PREPARE THE PATTERN

1. Locate the pivot point on the bodice back pattern by extending the foldlines at the center of the waist and shoulder darts until they intersect, as shown in **Dart Diagram 2.**

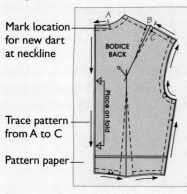

Mark location for new dart at neckline

Trace pattern from A to C

Pattern paper

Dart Diagram 2

■ **SEWING SECRET:** *When there is no waist dart, extend the center of the shoulder dart. Mark the pivot point 6½ to 7 inches from the shoulder seam.*

2. At the neckline, mark the location for the new dart as point A, as shown in **Dart Diagram 2,** and at the shoulder, mark points B and C—the dart lines at the back shoulder.

3. As shown in **Dart Diagram 2,** place the back pattern on top of a piece of pattern paper and insert a pin at the pivot point.

TRACE AND PIVOT

1. Beginning at point A and moving counterclockwise, trace the edges of the pattern to point C, as shown in **Dart Diagram 2.**

2. Pivot the pattern until point B is aligned with point C, as shown in **Dart Diagram 3,** and trace the rest of the pattern from point C to point A.

3. Remove the pin and the commercial pattern.

4. Transfer all of the pattern markings to the traced pattern. For instructions, see "How to Label a Pattern" on page 167.

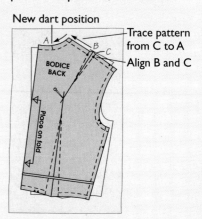

New dart position

Trace pattern from C to A

Align B and C

Dart Diagram 3

FINISH THE PATTERN

1. Mark the foldline at the dart center.

2. Mark the end of the new dart on the foldline so it is the same length as the original shoulder dart.

3. Measure the width of the old dart and plot the ends of the new dart lines.

4. Draw the new dart lines from the end of the dart to the point.

5. Label the pattern "Bodice Back—Cut 1."

6. True the dart and trim the excess paper, as shown in **Dart Diagram 4.** For instructions, see "Truing Darts" on page 170.

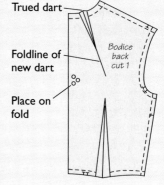

Trued dart

Bodice back cut 1

Foldline of new dart

Place on fold

Dart Diagram 4

Converting Darts to Seams

Darts are frequently converted to seams for design purposes and to improve the fit of a garment. Two of the most popular of these designs have yokes and princess seams. These directions for adding a back yoke can be adapted for creating seams with darts on the bodice front.

Prepare the Working Pattern

1. Analyze and sketch the design. Select a sloper to match your design.

2. On a piece of pattern paper, trace the back pattern. Cut it out.

◼ SEWING SECRET: If the pattern has ease instead of a shoulder dart, pin the front and back patterns together at the shoulder seams. Fold out and pin a dart at the center of the back shoulder so the back shoulder is the same length as the front shoulder, as shown in **Diagram 1.**

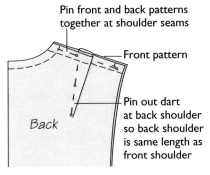

Pin front and back patterns together at shoulder seams

Front pattern

Pin out dart at back shoulder so back shoulder is same length as front shoulder

Back

Diagram 1

3. To mark the yoke line on the back pattern, square a line from

Shoulder darts have been converted to a back yoke on this rich linen jacket.

the center back 3 to 4 inches below the back neckline, and mark one matchpoint about 2 inches from the armscye, as shown in **Diagram 2.**

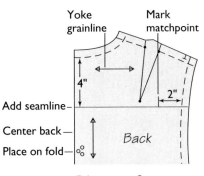

Yoke grainline

Mark matchpoint

Add seamline

4"

2"

Center back

Place on fold

Back

Diagram 2

4. Mark the grainlines on the yoke and back sections.

Transfer the Dart

1. Locate the dart line closest to the center back and slash it to the yoke line. Close the dart by matching the dart lines at the shoulder seam and taping the edges together. If the yoke is more than 4 inches below the neckline, extend the slash only ½ to 1 inch beyond the dart point.

2. Cut the pattern apart on the yoke seamline and, as shown in **Diagram 3**, tape each pattern piece to a piece of pattern paper.

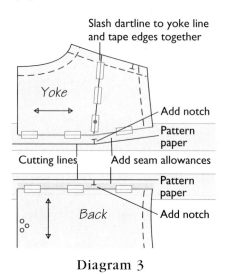

Slash dartline to yoke line and tape edges together

Yoke

Add notch

Pattern paper

Cutting lines

Add seam allowances

Pattern paper

Back

Add notch

Diagram 3

3. Add seam allowances and notches to both pattern pieces, as shown in **Diagram 3**. (For instructions on adding seam allowances, see "Adding a Seam" on page 201.)

4. Trim away the excess paper and examine the pattern pieces. The top of the back pattern piece is straight, while the bottom of the yoke pattern piece curves upward at the armscye. When the garment is worn, this seam will appear to be parallel to the floor.

■ SEWING SECRET: On striped fabrics, the yoke is more attractive when the lower edge of the yoke follows a color bar on the fabric. (For directions on how to make this adjustment, see "How to Subtract from and Add to Garment Sections" on page 209.)

Finish the Pattern

1. Trace the back pattern onto a piece of pattern paper.

2. To make a full pattern for the yoke, place the yoke pattern on a piece of pattern paper folded vertically, as shown in **Diagram 4**.

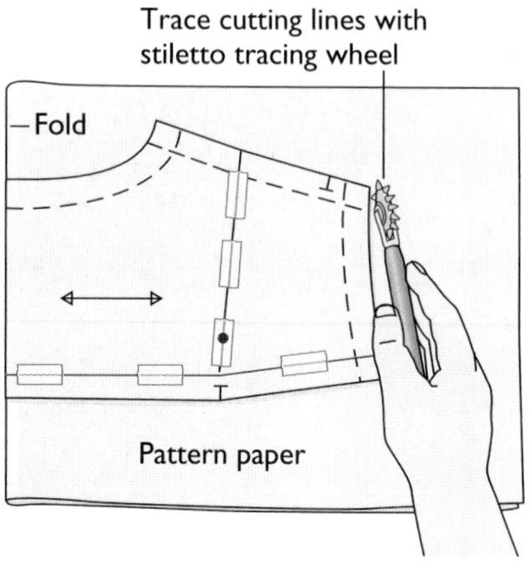

Trace cutting lines with stiletto tracing wheel

Fold

Pattern paper

Diagram 4

3. Align the fold and the center the back.

4. Trace the cutting lines with the stiletto tracing wheel, as shown in **Diagram 4**.

5. Mark the grainlines and the notches on both the yoke and the back pattern pieces. (For instructions, see "How to Draw Matchpoints and Notches" on page 165.)

6. Cut out the yoke and the back pattern sections.

7. Open the yoke pattern and label it "Cut 2," as shown in **Diagram 5.**

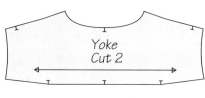

Yoke
Cut 2

Diagram 5

8. On the back pattern, mark the foldline and label the pattern following the directions in "How to Label a Pattern" on page 167.

How to *Add* a *Dart Seam* for *Fit*

On some designs, you can add a dart seam to improve the fit of the garment. One of my favorite designs is the back yoke. This design is not only pleasing to the eye, but it allows you to fit figures with rounded shoulders attractively, and it can be used with or without ease at the shoulder seam.

PREPARE THE WORKING PATTERN

1. Trace the back pattern onto a piece of pattern paper. Cut out the traced pattern.

2. Try on the traced back pattern, pinning it at the shoulder, underarm, back neck, and center back, as shown in **Seam Diagram 1**.

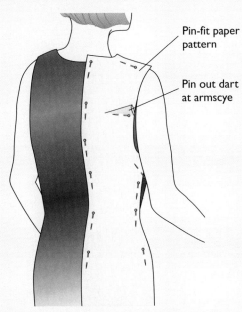

Pin-fit paper pattern

Pin out dart at armscye

Seam Diagram 1

■ **SEWING SECRET:** *To try on a pattern for a partial garment, pin it to your undergarments, a leotard, or a close-fitting T-shirt.*

3. Pin out a dart at the armscye to eliminate the gaping, but don't make the armscye skin-tight. Leave at least ¼ inch ease (about the thickness of your index finger),

between the pattern and your body.

4. Remove the pattern.

MARK THE PATTERN

1. Mark the dart lines at the pins.

2. Remove the pins.

3. Connect the marks to draw straight dart lines, as shown in **Seam Diagram 2**.

4. Square the yoke line from the end of the dart to the center back, as shown in **Seam Diagram 2**.

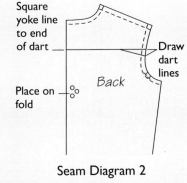

Square yoke line to end of dart

Place on fold

Draw dart lines

Back

Seam Diagram 2

5. For a more pleasing design, redraw the seamlines on the yoke and back following the instructions in "How to Subtract from and Add to Garment Sections" on page 209.

■ **SEWING SECRET:** *To provide additional shaping for rounded shoulders, pin a dart at the shoulder seams. Then convert the dart to ease following the instructions in "How to Convert Darts to Ease" on page 224.*

6. Cut the pattern along the yoke line.

7. Add seam allowances and matchpoints following the instructions in step 2 of "Transfer the Dart" on page 221.

8. Finish the pattern.

How to *Convert Darts* to *Ease*

Most small darts at the shoulder, armscye, elbow, and bustline can be easily converted to ease. This technique focuses on converting darts to ease at the back shoulder of a jacket. At the shoulder, ease is more aesthetically pleasing than the back shoulder dart. But ease can also be used with the shoulder dart to provide additional shaping for rounded shoulders or as a fitting tool to improve the fit at the back armscye or to tighten a V-shaped neckline.

1. Sketch the design. On the tailored jacket shown in **Ease Diagram 1,** the back shoulder darts were converted to ease at the shoulders.

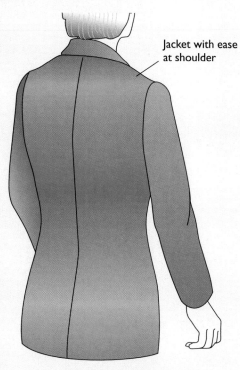

Jacket with ease at shoulder

Ease Diagram 1

2. Trace the jacket back pattern onto a piece of pattern paper.
3. Mark notches at each end of the shoulder ½ inch from the seamlines, following the instructions in "How to Draw Matchpoints and Notches" on page 165.
4. As shown in **Ease Diagram 2,** draw the new cutting line at the shoulder between the notches, using a curve as a guide.

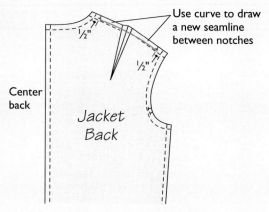

Use curve to draw a new seamline between notches

½"   ½"

Center back

Jacket Back

Ease Diagram 2

5. Repeat step 3 to mark the corresponding matchpoints on the front pattern.
6. To join the front and back garment sections together, baste the sections together, easing the longer back to the front.

■ **SEWING SECRET:** *To control ease on a garment section, set the machine at 10 to 12 spi (2.5 to 2.0 mm) and loosen the needle thread tension. With the right side of the garment up, stitch just inside the seamline. Then pull the bobbin thread to ease the fabric.*

Necklines

You can create countless designs by simply changing the neckline style on a garment. Move the neckline out or in, up or down to create an array of variations.

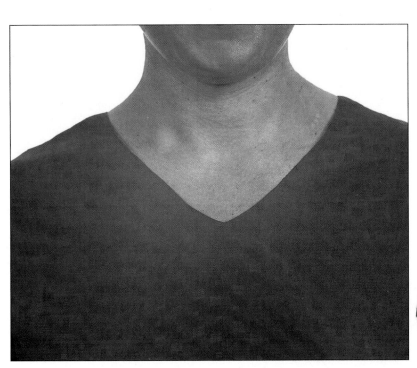

Look thinner instantly by altering your pattern to convert a rounded neckline to a V-neck.

Basic V-Neck

The basic V-neck is one of the most common necklines because it is very flattering for many figure types. This neckline will give you a slimmer look because the V-shape makes your neck look longer, thus making you look taller.

To restyle a neckline, simply start with the bodice included in the basic pattern set. This basic bodice features a close-fitting or

Tips for Creating Necklines

♦ When planning a neckline, consider the shape of your face. For example, squared necklines accentuate a square jaw and V-neck designs elongate the neck. V-necks also elongate the figure and make it look slimmer.

♦ To experiment with new necklines, pin the neckline in place on a basic bodice and examine the results, or cut a paper neckline and try it on.

♦ Necklines can be lowered at the garment centers and shoulders. Necklines that are cut away on the shoulders usually remain high at the center front and back.

♦ Plunging necklines are rarely used on both the front and back of a garment, because they won't stay in place.

♦ Lowered necklines frequently need to be tightened to fit the contours and hollows of the body, as shown. This can be done by pinning

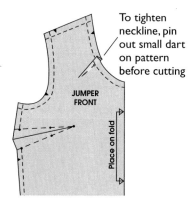

To tighten neckline, pin out small dart on pattern before cutting

JUMPER FRONT

Place on fold

out a small dart on the paper pattern before the garment is cut, by easing the neck edge to a stay tape, or by using a combination of these two methods.

♦ If the garment will be pulled over the head without a closure, the neckline must be at least as large the circumference of your head. Knit garments are an exception.

♦ On rounded or square necklines, the neckline should intersect at a right angle for $1/16$ inch at the center front to prevent the neckline from making a V-shaped dip at that point.

♦ Before finishing the neckline, check to be sure it crosses the shoulders smoothly without a jog or point.

---

jewel neck that hugs the natural curves of the neck. The front of this neckline barely covers the two bones on either side of the hollow at the base of the throat. The back of the neckline just covers the top of the bone at the nape of the neck.

Use your basic patterns block to experiment with all of the necklines in this section, which are a few of the most common and most flattering styles.

Plot the Front Neckline and Facing

1. Sketch the neckline.

2. On a piece of pattern paper,

trace the front bodice pattern.

3. Measure and mark Point A—the neckline depth—on the center front 4 inches below the neck, as shown in **Diagram 1**.

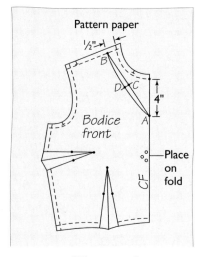

Pattern paper

½"

B

D C

4"

Bodice front

A

Place on fold

CF

Diagram 1

■ SEWING SECRET: If you have traced the pattern's seam allowances, measure from the stitching, not the cutting line.

4. Measure and mark Point B ½ inch from the shoulder point, as shown in **Diagram 1**.

5. Connect Points A and B and mark Point C at the center, as shown in **Diagram 1**.

6. Square a line from Point C and mark Point D ½ inch away, as shown in **Diagram 1**.

7. Connect Points A, D, and B with a curved line, as shown in **Diagram 1**, so the edge of the neckline will look straight when it is on the three-dimensional figure.

8. Add a seam allowance to the curved line and make sure you have marked the fold.

9. Outline the facing on the traced pattern so it is at least 2 inches wide, as shown in **Diagram 2**.

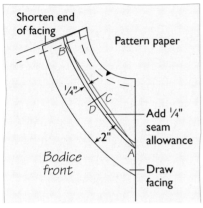

Diagram 2

10. Shorten the ends of the facing, as shown in **Diagram 2**, following the instructions in step 4 of "Plot the Facing Patterns" on page 211.

11. Trace the front facing pattern on a piece of pattern paper.

Plot the Back Neckline

1. On a piece of pattern paper, trace the back bodice pattern.

2. Measure and mark Point B ½ inch from the shoulder point, as shown in **Diagram 3**.

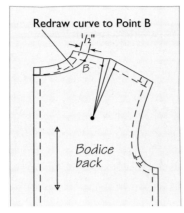

Diagram 3

3. Using a curve as a guide, redraw the curve of the back neckline to Point B, as shown in **Diagram 3**.

4. Plot the back facing following steps 9 and 10 of "Plot the Front Neckline and Facing" on the opposite page.

Finish the Patterns

1. True the patterns following the instructions in "Precision Patternmaking" on page 168.

2. Label all of the pattern pieces following the directions in "How to Label a Pattern" on page 167.

3. Cut out the pattern pieces.

design studio
secret

NECKLINE
SOLUTION

If you inadvertently make your neckline too low, you can make a small triangular dickey that you can snap to the facing. Make the dickey from the same fashion fabric as the garment or use a contrasting fabric or lace.

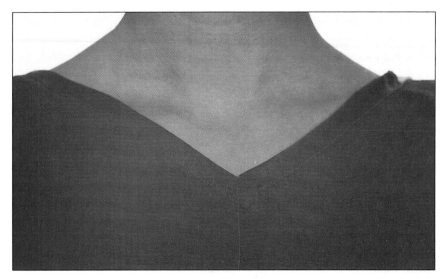

If you find a V-neck too revealing, draft a shallow V-shaped neckline.

Shallow V-Neck

The shallow V-neck on this blouse is cut away from the neck at the sides and lowered only slightly at the front and back.

The neck is large enough to slip over most heads, but check the pattern dimensions before making the actual blouse.

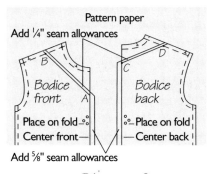

Diagram 1

Plot the Neckline

1. Sketch the neckline.

2. On a piece of pattern paper, trace the front and back bodice patterns.

3. Measure and mark Point A—the neckline depth—on the center front 3 inches below the neck stitching line. Measure 2 inches from the shoulder point and mark Point B. Connect Points A and B, as shown in **Diagram 1.**

4. Measure and mark Point C on the center back 2 inches below the neck stitching line. Measure 2 inches from the shoulder point and mark Point D. Connect Points C and D, as shown in **Diagram 1.**

5. Add ¼-inch seam allowances at the front and the back necklines and ⅝-inch seam allowances at the center front and the center back, as shown in **Diagram 2.**

6. Make a neckline facing following the instructions in "Plot the Front

design studio secrets

LINGERIE GUARDS
The shallow V-neck will be more attractive if you add lingerie guards on the inside of the garment at the shoulders. The guards will ensure that the blouse doesn't shift and slide off your shoulders. (For instructions, see "Lingerie Guards" on page 130.)

Diagram 2

Neckline Facing" on page 226 or finish the neckline with a bias strip following the instructions in "Bias Facing as a Trim" on page 25.

7. True, label, and cut out the patterns.

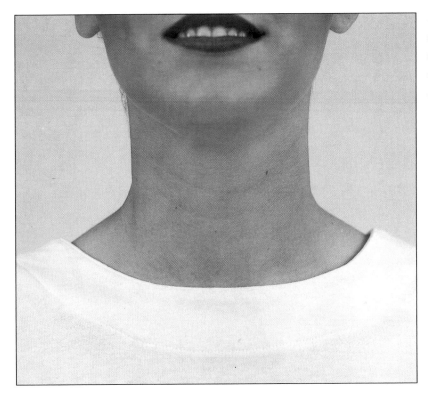

This shallow scoop neckline is cool and comfortable to wear during the hot summer months.

4. Measure and mark Point C on the center back 1¾ inches below the neck. Measure and mark Point D 1⅜ inches from the shoulder point. Connect Points C and D with a curve, as shown in **Diagram 1.**

5. Pin the stitching lines together at the shoulders. Check the neckline curve to be sure it crosses the shoulder gracefully.

Plot the Facings

1. As shown in **Diagram 2,** plot the neckline facings on the front and back patterns following the instructions in "Plot the Front Neckline and Facing" on page 226.

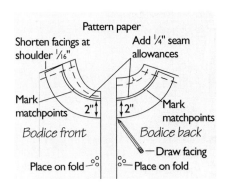

Diagram 2

2. Add ¼-inch seam allowances to the new front and back necklines, as shown in **Diagram 2,** and mark the matchpoints.

3. Trace the facing patterns onto a piece of pattern paper.

4. True the patterns, label all the pattern pieces, and cut out the patterns.

Cut-Away Scoop Neckline

This cut-away scoop neckline was traced from a lightweight Liz Claiborne knit blouse. I particularly like this neckline because it is cut away at the shoulders but not at the front and the back, making it cool and comfortable to wear during the summer, but not revealing.

Plot the Neckline

1. Sketch the neckline.

2. On a piece of pattern paper, trace the front and back bodice patterns.

3. Measure and mark Point A—

the neckline depth—on the center front about ½ inch below the neck stitching line. Measure and mark Point B 1⅜ inches from the shoulder point. Connect Points A and B with a curve, as shown in **Diagram 1.**

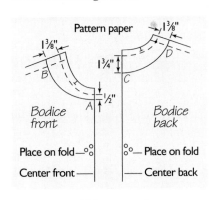

Diagram 1

Tucks

Tucks create an elegant, feminine design without being overly frilly. Soft, tailored tucks add interest to simple shapes and plain fabrics.

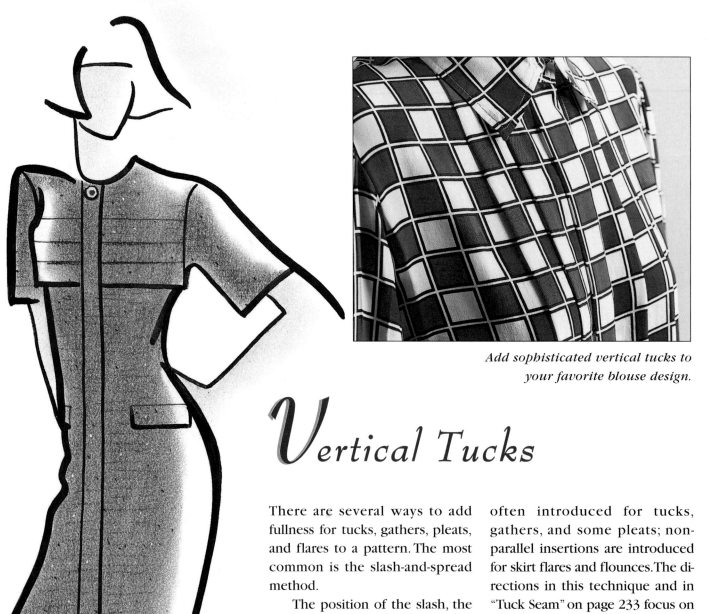

Add sophisticated vertical tucks to your favorite blouse design.

Vertical Tucks

There are several ways to add fullness for tucks, gathers, pleats, and flares to a pattern. The most common is the slash-and-spread method.

The position of the slash, the amount of fullness, and the kind of insertion determines the amount and location of the fullness in the finished garment.

Parallel insertions are most often introduced for tucks, gathers, and some pleats; non-parallel insertions are introduced for skirt flares and flounces. The directions in this technique and in "Tuck Seam" on page 233 focus on parallel insertions, but the instructions can be adapted for adding gathers or pleats. (For directions on adding flares, see "Double Flounce Collar" on page 79.)

Analyze the Design

1. Sketch the design.

2. Analyze the design. The basic shirt design in the photo on the opposite page has tucks on the front and is very flattering for figures with a small bust. The shirt has a forward shoulder seam, a two-piece shirt collar, and two tucks on each side of the opening. Each tuck is 1½ inches wide and the space between the tucks is 1⅜ inches. The first tuck begins ⅝ inch from the center front.

■ SEWING SECRET: The tucks on this design are called blind tucks. The space between the tucks is less than the tuck width, and one tuck covers the stitching line of the adjacent tuck.

Plot the Tucks on the Pattern

1. Select a blouse pattern and trace the front pattern onto pattern paper. To add a forward shoulder seam, see "Transferring a Seam" on page 207.

2. Draw a vertical tuck line on the traced pattern 1⅜ inches to the left of the foldline to mark the location of the first tuck, as shown in **Diagram 1**.

3. To mark the location of the second tuck, draw another vertical tuck line 1⅜ inches to the left of the first tuck line, as shown in **Diagram 1**.

■ SEWING SECRET: Tucks are frequently placed on the lengthwise grain or crossgrain, but they can be placed on the bias.

4. Square a guideline across the tuck lines, as shown in **Diagram 1**.

5. Number the blouse sections 1, 2, and 3, beginning at the center front, as shown in **Diagram 1**.

■ SEWING SECRET: For vertical tucks on the back and on other garment sections, begin numbering on the left-hand side. For horizontal darts, begin numbering the sections at the top.

Make the Tuck Strips

1. On another piece of pattern paper, draw Line A, as shown in **Diagram 2**. Draw Line B parallel to Line A and the width of the tuck—1½ inches—away. Repeat to draw Line C. To check your

pattern, measure the distance between Lines A and C at the top and bottom. The total distance should be 3 inches—twice the width of the tuck.

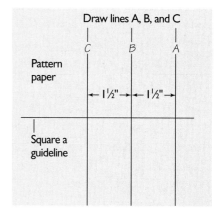

Diagram 2

2. Square a guideline across the strip, as shown in **Diagram 2**.

3. Repeat steps 1 and 2 to make another tuck strip.

Add the Tucks

1. Cut the pattern on the first tuck line.

2. Place Section 1 on one tuck strip, as shown in **Diagram 3**,

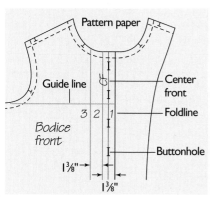

Diagram 1

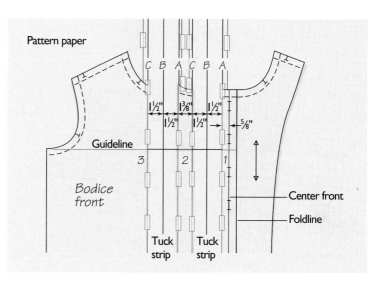

Diagram 3

aligning the horizontal guidelines.

3. Then align the vertical edge of Section 1 with Line A. Tape the pattern in place, as shown in **Diagram 3** on page 231.

4. Repeat step 2 to align blouse Section 2 with Line C.

5. Repeat steps 1 through 4 using the second tuck strip, as shown in **Diagram 3** on page 231.

6. For the right side of the blouse, fold the pattern along each Line A and align the folds with each Line C, as shown in **Diagram 4.** To make the tucks on the left side of the blouse, fold the pattern along each Line C and align the folds with each Line A.

7. To true the pattern, crease each tuck on Line B.

8. True the edges of the blouse front pattern at the neckline and the hemline and trim away the excess paper, as shown in **Diagram 5.**

Finish the Pattern

1. Trace and label the new blouse front pattern.

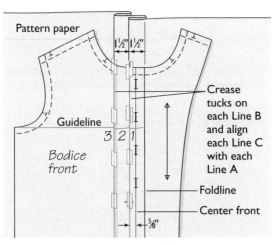

Diagram 4

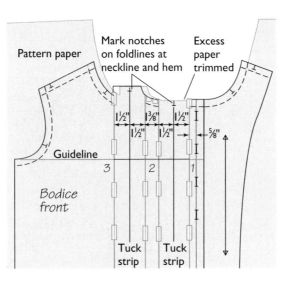

Diagram 5

2. Label the pattern "Cut 2."

3. Mark the stitching line for each tuck with a notch at the neckline.

4. Then mark the stitching line for each tuck with a notch at the hemline.

5. Cut out the pattern pieces.

design studio secret

FOLDING TUCKS ACCURATELY

Tucks are easy to fold when the fashion fabric is striped or has a design that can be used as a guide. Tucks usually are folded on the lengthwise or crosswise grain of the fabric, which allows you to press them flat. If you choose to place the fold on the bias, the tucks will not press as flat.

This smart tuck seam duplicates a classic design by Yves Saint Laurent.

Tuck Seam

The tuck seam looks like a tuck, but it has several advantages that a regular tuck doesn't have. The most striking is that you have the ability to manipulate the fabric pattern or to change the grain on one of the garment sections. The tuck seam also lies flatter because the fabric is cut instead of folded.

This classic shirt is a reproduction of an Yves Saint Laurent design. It has tucked seams on the front and back. On the back and the front, the yoke is cut on the crossgrain, and on the front, the tuck laps the pocket opening. When viewed from the side, the yokes are the same depth. When "snoop-shopping," I used my

hand to estimate the width of the yokes and the tucks. The stitching line for the yoke is 2¾ inches below the center front neck, and the tucks are 1 inch wide.

Add the Yoke Seamlines

1. Select a blouse pattern and trace the front and back pattern onto pattern paper.

2. To add the yoke seamline on the front pattern, square a line 2¾ inches below the center front neck stitching line to mark the stitching line, not the foldline, for the tuck. Draw a vertical guideline perpendicular to the stitching line, as shown in **Diagram 1.**

3. To make the yokes the same depth at the armscye, measure the distance from the shoulder seam to the stitching line on the front yoke. Measure the same distance on the back pattern, mark a point, and then draw the yoke seamline from that point perpendicular to the center back, as shown in **Diagram 1.** Draw a vertical guideline perpendicular to the yoke seamline.

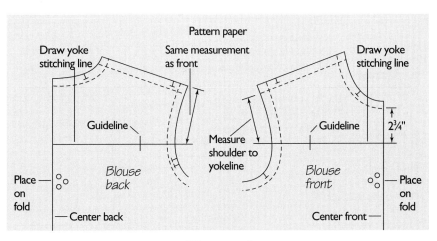

Diagram 1

design studio secrets

COMPLETE-FIGURE PATTERNS

Sometimes called full patterns, complete-figure patterns include one pattern piece for each garment section. The pieces are laid on a single layer of fabric, which is called an open lay in the fashion industry. After you invest the time to create complete-figure patterns, you can match printed and plaid fabrics faster and with greater accuracy. You can also create a tighter pattern layout on expensive fabrics.

Make the Tuck Seams

1. Make a tuck strip following the instructions in "Make the Tuck Strips" on page 231, placing the lines 1 inch apart. Mark a vertical guideline perpendicular to the lines on the tuck strip.

2. Cut out the front pattern, and slash it on the yoke seamline. Label the yoke pattern. Align and tape the tuck strip to the yoke section, as shown in **Diagram 2.** Tape the remaining bodice pattern to a piece of pattern paper.

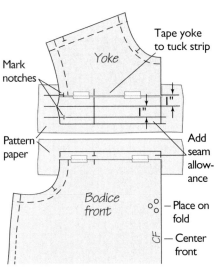

Diagram 2

3. Add seam allowances to the yoke pattern and to the remaining bodice pattern, as shown in **Diagram 2.** (See "Adding a Seam" on page 201 for directions. Mark notches at the tuck matchpoints and at the armscye.)

4. Fold the tuck in place.

5. Place the yoke pattern on top of the bodice pattern, and align and pin the stitching lines together.

6. To true the pattern, trim the edges of the pattern at the armscye and at the front opening. Remove the pins.

7. To finish the back pattern, repeat steps 1 through 6.

Finish the Blouse Patterns

1. Trace and label the pattern pieces.

2. Label the pattern pieces, indicate the grainlines and mark the notches at the ends of the stitching lines. (For instructions, see "How to Label a Pattern" on page 167.)

Sewing a Tuck Seam

1. With right sides together, stitch the yoke and front together with a ⅝-inch seam.

2. Fold the tuck in place with the wrong sides together and pin the tuck at the seamline, as shown in **Diagram 3.** Press the folded edge.

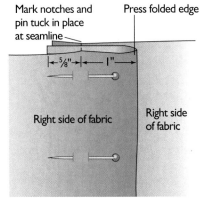

Diagram 3

3. Mark and stitch the tuck in place 1 inch from the fold.

4. Complete the garment.

Button Closures

Decorative as well as functional, button closures can easily change the appearance of a design.

To create the illusion of a slimmer figure, add a buttonhole opening to the front of a skirt design.

Adding Buttons and Buttonholes

You can add design interest to a simple garment or create the illusion of a slimmer figure by adding a button/buttonhole closure.

Although zippers are frequently used at garment openings, a button/buttonhole closure is more versatile because you can create a much longer opening—often to the hemline—than is possible with a zipper. Also, the button closure is a more supple closure and flows with the body's movements.

With the large variety of buttons available today, there is an infinite range of design possibilities. Buttons are usually spaced evenly, but they can be placed in pairs or groups to create a more interesting arrangement.

These instructions are for a center front closure, but they can

Tips for Button Closures

♦ Women's garments lap right over left and men's lap left over right.

♦ When garments are buttoned at the center front and back, buttons are located on the center line. On asymmetrical designs, they are located on the fitting line.

♦ The button diameter, thickness, shape, and texture determine the length of the buttonhole.

♦ The button diameter and garment quality determine the width of the button stand or extension—the distance between the garment center or fitting line and the garment edge. On better garments, the stand is equal to the diameter of the button.

♦ To determine the spacing between the buttons, first determine the locations of the top and bottom buttons and the number of buttons on the design. Then measure the space between the buttons and divide that measurement by the total number of buttons, minus one.

♦ On a design with lapels, the first button is placed at the breakpoint—the beginning of the lapel roll line.

♦ On designs with belts, space the buttons above and below the edges of the belt at least half the diameter of the button plus ¼ inch. On designs without a belt, place a button at the waistline.

♦ Buttonholes can be horizontal, vertical, or slanted.

♦ Most buttonholes are positioned horizontally on the crossgrain at right angles to the garment edge because in that position they are more secure and will gap less than vertical button placements.

♦ On a diagonal opening, buttonholes are generally positioned parallel to the floor, but they can be positioned perpendicular to the edge.

♦ Horizontal buttonholes lap the center front, or the fitting line if the closure is asymmetrical, at least ⅛ inch to extend into the button stand, as shown. The exact amount the buttonhole laps the center is determined by the size of the button shank or stem and the bar at the end of the buttonhole. If the holes on the buttons are widely spaced and the stem is thick, the buttonhole should lap the center more than ⅛ inch.

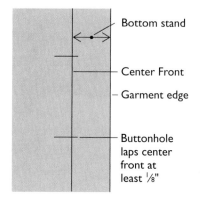

Bottom stand

Center Front

Garment edge

Buttonhole laps center front at least ⅛"

♦ On belts, tabs, bands, collars, and cuffs, buttonholes are placed parallel to the long edges.

♦ Vertical buttonholes are located on the center front or center back or on the fitting line of asymmetrical designs. Vertical buttonholes are more pleasing aesthetically on designs with vertical bands and tabs.

♦ Vertical buttonholes can be positioned so the button is set either at the top of the buttonhole or in the center. Many designers prefer the latter, except for the first button, because it allows the button to move a little in the buttonhole and eliminates a tight, pulled look.

also be applied to the center back and can be adapted for asymmetrical closures. You can choose whether to add an extended facing or a separate facing to the front pattern.

Analyze the Design

1. Sketch the garment.

2. Analyze the design. The basic straight skirt in the photo on page 235 fastens at the center front with six ¾-inch buttons, including the one on the waistband. The first button on the skirt is 2½ inches below the waistband, and the bottom button is 4⅜ inches above the hemline. The button stand—the distance between the center front and the garment edge—is ¾ inch wide.

3. Select a skirt pattern with the desired silhouette.

Define the Button Stand

1. On a piece of pattern paper, trace the skirt front pattern, leaving at least 5 inches between center front on the pattern and the right side of the paper.

2. Measure the diameter of the button and use this measurement as a guide when determining the width of the button stand.

■ SEWING SECRET: The minimum width of a button stand is one-half the button diameter plus ⅛ inch. However, when the buttons are small, the stand can be ⅛ to ¼ inch wider than the button diameter.

3. Draw the button stand parallel and to the right of the center front, as shown in **Diagram 1.** The button stand in Diagram 1 is ¾ inch wide.

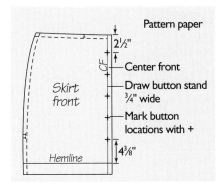

Diagram 1

4. Mark the placement for the top button and the bottom button.

5. Measure the space between the top and bottom buttons.

6. Divide that number by the number of buttons minus one, and mark the button locations with a plus sign.

■ SEWING SECRET: When marking placement of a top button, the minimum distance from a seam or garment edge is one-half the diameter of the button plus ⅛ inch, but it can be several inches, as on this skirt design. The placement of the bottom button varies. On a skirt it depends on how much leg you want to show and whether you are considering a different hem length in the future.

Usually the bottom button is placed at least 2 inches above the hemline.

7. Mark the grainline on the skirt front pattern.

Plot an Extended Facing Pattern

1. To add an extended facing to the front of the skirt, draw the facing parallel to the garment edge and 3 inches away, as shown in **Diagram 2.** The facing can be wider or narrower, but it should be wide enough to support the buttonhole. Mark the garment edge "Foldline."

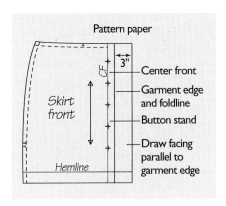

Diagram 2

2. Fold the pattern paper at the front edge.

3. True the edges of the skirt pattern at the waist and hem following the instructions in "Precision Patternmaking" on page 168.

4. Cut out the rest of the pattern.

■ SEWING SECRET: When sewing a skirt with a front opening or vent, always hem the skirt before finishing the facing so the hem will not show at the vertical edge, as shown in **Diagram 3.**

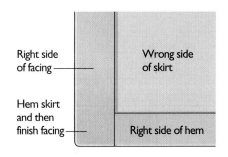

Diagram 3

Plot a Separate Facing Pattern

1. To add a separate facing to the skirt front pattern, add a ⅝-inch seam allowance to the front edge of the pattern, as shown in **Diagram 4.**

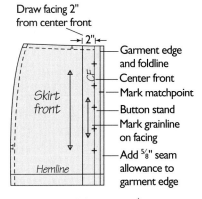

Diagram 4

2. Then draw the facing on the skirt front pattern 2 inches from the center front, as shown in **Diagram 4.** Mark a matchpoint on the foldline at the front edge.

3. Mark the grainline on the facing section parallel to the grainline on the skirt, as shown in **Diagram 4.**

4. Use a stiletto tracing wheel to trace the facing pattern onto a piece of pattern paper.

5. Cut out the front facing pattern.

Design Worksheet

DATE: _____

DESCRIPTION: _____
_____
_____
_____
_____

MASTER PATTERN: _____

FABRIC/FIBER CONTENT	WIDTH	LENGTH

INTERFACINGS: _____
_____

BACKINGS/LININGS: _____
_____

TRIMS: _____
_____

OTHER MATERIALS: _____

GARMENT CARE: _____
_____

TOTAL COST: _____

NOTES: _____
_____

Fabric Swatches:

SOURCE: *High-Fashion Sewing Secrets from the World's Best Designers*, Rodale Press © 1997. All rights reserved.
Design figure courtesy of Victor Costa. Rodale Press grants individuals permission to photocopy the design worksheet for personal use only. All rights reserved.

Acknowledgments

I want to thank the following people and businesses for their help and cooperation in researching and producing this book.

Jeanne Allen and Marc Grant at Jeanne Marc

Allentown Sewing Machine Outlet

Helen Armstrong

Geoffrey Beene

Barbara Blom at Sawyer Brook Distinctive Fabrics

Butterick

Clotilde

Victor Costa

Dick Blick Art Materials

Eisenhower Medical Center's Collector Corner volunteers

Fabric Mart of Bethlehem

Todd Fisher Textiles

Gingher

Greenberg & Hammer

The late Adeline Guintini

High School of Fashion Industries

Nel Howard at Juki America

HTC-Handler Textile

Charles Kleibacker

Koret of California

Linda Lee at The Sewing Workshop

LivingSoft

Jon Moore at Hardy Amies

Newark Dressmaker Supply

Richard Nott at Workers for Freedom

Michael Novarese

The Personality Shoppe

Emilio Pucci

Zandra Rhodes

David Sassoon at Belleville Sassoon

Lucy Spector at Britex Fabrics

Taunton Press

Web of Thread

Yves Saint Laurent

Photo Credits

The photo on page 1 was provided by Joe Gafney, Archives Givenchy s.a.
Special thanks to Natasha D. Crittle at Marion Greenberg

The photo on page 153 was provided by The Fashion Group

The photo on page 173 was provided by UPI/Bettmann

Glossary

Armhole: The garment opening for the arm and the sleeve.

Armscye: The armhole.

Baste-fuse: To steam press only 3 to 5 seconds and then pat the interfacing gently to fuse the interfacing to the fabric.

Basting: Hand or machine temporary stitches used to hold two or more fabric layers together for fitting or sewing.

Bias: Any line that extends diagonally across the lengthwise and crosswise grains of a fabric.

Binding: A strip of fabric that encases the edge of a piece of fabric.

Blind catchstitch: A stitch placed between the hem allowance and garment; a catchstitch used as a hemming stitch.

Blind-hem stitch: A stitch used to secure the hem. It can be done by hand or by machine.

Breakpoint: The beginning of the roll line at or just above the top button.

Butt: To place two edges together so that they touch.

Button stand or extension: The distance between the center front and the garment edge. It is the same as the width of the underlap.

Ditch-stitch: To stitch in the crack of a seam or very close to a seamline.

Double hem: Two rows of hemming stitches—one in the middle of the hem allowance and one in the usual position.

Center back: A vertical line that runs the length of the body in the middle of the back.

Center front: A vertical line that runs the length of the body in the middle of the front.

Clip: A small cut made in the seam allowance used for marking pleats, darts, garment centers, and notches. During construction, clips are used on curves and corners to allow the fabric to lie flat.

Closure: A finished opening or device, such as buttons and buttonholes, loops, hooks and eyes, snaps, hook-and-loop tape, and zippers; used to facilitate dressing and undressing.

Crossgrain: The threads that run from selvage to selvage at right angles to the selvage.

Dart: A stitched fold of fabric that is used to provide shaping. Darts are usually stitched on the inside of the garment and taper to a point on one or both ends. Stand-up darts are used as a decorative detail on the right side of the garment.

Ease: (1) The minimum ease in garment design that allows for movement. (2) The small amount of fullness on a longer section of fabric that is sewn to a shorter section.

Ease-baste: The basting used to control the fullness on a longer section of fabric so it will fit a shorter section.

Edgestitch: To stitch $1/16$ inch from the edge of the garment or garment section.

Finger-press: To press with your fingers instead of an iron to flatten a seam or section.

Float: An evening wrap originally designed by Charles Kleibacker and made from shocking pink silk gauze.

Fusible web: Polyester resin or polyamide that melts when pressed with heat and moisture. It is available as a web or on as a nonstick release paper.

Grainline: The lengthwise and crosswise threads of the fabric. On patterns, the lengthwise grain is marked with a double-headed arrow.

Hemline: The line at the lower edge of the finished garment. On patterns, it indicates the hem fold or seamline.

Hera: A wooden or molded plastic tool used for marking fabric.

Jogline: The edge that must change direction when there is a fold in the fabric.

Key: A guideline on two sections to facilitate matching them during the garment's construction.

Knock-off: An adaptation of a ready-made and usually more expensive garment.

Lapel: The part of a jacket front that is finished with a facing and turned back onto itself between the neckline and the first button.

Layout: The position of pattern pieces on uncut fabric that has been prepared for cutting.

Lengthwise grain: See straight grain.

Lining: The fabric section used to cover the wrong side of a garment.

Matchpoints: The marked points used to facilitate sewing the garment sections quickly and accurately. On commercial patterns, they are represented as circles, triangles, squares, or notches.

Open lay: A fashion industry term for a layout on a single layer of fabric.

Pin-baste: To baste with pins.

Placket: The finished opening used to facilitate garment openings at the neckline, waistline, or lower edge of sleeves.

Preshrink: To wash and dry, steam, or dry-clean fabric prior to cutting garment sections.

Pret-a-porter: A French term for ready-to-wear; literally means ready to carry. The English term is "off the peg."

Ruana: An ethnic design wrap with a long slit at one end.

Seam allowance: The amount of fabric between the seamline and the raw edge; usually ⅝ inch in home sewing.

Seamline: The position of the seam of the garment. On the pattern, it designates the stitching line for the garment seam.

Self-fabric: The same fabric as the garment itself.

Self-threading needle: A calyx-eyed needle that is open at the top for easy threading.

Serge-finish: A thread casing stitched on raw edges of the fabric with a serger to neaten the edges and prevent raveling.

Skimmer: A fashion silhouette that follows the curves of the figure without fitting it closely.

Sloper: A basic styled pattern used as a template to make new patterns.

Spottack: To sew several machine stitches one on top of another.

Stabstitch: A permanent stitch used when sewing thick sections together.

Stay: (1) Narrow, firmly woven tape used to maintain the seam length or to hold in fullness; (2) the garment section positioned inside a garment to control the shape and drape of the garment.

Staystitch: A regular machine stitch placed just inside the seamline or ⅛ inch away.

Stiletto tracing wheel: A tracing wheel with sharp needle points for patternmaking and fabric marking.

Straight grain: The lengthwise grain of the fabric parallel to the selvage.

spi: The abbreviation for stitches per inch.

Tension: The amount of pressure on the needle and bobbin threads. Stitching tension is balanced when the threads lock at the center of the fabric layers.

True bias: A diagonal line located at a 45-degree angle to the selvage. It has the greatest amount of stretch and the least amount of fraying.

Weft-insertion interfacing: Fusible knit interfacing with additional threads inserted on the crossgrain.

Wigan: Firmly woven cotton interfacing material similar to muslin used in tailoring.

Bibliography

Amig, Marya Kissinger, ed., et al. *The Experts' Book of Sewing Tips & Techniques.* Emmaus, Pa.: Rodale Press, 1995.

Andrews, Robert. *The Columbia Dictionary of Quotations.* New York: Columbia University Press, 1993.

Armstrong, Helen. *Patternmaking for Fashion Design 2nd Edition.* New York: Harper Collins College Publishers, 1995.

Current Biography. "James Galanos." 148–151. Bronx, New York: H. W. Wilson, 1970.

King, Judith E. *Patterns from Ready-to-wear: Pants.* Dayton, Ohio: Designing Lady Studio, 1988.

Lambert, Eleanor. *World of Fashion: People, Places, Resources.* New York: R. R. Bowker, 1976.

Fleming, Nancy. *Vogue and Butterick's Designer Sewing.* New York: Simon & Schuster, 1994.

McDowell, Colin. *McDowell's Directory of Twentieth Century Fashion.* Englewood Cliffs, N.J.: Prentice-Hall, 1985.

Milbank, Caroline Rennolds. *Couture: The Great Designers.* New York: Stewart, Tabori & Chang, 1985.

———. *New York Fashion: The Evolution of American Style.* New York: Harry N. Abrams, 1989.

More Creative Sewing Ideas, Singer Sewing Reference Library. Minnetonka, Minn.: Cy DeCosse, 1992.

O'Hara, Georgina. *The Encyclopaedia of Fashion from 1840 to the 1980s.* New York: Harry N. Abrams, 1986.

Shaeffer, Claire. "Borrowing from Calvin Klein," *Threads,* 56 (December 1994): 44–47.

———. *Claire Shaeffer's Fabric Sewing Guide—Updated Edition.* Radnor, Pa.: Chilton, 1994.

———. "Clothing Connections—Variations on a Seam," *Threads,* 22 (April 1989): 24–29.

———. *Couture Sewing Techniques.* Newtown, Conn.: Taunton Press, 1994.

———. "The Comfortable Side of Couture." *Great Sewn Clothes From Threads Magazine.* Newtown, Conn.: Taunton Press, 1991.

———. *The Complete Book of Sewing Shortcuts.* New York: Sterling, 1981.

———. "A Do-It-Yourself Chanel-Style Skirt," *Threads,* 44 (December 1992): 62–69.

———. "Elegant, Functional Bindings," *Threads,* 53 (June 1994): 46–51.

———. *Sew Any Patch Pocket.* Radnor, Pa.: Chilton, 1992.

———. *Sew Any Set-In Pocket.* Radnor, Pa.: Chilton, 1994.

———. *Sew Successful.* New York: Avon Books, 1984.

———. *Sewing for the Apparel Industry: Industrial Sewing Techniques.* New York: Fairchild Books, 1997.

———. "A Stay Tape Prevents Stretch," *Threads,* 60 (September 1995): 44–48.

———. "Techniques and Tips from Dior's Ready-to-Wear." *Jackets, Coats and Suits from Threads Magazine.* Newtown, Conn.: Taunton Press, 1991.

———. "Zandra Rhodes' Couture," *Threads,* 29 (June 1990): 40–45.

Shoben, Martin. *Patterns From Your Favorite Clothes.* Oxford: Heinemann Professional Publishing, 1988.

Stegemeyer, Anne. *Who's Who in Fashion.* New York: Fairchild Publications, 1996.

Young, Tammy and Lori Bottom. *ABCs of Serging.* Radnor, Pa.: Chilton, 1992.

Resources

Allentown Sewing Machine Outlet
725 N. 15th Street (Rear)
Allentown, PA 18102
(610) 434-8777
(800) 290-8484
   Sewing machines, sergers, and accessories

Butterick Company
161 Avenue of the Americas
New York, NY 10013
(212) 620-2500
   Patterns

Dick Blick Art Materials
702 Broad Street
Emmaus, PA 18049
(610) 965-6051
   Drafting tools and art supplies

Clotilde
2 Sew Smart Way B8031
Stevens Point, WI 54481-8031
(800) 772-2891
   Mail order: notions, Swedish tracing paper, and double tracing wheel

Fabric Mart of Bethlehem
2485 Willow Park Road
Bethlehem, PA 18017
(610) 866-3400
   Fine dressmaking fabrics and quilting cottons

Gingher
322-D Edwardia Drive
Greensboro, NC 27409
(800) 446-4437
   Dressmaking shears

Greenberg & Hammer
24 W. 57th Street
New York, NY 10019-3918
(800) 955-5135
   Mail order: drafting tools, interfacing, pressing supplies, stiletto tracing wheel, notions, and wadding

HTC-Handler Textile
Consumer Products Division
24 Empire Boulevard
Moonachie, NJ 07074
(201) 641-4500
   Space Board, Touch 'o Gold, and lightweight fusible interfacing

Newark Dressmaker Supply
6473 Ruch Road
P.O. Box 20730
Lehigh Valley, PA 18002-0730
(800) 736-6783
   Mail order: notions

The Personality Shoppe
1655 Hausman Road
Allentown, PA 18104
(610) 395-2067
   Bridal gowns and after-five dresses

Claire Shaeffer
P.O. Box 157
Palm Springs, CA 92263
   Mail order: stiletto tracing wheel, seam binding, *Threads* and Claire Shaeffer books

Sawyer Brook Distinctive Fabrics
P.O. Box 1800
Clinton, MA 01510-0813
(508) 368-3133
(800) 290-2739
   Mail order: designer fabric

Todd Fisher Textiles
53 Mertz Lane
Allentown, PA 18104
(610) 391-9000
   Fabric

Web of Thread
1410 Broadway
Paducah, KY 42001
(502) 575-9700
(800) 955-8185
   Mail order: silk thread

Index

A

Adolfo, 72
Akker, Koos van den, 4
Allard, Linda, 85
Allen, Jeanne, 12
Armani, Giorgio, 66

B

Balmain, Pierre, 117
Baste-fusing, 58
Basting, 6, 14
Basting tape, doublestick, 14
Beene, Geoffrey, 33, 34, 69
Bias
   defined, 5
   facings, 25–26
   strips, 5, 13
   tape, making, 50
Bindings
   on curves, 13, 47
   double, 51
   finishing ends of, 48
   French (double), 45–48
   neckline, 47
   one-step, 49–51
   seam, 12–14
   in soft fabrics, 49–50
Blanket stitch, 39
Block-fusing, 86
Bow, tying, 74
Button closures, 235–37
Buttonholes
   adding, 235–37
   bound, 105–10
Button loops, 97–100
Buttons, placement of, 237

C

Chain stitching, 19, 21
Chanel, Coco, 27, 72
Collars
   double flounce, 79–81
   drafting patterns for, 72, 76, 80
   notched, 85–87
   tie, 71–74
   turtleneck, detachable, 75–78
Copying garments
   measuring method for, 180–83
   pants, 199
   procedure for, 176–78
   rub-off method for, 192–97
   sleeves, 190–91, 198
   tools for, 173–75

tracing method for, 186–91
Costa, Victor, 109
Curves
   binding, 13, 47
   measuring, 76, 169
   piping, 17
   stitching, 22, 119

D

Darts
   converting to dart tucks, 219
   converting to ease, 224
   converting to seams, 221–22
   converting seams to, 205
   copying, 193, 195
   replacing seams with, 205
   sewing tips for, 218
   in skirt lining, 149
   take-up, defined, 217
   transferring (manipulating)
      216–17, 220
   truing, 170
Dart seams, 223
de la Renta, Oscar, 46, 117
Design worksheet, 238
Ditch-stitching, 48, 147

E

Ease, converting darts to, 224
Edgestitching, 6, 51
Ellen Tracy, 85
Ellis, Perry, 43

F

Facings
   all-in-one (neckline-armhole),
      213–15
   bias, 25–26
   for bound buttonholes, 107
   drafting patterns for, 89, 210–11
   extended, interfaced, 212
   interfacing, 28
   ribbon, 32
   for slot zipper, 113
   topstitched, 20–24
   as trim, 25–32, 211
Figure problems, 55
Folder (machine attachment), 49
Fringe, as piping, 17

G

Galanos, James, 97, 128
Gathers, 116, 123
Glossary, 240–41

Glue sticks, 14
Godets, 183–85
Grainline
   copying garments and, 176, 177,
      194
   fabric give and direction of, 166
   for facing pattern, 211
   marking on patterns, 203
   for tucks, 231
Grant, Marc, 12
Gregory Pal, 15, 25

H

Hand sewing techniques, 8, 116, 147
Hanger loops, 130, 131
Hayes, David, 105
Hems
   adding, 208
   band, 43–44
   blanket-stitched, 38–39
   chiffon (machine-rolled), 40–41
   fusing, 146
   hand-rolled, 125
   hand-stitched, 8, 42, 125
   overlock, gold, 36–37
   pin, 42
   preventing roll of, 36
   satin-stitched, 80–81
   in skirt linings, 148–49, 150
   in skirts with vent or front
      opening, 237
   topstitched, 33–35
   truing, 171

I

Interfacing
   applying, 28, 136–39
   block-fusing, 86
   preshrinking, 137
   tips for using, 28, 34, 60

J

Jackets
   eliminating seams on, 206
   fuse-hemming, 146
   interfacing, 136–39
   lining for, 140–47
   pockets for, 53–56, 63
Jeanne Marc, 12, 36

K

Klein, Calvin, 58, 148

L

Lace inserts, 118–19

Landmarks, 177
Lapels, 82–84, 87
Lauren, Ralph, 38
Layout, open, 166, 179
Lingerie guards, 130, 228
Lining
    for jacket, 140–47
    for shoulder pads, 141
    for skirt, 148–51
Liz Claiborne, 21

M

Marking
    darts, seams, edges, 195
    garments for copying, 177
    tools for, testing, 90
Matchpoints, 165, 187, 208
Measuring tools, 159, 181
Muir, Jean, 35

N

Necklines. *See also* Facings; Plackets
    binding, 47
    cowl, 134–35
    creating, tips for, 226
    scoop, 229
V-neck, 225–28
Needle lubricant, 23
Needles
    hand, 24, 39, 128
    machine, 35, 37, 139
Neiman Marcus, 121
Notches, 165, 187
Nott, Richard, 7
Novarese, Michael, 32, 118

O

Overlocking. *See* Sergers, over-
    locking with

P

Pants
    copying, 199
    inseam pocket for, 66–68
Patternmaking. *See also* Copying gar-
    ments; specific garment or pattern
    piece
    drafting techniques for, 160–62
    labeling patterns, 167
    landmarks used in, 177
    mistakes in, common, 202
    patterns for, 158–59
    procedure for, 163–66
    tools for, 155–56
    truing, 168–71
Patterns
    duplicating, 54
    full, 10, 166
    for patternmaking, 158–59
    preserving, 138
    reshaping, 209
    trying on, 70, 223

Piping, 15–17, 44, 55
Plackets
    bound, 92–94
    fly (concealed), 101–4
    keyhole (slashed), 88–91
Pleats, marking, 135
Pockets
    double-welt, 57–59
    inseam, with faux flap, 69–70
    inseam, with zipper, 66–68
    inside jacket, 63
    patch, piped, 53–56
    porthole, 64–65
    windowpane opening for, 60–62
Preshrinking
    interfacing, 137
    trim, 32
Pressing, 30
Private label, defined, 75

R

Resources, 243
Rhodes, Zandra, 32, 92
Ribbon
    making facings with, 32
    trimming zippers with, 95
    used inside garments, 130–31
Roll line, 87
Roses, fabric, 115–17
Rotary cutter, 121

S

Saint Laurent, Yves, 54, 139
Seam allowances
    trimming, 6, 19, 21
    width of, 189, 202
    working with, 217
Seams
    adding, 201–3
    baby, 18–19
    bias bound, stand-up, 12–14
    eliminating, 204–6
    French, raised, 7–8
    marking, 195
    overlock, raised, 9–11
    piped, 15–16
    replacing darts with, 221–22
    shoulder, 21, 207
    strap, 3–6, 14
    test, 26
    transferring, 207–9
    truing, 169–70
Sergers
    overlocking with, 9–11, 36–37
    trimming with, 6
    using rayon thread with, 37
Shawl, ruffled, 122–23
Shoulder pads, lining, 141
Simpson, Adele, 40
Skirts
    double-welt pocket on, 57–59

eliminating seams on, 205
    godets in, 183–85
    lining for, 148–51
Sleeve heads, 144
Sleeves
    copying, 190–91, 198
    placket for, 92
Stays
    blouse, 132–33
    cowl, 134–35
    waist, 127–29
Staystitching, 98
Stitches, skipped, 35
Stitch-in-the-ditch, 48, 147

T

Tacks
    French, 151
        machine, 34
Tailor's knot, 35
Thread
    for overlocking, 10, 11, 37
    quality of, 11
    for topstitching, 30
Thread ends
    fastening, 35, 90
    hiding, 24, 37
Topstitching
    facings, 20–24
    hems, 33–35
    placement of, 20–21
    thread for, 30
    tips for, 23, 24
Travilla, Bill, 19
Trim
    facings as, 25–32, 211
    lace inserts, 118–19
    preshrinking, 32
    roses, fabric, 115–17
Tubing, self-filled, 99
Tucks, 230–32
Tuck seam, 233–34

U

Understitching, 22

V

Valentino, 101

W

Waistbands, 129, 150
Windowpane opening, 60–62
Workers for Freedom, 7
Wraps
    cocoon, 120–21
    evening, 124

Y

Yardage, estimating, 179

Z

Zippers, 66–68, 94–96, 111–13

If you've enjoyed this book,
you may be interested in these other fine books from Rodale Press.

Christmas with Jinny Beyer

DECORATE YOUR HOME FOR THE HOLIDAYS WITH BEAUTIFUL QUILTS, WREATHS, ARRANGEMENTS, ORNAMENTS, AND MORE
by Jinny Beyer

Renowned quilt designer Jinny Beyer shares her ideas and techniques for making over 50 holiday projects, suitable for any skill level. Complete instructions and full-color illustrations accompany every project.

Hardcover   ISBN 0-87596-716-7

Sew It Tonight, Give It Tomorrow

50 FAST, FUN, AND FABULOUS GIFTS TO MAKE IN AN EVENING
edited by Stacey L. Klaman

Make one-of-a-kind gifts in no time at all. The projects, from golf club covers and a tea cozy to crib bumpers and holiday ornaments, are appropriate for sewers of all levels.

Hardcover   ISBN 0-87596-645-4

The Experts' Book of Sewing Tips & Techniques

FROM THE SEWING STARS OF AMERICA—HUNDREDS OF WAYS TO SEW BETTER, FASTER, & EASIER
edited by Marya Kissinger Amig, Barbara Fimbel, Stacey L. Klaman, Karen Kunkel, and Susan Weaver

Learn the trade secrets of the top sewing experts in this easy-to-use guide. Hints and tips, from appliqué to zippers, are covered in alphabetical order.

Hardcover   ISBN 0-87596-682-9

No Time to Sew

FAST & FABULOUS TIPS & TECHNIQUES FOR SEWING A FIGURE-FLATTERING WARDROBE
by Sandra Betzina

Sandra Betzina, star of the television series "Sew Perfect," helps you to sew in record time, offering stylish patterns, step-by-step instructions, time-saving tips, and wardrobe advice. A complete set of multi-sized patterns is included with the book.

Hardcover   ISBN 0-87596-744-2

Sewing Secrets from the Fashion Industry

PROVEN METHODS TO HELP YOU SEW LIKE THE PROS
edited by Susan Huxley

Learn the same tips and techniques that the industry professionals use in their sample rooms and production factories. Over 800 full-color photographs accompany the step-by-step directions.

Hardcover   ISBN -0-87596-719-1

Secrets for Successful Sewing

TECHNIQUES FOR MASTERING YOUR SEWING MACHINE AND SERGER
by Barbara Weiland

The ultimate owner's manual, full of tips and techniques for mastering a machine—regardless of brand. Includes a comprehensive look at machines and their accessories plus step-by-step instructions for the most popular and unique serger and sewing machine techniques. Barbara Weiland is the former editor of *Sew News*.

Hardcover   ISBN 0-87596-776-0

 FOR MORE INFORMATION OR TO ORDER ANY OF THESE BOOKS, CALL **1-800-848-4735** OR FAX US ANYTIME AT **1-800-813-6627.**
OR VISIT OUR WORLD WIDE WEB SITE AT: http://www.rodalepress.com